AVON CONNECTICUT'S FIRST CENTURY

VISIONARIES AND VICTIMS

SCOTT R. LEWIS

THE History PRESS

Published by The History Press
An imprint of Arcadia Publishing
Charleston, SC
www.historypress.com

First published 2025

Manufactured in the United States

ISBN 9781467170147

Library of Congress Control Number: 2025941487

In memory of my dad, Kenneth Deane Lewis, a writer

CONTENTS

Contents

FOREWORD

Scott Lewis's *Avon, Connecticut's First Century: Visionaries and Victims* is a page-turner of stories about Avon from 1830 to 1930. The book's publisher is the venerable History Press, printer of local history treasures from all fifty states. This is a History Press triumph, truly one of its "valued touchstones for community identity." Scott's work beautifully achieves the publisher's mission to discover, document and deliver history.

Terri Wilson, president of the Avon Historical Society, noted especially the author's "keen way of connecting dots in history, whether it's between two people or the circumstances that occurred in our town's history. He is to be commended for bringing these stories to life."

Visionaries and Victims adds rich details to the documented history of Avon. It builds on Mary-Frances MacKie's *Avon, Connecticut, an Historical Story* and Dr. Christopher P. Bickford's *Farmington in Connecticut*, as well as my books *Catch'd on Fire: The Journals of Rufus Hawley, 1763–1812*; *Avon*, in Arcadia Publishing's Images of America series; and *A Tale of Two Meetinghouses*, coauthored with Marjorie P. Bender and Jean T. Parker.

The earliest inhabitants of the land that became Avon were Native Americans who kept seasonal villages along the banks of the Farmington River. The first evidence of Paleo-Indian presence in Avon was discovered in 2019 near the Old Farms Road bridge and documented by archaeologists to at least 12,500 years ago; the second is the Tunxis tribe of Farmington, whose members belonged to the Algonquin family of tribes that came to New England around one thousand years ago.

Foreword

Avon was incorporated as a separate town from Farmington in 1830, and for its first one hundred years, the town had only a small population of 900–1,300 people. Nevertheless, Avon punches above its weight with stories that will inspire, inform, amuse, amaze—and horrify. Here are ordinary people getting through the day and visionary leaders dedicated to expanding knowledge, creating advancement and making change.

Avon's history parallels American history in these stories. Avon had leaders in manufacturing, arts, religion and education. Some fought for social reform—the abolition of slavery, women's suffrage and immigrant rights. The feast goes on with stories of those who built the towers on Avon Mountain, collected rare books, manufactured safety fuse, surveyed the land and faced scandal in the ministry.

There are stories about the Underground Railroad and of Civil War soldiers, Black and white. The author writes about Avon Old Farms School, Eleanor Roosevelt's connection to the town, spectacular gardens and an annual fair with daredevil stunts. In addition to covering crimes and disasters, the book tells of the political activism of the Alsop family and the story of Yung Wing, a Chinese immigrant and education advocate who married an Avon woman.

When Avon became an incorporated town in 1830, it was on a path to radically transform itself from the farming parish that had been led by its minister Reverend Rufus Hawley from 1769 to 1817. Scott Lewis was able to expertly mine the journals and papers of Hawley's grandson Edward Eugene Hawley and other residents from the time period covered by *Visionaries and Victims*. It was akin to the author finding buried treasure.

Visionaries and Victims will be appreciated for generations to come, inspiring further reading about Avon and contributing mightily to future research by students and scholars. The author's extensive research and his knack for storytelling are superb. This book's achievement is how brilliantly it documents and honors local events and people's complicated lives. Our understanding of Avon is heightened. The sense of our own particular place in this community—and in our own time—is supremely enriched.

The facts will stand; these new stories will endure. There is no greater calling for a book on local history.

—Nora Oakes Howard
Historian, Town of Avon, and
Historian of the Avon Congregational Church

ACKNOWLEDGEMENTS

Shortly after I moved with my family to Avon, Connecticut, in 1999, I began building and maintaining hiking trails for the Avon Land Trust. One day in 2022, I decided I would like to know more about the history of the land on the west slope of Avon Mountain. Little did I know that the mountain had such a storied past. I learned that there were three predecessor towers to the Heublein Tower and that those towers were in Avon, not in Simsbury. I became fascinated with the stories of the people who built the Avon towers, and it piqued my interest to learn more about the history of other parts of town.

Certainly, the beginning of my research was Mary-Frances MacKie's history of the town written in 1988 titled *Avon, Connecticut, an Historical Story*, as well as Nora Oakes Howard's *Catch'd on Fire*, an excellent account of the life of the Reverend Rufus Hawley. Many of the stories I have written about were briefly mentioned in MacKie's timeless work, but I thought they deserved to be told in richer detail.

One of the most remarkable things I found during my research was how many times a character in one story unexpectedly appeared in another. Perhaps that is not so unusual for what had been a town of fewer than two thousand people during Avon's first one hundred years, but what clearly emerged was a series of stories that are more closely connected than I expected.

I have so many people to thank for providing me with the support to write this book. Principal among them is Tina Panik, reference manager at the Avon Free Public Library, who was invaluable in helping me track down source material that was difficult to find and who has a wealth of knowledge about the material available in the Marian Hunter Local History room at the library. Her mother, Heddy Panik, provided critical support as well, always willing to give me a hand. I also must thank people who have a deep knowledge of Avon's history and who steered me in the right direction, offering support when needed, including Nora Oakes Howard, historian of the town of Avon and Avon Congregational Church; Terri Wilson, president of the Avon Historical Society; and Janet Conner, historian for the Avon Land Trust. In addition to her overall extensive knowledge of Avon history, Nora was especially helpful to me in her excellent in-depth review of all the stories and her research of Corinne and Joseph Alsop.

I am also grateful for the many excellent archivists who assisted me at libraries and museums where source material for this book was located, including Melanie Bourbeau, senior curator at the Hill-Stead Museum; Sierra Dixon of the Connecticut Museum of Culture and History in Hartford; Sarah Neagoy and Tara Willerup, research librarians of the Simsbury Free Library; and Melissa Graham, director of information services at the Town of Farmington libraries. Also providing indispensable support were the archivists at the Houghton Library at Harvard University, the Beinecke Library at Yale University, the Watkinson Library at Trinity College in Hartford and the archivists at the University of Connecticut in Storrs. Other local resources who helped to validate key facts on local history included Tina Amato, assistant town clerk for Avon; Sarah Jean Willett, historian of the First Church of Christ, Congregational, Farmington; Arthur Custer, historian for Avon Old Farms School; Jay Willerup, president of Friends of Heublein Tower; Erin Monroe, Krieble Curator of American Paintings and Sculpture at the Wadsworth Atheneum Museum of Art; Chloe Collins of the Auerbach Art Library and Museum Archives, Wadsworth Atheneum Museum of Art; Sarah Cremeans of the Golf Club of Avon; and Earle Stone of the Church of Jesus Christ of Latter-day Saints.

I am indebted to those who dedicated time to helping edit this work, including Nora Howard, Terri Wilson, Tina Panik, Carol Genco, Rick Dubiel and Risa Lewis. I am also grateful for Bill Crofton's invaluable assistance with the photos and other images. In addition, I appreciate all the guidance I received from my publisher, The History Press, including the support of Mike Kinsella and Abigail Fleming.

Acknowledgements

Most of all, I must thank my wife, Ruth Lewis, who encouraged me on this project and had the patience to stick with me while I worked tirelessly to finish the research. I love the town of Avon for its beauty and its people, and this work is my appreciation for what the town has given me.

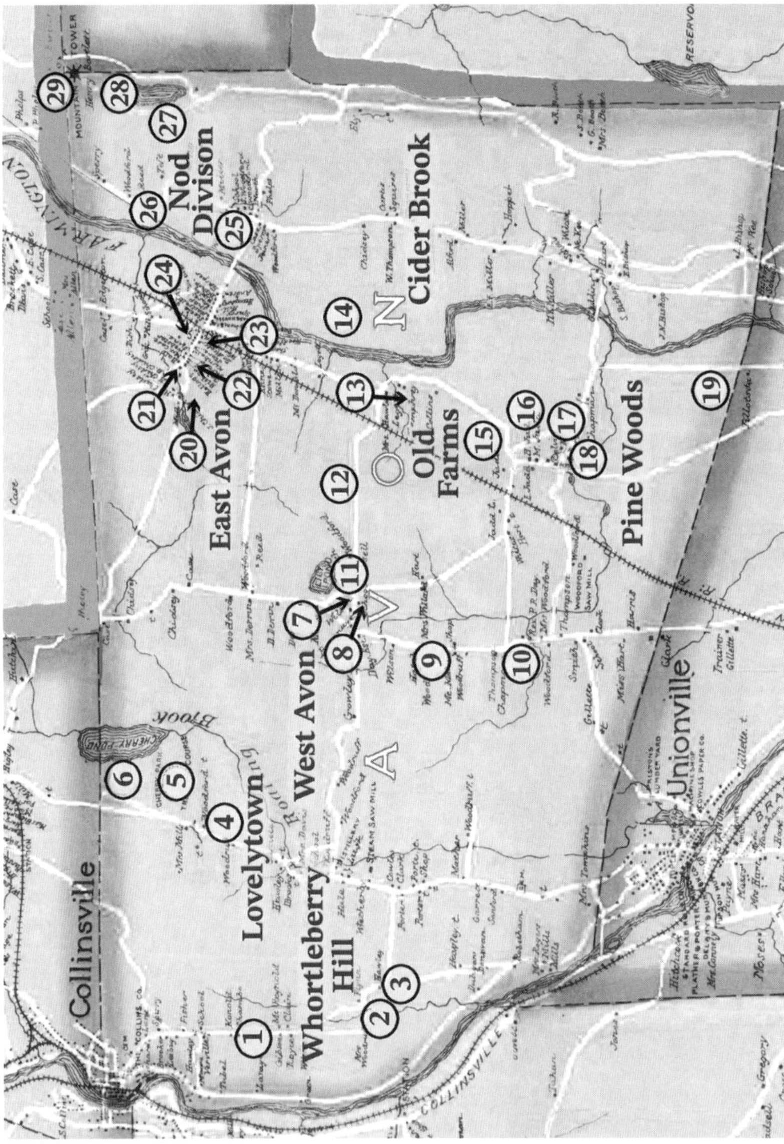

Derived from 1884 Driving Chart of Hartford and vicinity. *Albert A. Hyde & Co.*

Key to Map of Avon: Points of Interest

Whortleberry Hill

1. Orson and Cornelia Woodford's home
2. Romanta and Hannah Woodruff's home
3. Orrin and Diana Woodford's home

Lovelytown

4. Enslavers Shubael and Romanta Tillotson's summer home
5. Cherry Park Fairgrounds
6. Secret Lake (aka Cherry Pond)

West Avon

7. David W. and Matthew Henry Bartlett's childhood home
8. Center School House
9. Sunshine Farm (originally the home of Eldad Woodruff)
10. Edgar and Mary Woodford's home
11. West Avon Congregational Church (original site)
12. Stilwell Farm (later Golf Club of Avon)

Old Farms and Cider Brook

13. Reverend Rufus Hawley's home
14. The Lord's Barn
15. Sherman Eddy's Tow Path Lodge
16. Avon Old Farms School
17. Aphek Woodruff's mill
18. Wilford Woodruff's boyhood home

Pine Woods

19. Pine Woods Farm (Fanny and Seth Tillotson)

East Avon

20. Chidsey house (Dickman's boardinghouse)
21. Climax Fuse factory
22. Bela Crocker Kellogg's home (Yung Wing and Mary Louise's residence in the 1870s)
23. Tally Ho Tavern (later, the Avon Hotel)
24. Avon Congregational Church

Nod Division

25. Wood Ford Farm (home of Amasa Woodford and later, Joe and Corrine Alsop)
26. Chester Woodford's home
27. Monte Video (Wadsworth estate, then David Collins and later Robert Hoe)
28. Wadsworth Towers
29. Bartlett Tower in Avon

PART I

SPIRIT OF INDEPENDENCE

1

ACRIMONY AMONG THE FAITHFUL

The Split of the Church

On a cold wintry day in December 1817, the white-haired Reverend Rufus Hawley was contemplating the future—his own future, certainly, but also that of the church of which he had been pastor for the past forty-eight years. Known for his "sound doctrine and plain speech,"[1] Hawley was of the utmost integrity. And on this December day, the seventy-six-year-old minister desperately wished that the dissension that had plagued his church for the last twelve years would be healed. Constructed in 1754, the "Lord's Barn," as the Congregational church in Northington was called, was pitifully inadequate, small and run-down. Church members universally agreed that they needed a new house of worship, but there was one matter that prevented them from moving forward with replacing the structure. The parishioners could not agree on where to build the new church, and the impasse led to outright hostility. Despite all his efforts, Reverend Rufus Hawley couldn't guide his congregation to reach a compromise.

For the reverend, at least, there was resolution of one long-outstanding matter—his own retirement from the pulpit. On December 11, 1817, Hawley gave his written resignation with the agreement that he would receive his overdue salary of $150 and fifteen cords of wood. After he consented to help with the transition to a new minister, the seemingly insolvable dispute that had roiled his church for so long would now be someone else's problem.

Then, less than three weeks later, sometime between the evening of Sunday, December 28, and the early morning hours of Wednesday, December 31, 1817, the Lord's Barn mysteriously burned to the ground.

Reverend Rufus Hawley had served as minister for so long, his life was interwoven with the history of the town, since nearly the time it became a separate parish within Farmington called Northington (now Avon). Educated at Yale College, Hawley became pastor of the Northington Parish in December 1769, just eighteen years after the Northington society was formed.

As Northington was once part of Farmington, the town's history traces back to when Farmington was first settled in 1640. The earliest known English colonist to make his homestead along the Farmington River in what is now Avon was Stephen Hart. He was the son of Deacon Stephen Hart, who was one of the first twenty-five Englishmen who explored the Hartford area in 1635 prior to Reverend Thomas Hooker's arrival in 1636. Much of the land that became Farmington, including Northington, had been inhabited by the Native American Tunxis-Sepus tribe. As part of a 1650 conveyance of land to the English, the Tunxis-Sepus were relegated to a strip of property along the Farmington River the colonists later called "Indian Neck,"[2] though even that land would later be claimed by the settlers.

Native Americans had lived in the Farmington Valley for thousands of years prior to the arrival of the English, with one Paleo-Indian archaeological site in Avon dating back more than 12,500 years. For centuries, the Tunxis-Sepus had seasonal camps along the Farmington River where they fished, farmed and hunted along its riverbanks. Forced out by the continued influx of English colonists, what was left of the tribe moved to upstate New York and eventually to Wisconsin.

By the early eighteenth century, more English settlers had moved to the area along the river north of and downstream from the center of Farmington. It was not long before they began to complain about the distance required to attend church services, especially in winter when roads could become nearly impassable. Staying home was not an option. If parishioners did not attend church, they could be excommunicated and would be ostracized from society.

In 1746, twenty-three years before Reverend Hawley began his ministry, there were thirty-one families of English colonists living in what would become Avon. Frustrated by the inability to form their own parish, Joseph Woodford Jr., grandson of one of Farmington's original settlers, and other residents of the area began attending church services in nearby Simsbury. When they petitioned the Connecticut General Assembly to let them be annexed by Simsbury, however, they were rebuffed.

Yet the challenge of traveling to church in winter did not go away. Finally, by majority vote at a meeting on May 12, 1746, the Congregational Church in Farmington granted winter privileges for families living north of the village described as "both sides of ye River to Simsbary [*sic*] line" and "on ye West Side of ye mountain." Permission was granted provided they "procuer [*sic*] an orthodox preacher…& obtain ye Confirmation…by ye General assembly."[3] This time, the General Assembly approved the plan, and winter privileges went into effect in the late fall of 1746.

Enjoying their new arrangement, residents who settled in the "Cider Brook"[4] area on the east bank of the river decided to petition the General Assembly again in early 1750, this time asking to hold services year-round in the winter location. With the consent of Farmington, the General Assembly granted their request, and the Northington Parish, or Second Ecclesiastical Society of Farmington, was born.

Needing a pastor, Northington parishioners installed a man named Ebeneezer Booge, who gave his first sermon on Sunday, November 28, 1751. Three years later, the congregation constructed a small church along the river at the end of present-day Reverknolls, a simple meetinghouse with box pews. After Reverend Booge's premature death in February 1767, they spent nearly two years looking for a new minister, finally settling on Rufus Hawley. Hawley would end up serving as pastor of the Northington Parish for the next forty-eight years.

Around 1805, members attending the Northington meetinghouse near Cider Brook began complaining about the poor condition of their house of worship and the need to replace it. In 1815, parishioners started referring to their church as the "Lord's Barn"[5] because sheep took shelter under it during storms. Visitors described the structure as drafty, dilapidated and smaller than many homes. As Yale Professor Benjamin Silliman wrote after attending a church service there, the building, enveloped by large trees, had "gray, unpainted shingles and clapboards with many water-worn channels, and it seemed as if it would soon fall."[6] And services in the Lord's Barn during the winter could be unbearably cold, even with the use of foot stoves.

Underlying their grievance about the aging meetinghouse, however, was a more concerning problem. As more families began to settle in West Avon and the Old Farms area west of the Farmington River, residents there found it burdensome to have to travel across to the east side of the river to attend church. Given that church attendance was mandatory, it was this very concern over having to travel too far to worship that resulted in Northington being established as a separate ecclesiastical society from Farmington in 1750.

In 1808, parishioners turned to the Hartford County Court to advise them on where to locate a new meetinghouse but rejected the court's recommendation to build the structure in the Old Farms area, about halfway between East Avon and West Avon. Then, in November 1809, the membership passed a resolution stating that the church would be located at a site chosen by whichever group (East Avon, West Avon or Old Farms) was first able to pledge $3,000 toward the building of the new meetinghouse, provided the location was approved by the Hartford County Court. Perhaps because no group was able to meet the financial commitment, this plan of action did not resolve the matter.

Eventually, the balance of power within the church shifted as more residents settled in the far western part of town along Lovely Street and on Whortleberry Hill (now known as Huckleberry Hill). In 1815, Lot Hawley, first cousin once removed of Reverend Hawley, and other residents of that area petitioned the Connecticut General Assembly to allow them to join the Northington society. East Avon residents, upset with the request, passed a resolution stating that "we are opposed to said petitioners… being annexed to this society, because…such annexation…will have a tendency to increase the unhappy division that now exists in the society."[7] Despite their objections, the Connecticut General Assembly approved the petition, and as the year turned to 1817, residents living west of the river now held the majority, a state of affairs that likely triggered the incendiary developments to come.

At a tempestuous meeting at the Lord's Barn in June 1817, East Avon parishioners refused to abide by a vote to build the new meetinghouse near the true geographical "center of the society"[8] at the intersection of present-day Country Club and Burnham Roads. In September 1817, the dissension prompted a few members, including Amasa Woodford and Ozem Woodruff, to split off, forming the Union Baptist Society. Two months later, seeking to break the impasse, the congregation voted on a proposal to build at a site on present-day Old Farms Road just north of its intersection with present-day Country Club Road, but that motion was narrowly defeated by a tally of 38 to 37. Decades later, Reverend Joel Grant of the West Avon Congregational Church said of the Lord's Barn, "Instead of being a dwelling house for the prince of peace, it had become an arena for angry combatants."[9]

On December 17, 1817, Reverend Rufus Hawley gave his resignation, unable to keep up with the daily rigors of the job. Then, shocking the community, shortly before or on the morning of New Year's Eve, word quickly spread that the Lord's Barn had caught fire and had been reduced to ashes. On December 31, a meeting was hastily called at the residence of parishioner Silas Goff in East Avon and a resolution was made to "offer a suitable reward for apprehending the person or persons that caused the meeting house to be burned in Northington."[10] Clearly, in the opinion of parishioners, on inspecting the ruins, the fire was an act of arson.

Writing seven years after the Lord's Barn had been destroyed by fire, Benjamin Silliman reflected on the hostility that had divided other communities in Connecticut as well: "Happier it would be, if these separations had always been free from animosity—if they had not sometimes laid the foundation of permanent discord, and if there had been no instance of outrageous violence."[11] Rumors swirled around town about who had committed the act of "outrageous violence," but no suspects were ever named or tried.

Rather than bringing the congregation closer together, the burning of the Lord's Barn deepened the animosity. At the December 31 meeting, parishioners from West Avon put forward a resolution to build the new church in their section of town, and while the motion passed, it became clear that East Avon residents were threatening to defect.

Finally, on March 2, 1818, by an affirmative vote of 43 to 37, the issue was settled. The Second Ecclesiastical Society of Farmington, known as the Northington Parish, resolved to build their new meetinghouse near the Center School House on a parcel at the northeast corner of present-day Burnham and Country Club Roads. After Avon became a separate town in 1830, that church would come to be known as the West Avon Congregational Church, which, in 1969, was moved to the other side of Burnham Road.

Unwilling to travel to West Avon, fourteen of the thirty-seven male members from East Avon who lost the vote decided to split off and form their own church. In October 1818, the men agreed they would raise money to build a meetinghouse just east of Amos Wheeler's mill on Nod Brook along the Albany Turnpike (present-day 6 West Main Street). With construction of their new church underway, in March 1819, the North Consociation of Hartford County approved the defectors' application to form the Third Ecclesiastical Society of Farmington, later renamed the Avon Congregational Church. The membership installed as its first pastor the Reverend Bela Kellogg, who grew up in Amherst, Massachusetts, and had most recently been the minister in Seymour, Connecticut. In establishing their new meetinghouse, the group voted unanimously to "retain no unchristian feelings towards the members of [the West Avon] church—that we wish to be separated from them in brotherly love, & to continue in the exercise of charity & Christian communion with them."[12] Now that they were going their own way, East Avon parishioners found it easier to be gracious.

To fund the building of their new edifice, the East Avon congregation asked for pledges from its parishioners, with the largest contribution of $500 received from Obadiah Gillet, who operated the Tally Ho Tavern, which was across the street from where the Avon Congregational Church was being built. Congregants were also asked to rent their pews, though one member, Elijah Miller, who pledged $425 to build the church, refused, saying, "Damned if I'll give…to build the church and then pay to sit in a seat on the Sabbath Day!"[13] He was true to his word; instead of renting a pew, he brought his own chair and sat in the aisle.

Reverend Rufus Hawley elected to stay with the Second Ecclesiastical Society of Farmington after it moved to West Avon and would occasionally give sermons during his retirement. After guiding the community through a tumultuous time in its history, Reverend Hawley passed away in January 1826 at the age of eighty-four with the harmony he long sought solved by separation.

Assuming the act was arson, no one was ever identified as having burned the Lord's Barn to the ground. Given he was stepping down from the ministry, it seems unlikely that Reverend Hawley had a strong motive. Perhaps Obadiah Gillet or another East Avon parishioner set the fire, unhappy that the majority faction from West Avon was unwilling to locate the new meetinghouse closer to the Albany Turnpike. More likely, it was a church member from west of the river, such as Lot Hawley or Ashbel Tillotson from Lovelytown, who concluded that an insuperable vote to move the church to West Avon remained unlikely as long as the Lord's Barn remained standing. For all the speculation, the true origin of the fire will likely never be known. Benjamin Silliman could only express sorrow and bewilderment about the divisions happening in so many church parishes at the time, commenting, "It would be easy to give a considerable list of towns in Connecticut, where two spires rise instead of one, because the people could not agree where the *one* should be placed."[14]

2

INDEPENDENCE AT LAST

The Town of Avon Is Born

With the controversy over the Lord's Barn behind them, Northington inhabitants turned their attention to another issue that divided town citizens. While many still felt a strong attachment to Farmington, a growing number of residents believed that Northington was too far from Farmington center and, as a result, complained that they were underrepresented by town government. Leaders in Northington demanded that town meetings alternate between Farmington center and Northington, but town officials in Farmington rejected that idea.

In November 1828, Amasa Woodford of Nod Road was selected by his peers to moderate a meeting of Northington residents to consider whether they should petition the Connecticut General Assembly to be incorporated as a separate town from Farmington. Amasa was an excellent choice as moderator. While he himself was in favor of separation, as the great-great-grandson of one of Northington's founding fathers, he had the respect of town citizens because he understood the strong connection many still had to Farmington. Other nearby towns had declared their independence from Farmington, including Southington in 1779 and both Bristol and Berlin in 1785, and the time seemed ripe to consider the question.

Working with Amasa was a man named Truman Hawley, brother of Lot Hawley, and together they pursued a path to independence. It wasn't just the hassle of traveling such a far distance that prompted the call for separation. With an increase in commerce along the Albany Turnpike and, more significantly, the opening of the Farmington Canal in 1828, Northington had established its own town center and with it, its own identity. Through Amasa and Truman's persistence, in December 1828, they convinced the majority of Farmington residents, including those living in the Northington Parish, to move forward with separation and, in early 1829, petitioned the Connecticut General Assembly. When the assembly failed to act on their petition, Amasa and Truman were disappointed, but they were not going to give up.

As early as 1801, residents of the Northington section of Farmington had appealed to the Connecticut General Assembly to become an independent town. They made a second request in 1811, but the Assembly, with Farmington native John Treadwell serving as moderator, declined to consider the petition. In the meantime, town residents were deeply embroiled in the question of where to build a new meetinghouse to replace the Lord's Barn, so no action was taken on the idea of separating from Farmington for the next seventeen years.

Shortly after the Farmington Canal opened in 1828, a village formed near the warehouse built along the west side of the canal and Northington inhabitants had a town center to call their own. While the project to build the canal had begun in the early 1820s, it had taken a while for residents to warm up to the idea of a waterway cutting through their farmland. To appease the concerns of farmers and gain momentum behind the canal project, on July 4, 1825, Farmington Canal Company president James Hillhouse of New Haven toured the route on a wheeled boat pulled by horses as throngs of people along the way waved flags and handkerchiefs. Three years later, after Irish immigrants and other laborers toiled to dig the nearly sixty-mile length of the canal from New Haven to the Massachusetts state line, a great multitude gathered in Northington on June 20, 1828, to witness the grand opening of Northington's section of the canal as church bells rang in celebration. With frequent deliveries of goods from warehouses in New Haven and an increase in people traveling through the village via either the Albany Turnpike or the canal, businesses sprang up in the village.

By the late 1820s, the development of a commercial center to serve canal traffic likely helped tip the scales in favor of independence. Recognizing this new reality, in December 1828, the town of Farmington acknowledged that the proposed town borders for Avon "would be equal, in extent, to many

& perhaps most of the towns in the state"[15] and gave its support for the separation, with 162 of 210 eligible voters giving their approval. That same month, Northington residents also declared their support for independence, voting 59 to 44 in favor.

After more than a year passed, on March 4, 1830, Truman Hawley submitted yet another petition to the Connecticut General Assembly, noting "that great inconveniences are experienced" in traveling to the "electors' meeting…the school-house and churches," and arguing that the "public interest in general" would be advanced by separation.[16] This time the petition was successful, and on May 5, 1830, the General Assembly, meeting in New Haven, approved the plan. The state assembly declared that "the inhabitants therein be and the same is hereby incorporated into a district Town of Avon, and the inhabitants…shall have and enjoy all the powers, privileges, and immunities which are enjoyed by other towns in this state."[17] Meeting the demands of the mother town, Avon assumed its share of Farmington's debts and agreed to pay a proportionate share of common expenses, including that of the common jail and poorhouse in Farmington. The day after the state assembly announced its decision, the split was ratified by Farmington and the path to independence was finally complete.

With separation achieved, Amasa Woodford served as chairman presiding over the first Avon town meeting on Tuesday, June 21, 1830, with many of the town's 1,025 residents assembling at the West Avon Congregational Church. Town meetings alternated between Avon's two Congregational churches for the next sixty-one years until the first town hall was built in 1891.

Town leaders adopted the name Avon,[18] since residents had been using that name as early as 1753 and it was already more familiar to them than the name Northington. Why residents of the area started using the name Avon in the eighteenth century is not known. Perhaps the fertile land along the Farmington River reminded English colonists of towns along the River Avon in England. For its first one hundred years, independently minded Avon would remain a tight-knit community, rooted in agriculture.

3

CHESTER WOODFORD'S WISE COUNSEL

On October 25, 1914, the day before his one hundredth birthday, farmer Chester Randolph Woodford sat comfortably in his living room on Nod Road in Avon talking with a reporter from the *Hartford Courant* about his remarkable life. Chester had seen extraordinary changes over the course of a century. Just a few days earlier, his daughter had taken him with some friends to Hartford in an automobile, a thrill for Chester, who had spent his life traveling on horseback or by stagecoach. Now, as he told the reporter, he would soon be getting his house wired for electricity.

Born sixteen years before Avon separated from Farmington, Chester was the embodiment of Avon's history, a nephew of Amasa Woodford, one of the town's founders. A farmer who tilled the land like his ancestors, he grew produce, had dairy cows and became the first farmer in Avon to grow tobacco. A sixth-generation descendant of Joseph Woodford, one of the first settlers in what became Avon, Chester had deep roots in the town's earliest formation. A teenager when Avon separated from Farmington, Chester was born three years before the Lord's Barn burned to the ground.

On the eve of his 100th birthday, he told the *Hartford Courant* reporter a story he had recounted many times before and would repeat each year until he passed away in 1921 at age 107. As Chester remembered it, when he was a young man, he and his uncle Joseph Bishop left their farms in Avon to become traveling clock salesmen. Unable to sell enough clocks along the Mid-Atlantic coastline, they headed out to Illinois, where they were arrested for selling clocks without a permit. In need of legal counsel, Chester related

AVON'S GRAND OLD MAN 105 YEARS OLD TODAY

Chester Randolph Woodford, Oldest Living Legislator, Has Held Every Public Office in Town—In Fine Health.

(Special to The Courant.)

AVON, Sunday, Oct. 26.

Chester Randolph Woodford, Avon's grand old man is 105 years old today and to celebrate the occasion his daughters will keep open house so that all their father's friends may greet him.

It was on Thursday, just two days before his birthday that one of "The Courant's" representatives called to see him and "interview" is entirely too cold and formal a word to apply to the visit. Mr. Woodford's home fairly radiates hospitality and the heart of it all is Mr. Woodford him-

CHESTER R. WOODFORD

105 Years Old.

company and these were the thrilling

Chester Randolph Woodford. *From the* Hartford Courant.

that he hired a struggling young lawyer trying to build up his legal practice—a man named Abraham Lincoln. He was impressed with Abe, who won the case by successfully arguing that the clocks Chester and Joseph were selling were assembled in Illinois and, therefore, did not require a license. Chester boasted that Abe earned praise among the bar for his defense of the case, and as a result, Lincoln's reputation and his practice grew.

Proud of his life, the story Chester told about being represented by Abraham Lincoln was certainly a good one that made headlines. But was it really true?

With the population along the Mississippi River rapidly expanding, in 1839, Eli Preston of Unionville, Connecticut, and his business associates looked to expand sales of their shelf clocks out west. They were partners of Williams, Orton, Preston's & Co., one of many shelf clock manufacturers established in Connecticut in the first half of the nineteenth century.

After Eli Terry of Connecticut found a way to manufacture clocks with interchangeable parts so that clocks could be mass produced, shelf clock manufacturers sprang up all over Hartford and Litchfield Counties. In time, Connecticut would become known for its clock manufacturing, with Seth Thomas establishing his company in Plymouth in 1853 and other producers forming in Bristol and Waterbury.

When Chester was a young man, there was a canal in Unionville that diverted water from the Farmington River to the center of town, and mills popped up along the canal. One of the mills belonged to the firm of Williams, Orton, Preston's & Co., which manufactured shelf clocks, both those made of brass clock components using locally rolled sheet brass as well as less expensive clocks manufactured with wooden clock movements.

To grow his business in the West, Eli Preston knew he needed to set up an operation in what was then the western part of the country to coordinate sales efforts and to assemble the clocks using parts shipped from Unionville. He decided to establish a branch agency in Alton, Illinois, along the banks of the Mississippi River. Although perhaps better known as the site where abolitionist publisher Elijah Lovejoy was murdered in 1837, Alton had become an important steamboat depot, as it was near the confluences of both the Missouri and Illinois Rivers at the point where they feed into the Mississippi.

Rather than try to hire people in Illinois they didn't know, Eli Preston and his partners contracted with two agents from Avon, twenty-four-year-old Chester Woodford and Chester's uncle, twenty-eight-year-old Joseph Bishop. Chester and Joseph created their own sales agency firm called Bishop, Woodford & Co., which, in September 1838, entered into a formal contract with the Unionville clockmaker. To get to Illinois, Chester and Joseph agreed to "furnish themselves with two good horses & two Wagons & harness to be driven by themselves."[19] In return, they would get a share of the profits from each clock sold and have their expenses paid.

On September 21, 1838, Chester and Joseph pulled together the provisions they would need to make the trip and brought along two of Chester's cousins, Samuel and Amherst Woodford. Accompanying them were two other men, James Gillet and Erastus Higley, who were hired to peddle clocks.

After setting up their office in Alton, the sales force of Bishop, Woodford & Co. began peddling clocks around the region. While they had early success, selling ten clocks in January 1839, the profit margins were thin. Depending on whether the mechanical clock movements were made of brass or less expensive wood, the firm sold clocks at prices ranging from $16 to $25, and as competition increased and demand waned, they eventually may have had to sell some clocks at a loss. Not long after they began peddling clocks, the sales firm ran into legal trouble. Four years earlier, in 1835, the State of Illinois had passed a law to protect domestic clock producers, requiring peddlers to obtain a license if they wished to sell clocks manufactured outside of Illinois. Sometime in late 1839, Chester and Joseph's employee Erastus Higley was peddling his wares when he was approached by a man named Abraham Fishbourne who became angry that an out-of-towner was selling clocks without a license as prescribed by the law. Fishbourne informed the justice of the peace, and Higley was fined $50. To contest the fine, Erastus retained the services of a highly respected lawyer in Springfield, Illinois, named Stephen Logan.

Williams, Orton, Preston's & Co. shelf clock, circa 1840. *Courtesy of New Hampshire Historical Society.*

Many regarded Stephen Logan as the most talented lawyer in Sangamon County, if not in all of Illinois. He was known to have mastered the art of convincing a jury of his side of the case, methodically crafting his arguments using facts favorable to his client. In 1841, tired of traveling from town to town on the Eighth Judicial Circuit, Stephen looked to hire a junior law partner and reached out to young Abraham Lincoln, who was then working with John Todd Stuart in Springfield. As early as 1832, Lincoln had impressed Stephen with his acuity and superior speaking ability. Though Logan noted that Abe was "a very tall and gawky and rough looking fellow,"[20] all that mattered to Stephen was Lincoln's intellect. Abraham Lincoln jumped at the chance to work with Logan, knowing he would learn a great deal from him.

Abe proved to be a natural in court who, as Stephen Logan remembered, "put himself at once on an equality with everybody."[21] When Lincoln joined in partnership with Logan in 1841, Erastus Higley had just lost at the circuit court level and the case was on appeal to the Illinois Supreme

Court. According to Dan Bannister, a Lincoln scholar who studied Illinois Supreme Court cases of the period, the future U.S. president had at least some involvement in *all* of the cases argued by Logan's firm before the Illinois Supreme Court, which would have included the Erastus Higley case. Hence, Chester had some basis for asserting that he and his uncle, or at least their employee, had been represented by Abraham Lincoln.

When Logan and Lincoln were getting ready to try the Higley case before the Illinois Supreme Court, they were prepared to forcefully argue that the Williams, Orton, Preston's & Co. clocks were, in fact, produced in the state of Illinois since they did not come from Connecticut completed—they had to be assembled in Alton. At trial in January 1842, they ended up winning the case for Higley on a technicality, the court ruling that the action should have been brought in the name of Fishbourne and not on behalf of the people of the State of Illinois. No matter, Logan and Lincoln won the case.

However, even before the Illinois Supreme Court decided the Erastus Higley case, the firm of Williams, Orton, Preston's & Co. had run into financial difficulty. The principals of the company, along with Chester Woodford and Joseph Bishop, were defendants in a lawsuit for failure to pay a promissory note due in June 1841, and to settle the debt, the clock manufacturing firm assigned its assets for the benefit of the note issuer.

Left: Stephen Logan. *Illinois Historical Society.*

Right: Abraham Lincoln, by Alexander Gardner. *Library of Congress.*

The lawsuit convinced Chester Woodford that it was time to get out of the business. Fortunately for him, Erastus Higley, emboldened by his victory at the Illinois Supreme Court, was willing to take over as a partner of Bishop, Woodford & Co., allowing Chester to exit the venture. In March 1842, Chester Woodford was back in Connecticut when Joseph Bishop wrote to him telling him that he, too, was selling his interest in the sales firm to Erastus, ending his involvement.

It is unclear whether Chester or Joseph had to liquidate any of their personal assets to settle their debts, but by the summer of 1842, the pair were back in Avon for good, returning to their lives as farmers. Finally, in August 1846, Erastus Higley, still living and working in Illinois, sent a final distribution to the two, officially ending their days as clock peddlers.

Chester's version of his clock peddling story was that, unsure of what to do when he was accused of selling clocks illegally, he saw a sign on a shingle that said "Abraham Lincoln, Lawyer."[22] Deciding he liked the sound of the name, he asked Abe to handle his case. But while Lincoln worked in the Stuart and Lincoln partnership from 1837 to 1841 and then with Logan and Lincoln from 1841 to 1844, he never practiced law as a sole proprietor.

Without a record of a case involving Chester Woodford or Joseph Bishop directly, perhaps Chester's account of the story can't be refuted entirely. But there is no indication that the Erastus Higley suit was a particular threshold case that helped launch Abe Lincoln's career. In a legend, however, the argument works just fine.

Chester told many a newspaper reporter that he had corresponded with Abraham Lincoln and claimed to have saved a few letters from Honest Abe. Unfortunately, after Chester died, his daughters inadvertently threw out the letters during a spring cleaning at the Woodford Farm on Nod Road. And with the loss of those letters was the loss of the full picture of Chester's interaction with Lincoln.

While the nature and extent to which Chester benefited from Abraham Lincoln's wise counsel is unclear, he nonetheless showed the wisdom of his age. When asked how he managed to live to be a centenarian, Chester was quoted as saying: "If you wish to live long, keep your mind free from worry."[23] Wise counsel indeed.

PART II

HOOCH AND HORRORS ON HUCKLEBERRY HILL

4

DISTILLER OF WHORTLEBERRY HILL

Romanta Woodruff

Not yet married a year to his bride Esther Hinman, twenty-one-year-old Romanta Woodruff of Whortleberry Hill was cautiously optimistic in the waning summer of 1809. When Esther fell ill in the spring, she had traveled back to the Hinman family home in Hartford to recuperate. Benefiting from the warm summer weather, she recovered enough to join Romanta on the farm by early fall. But with the arrival of autumn, Esther's condition deteriorated, and on October 2, their first wedding anniversary, Romanta called for the doctor, telling him that Esther was "very sick,"[24] suffering from a severe headache. As her condition declined further, Romanta's hopes waned, and by early November it became clear that she would not recover. To ease her suffering, the doctor advised giving Esther laudanum, a tincture of opium, every hour, and on November 7, 1809, Esther passed away at age twenty-one. Romanta lamented, "This day a widower; a day of trial

Romanta Woodruff, by Samuel Broadbent, 1819. *Connecticut Museum of Culture and History, gift of Charles E. Bissel.*

and affliction. My wife with the dropsy of the head expired about [eight] o'clock. She died like the withering of a flower…oh, the sting of parting."[25]

Premature death of a family member was experienced by nearly everyone in the early 1800s, yet life went on. As Charlotte Cowles, a young Farmington woman of the time, put it, "Oh the world is full of suffering, and yet every scene of gayety and festivity goes on as if there were no such thing as death—as if we had never heard of sorrow."[26]

After about a year of mourning, on January 7, 1811, Romanta met twenty-two-year-old Hannah Robbins of Wethersfield, and after visiting her again in April, they began a courtship that continued through the summer. The relationship grew stronger during the month of August, and on October 3, 1811, a few days after his twenty-fourth birthday, Romanta noted in his diary: "was married to Miss Hannah Robbins exceedingly pleasant and a very large and agreeable company of both sexes."[27] Hannah and Romanta would raise nine children together, giving the name Esther to their first daughter.

Hannah Robbins Woodruff, by Samuel Broadbent, 1819. *Connecticut Museum of Culture and History, gift of Charles E. Bissel.*

Before they married in the fall, Romanta's father, John Woodruff, built a house on present-day Edwards Road as a wedding present, and with its three hundred acres, Romanta had plenty of land for his farm. In the early 1800s, the land west of present-day Huckleberry Hill Road was part of the West Britain Ecclesiastical Society, a parish within Burlington until it was annexed by Avon in 1845. Much of Romanta's land was within that parish.

While Romanta worked hard to maintain the farm, his favorite activity, as much a pastime as a job, was operating his distillery. Located in present-day Countryside Park between Edwards Road and the dam that separates the upper and lower ponds, the distillery had its own mill and produced hard cider and brandy that Romanta brought himself to Hartford, Wethersfield and other towns for sale. Before the Farmington Canal opened in 1828, those who traveled by stagecoach on the Albany Turnpike stopped about every ten miles to exchange horses and partake of a beverage at a local tavern, often apple brandy, Romanta's specialty.

Commissioned as a sergeant in the Fifteenth Connecticut Infantry, Romanta weathered the hardships of life on a farm. Once he survived being dragged nearly four hundred yards when his horse fell through ice and Romanta's foot got caught, "hung fast in the stirrup."[28] Active in the community, he cultivated relationships with many business partners to sell his cider and brandy. He exported apples and butternuts "to sell them in the West Indies"[29] and, in return, imported sugar, molasses and rum that was produced by enslaved labor in the Caribbean. In his business dealings, Romanta bemoaned that he had to bear "some losses and some crosses,"[30] referencing the old Puritan adage.

Though Romanta was certainly industrious and worked long hours, the Woodruffs were clearly part of the upper class of society, often traveling to social functions in neighboring towns as well as inviting guests to their home. On the second floor of their house, the Woodruffs hosted family and friends in their own ballroom, and it soon became known as the social center of the western district of town.

As his distillery business grew, it became increasingly difficult for Romanta to manage both his farm and his distillery. Shortly before his marriage to Hannah, Romanta secured the services of a biracial young man named Henry Fairchild, who was bound to Romanta until he reached the age of twenty-one.

Given the indenture agreement was dated June 7, 1810, when Henry was not yet three years old, it raises questions about how this arrangement came to be. Henry was the son of a woman named Sume, who may have been a Native American woman whom Reverend Hawley attended to before she passed away in May 1807. Assuming Sume died in childbirth, it would explain why Henry was an orphan at age three. Orphaned children were often indentured to other families in early America, although it is also possible that Romanta was Henry's father.

In any event, Henry Fairchild worked diligently and faithfully for Romanta for many years. While shy, he was always courteous, with "a good disposition."[31] With his slender build, the hard manual labor on the farm was toilsome and even dangerous for Henry, and one day he badly injured his left leg just above the ankle.

Then, on a day in July 1826, just two years shy of reaching his twenty-first birthday, Henry left Woodruff's farm on Whortleberry Hill without notice. He walked away with only the clothes he was wearing—a vest and pantaloons covered by a well-worn "broadcloth coat."[32] Perhaps Henry was trying to escape harsh treatment or had gotten into an argument with Romanta. Whatever the case, leaving the Woodruff farm was a huge risk for him. If captured, indentured servants could have their period of servitude extended or be prosecuted under the law.

Concerned and angry, on July 31, 1826, Romanta placed an advertisement on the first page of the *Connecticut Courant* offering a reward to "whoever will apprehend said boy and return him to me" or to "whoever shall give information where he can be found."[33] And then Romanta gave a warning at the end of his plea that made it clear that indentured servants were treated much like enslaved people: "All persons are forbid harboring or trusting said boy by penalty of the law."[34] Whatever happened to Henry after he left is not known, but by 1830, he was no longer living with the Woodruffs on Whortleberry Hill.

After Romanta died in 1837, Hannah Robbins Woodruff continued to live on the farm with her children, transferring title of the farm and distillery to her adult son Daniel in 1844. Life was quiet on the farm, and not much of consequence happened on Whortleberry Hill until one day in July 1845 when Hannah's next-door neighbor, Sarah Walker, knocked on the front door. Terror-stricken and out of breath, Sarah was in shock as she hurriedly explained to Hannah that there was word of an unspeakable crime at a neighbor's house down the road. On hearing the news, Hannah told her adult sons Daniel and Martin, and they sprinted to the scene.

5

THE INSANITY OF IT ALL

The Murder of Diana Derrin Woodford

While Orrin Woodford generally got along fine with the residents of Whortleberry Hill, his closest neighbors knew that something wasn't quite right in the Woodford household. As summer approached in 1845, Orrin was becoming unstable, and his wife, Diana, bore the brunt of it. At eleven o'clock on a warm night in mid-June, neighbor Sarah Walker was awakened by a knock on the door. It was Orrin Woodford, imploring her to come to his house down the road. Worried, he told her he had thrown his wife, Diana, to the floor and was afraid she might die from her injuries. Sarah knew this was not the first incident, and Orrin apologized profusely to her, urging Sarah to come with him. She hesitated, afraid to go alone with such a violent man late at night. But her husband, who evidently couldn't be bothered, encouraged her to help.

When Sarah arrived at the Woodford home, she was shocked by Diana's condition, "her face badly bruised and swollen, and her eye badly hurt." When Diana told Sarah that her husband had kicked her, Orrin said to Diana, "Ma, you ought to hide my faults." Exasperated and in pain, Diana replied that she had lied for Orrin long enough. Sarah stayed with her all through the night, with Diana confiding that "when he was Orrin Woodford, he was as kind a man as any woman need to live with; but when he was rum and cider, his conduct showed what he was."[35] The next day, a penitent Orrin promised Sarah Walker he would never abuse Diana again.

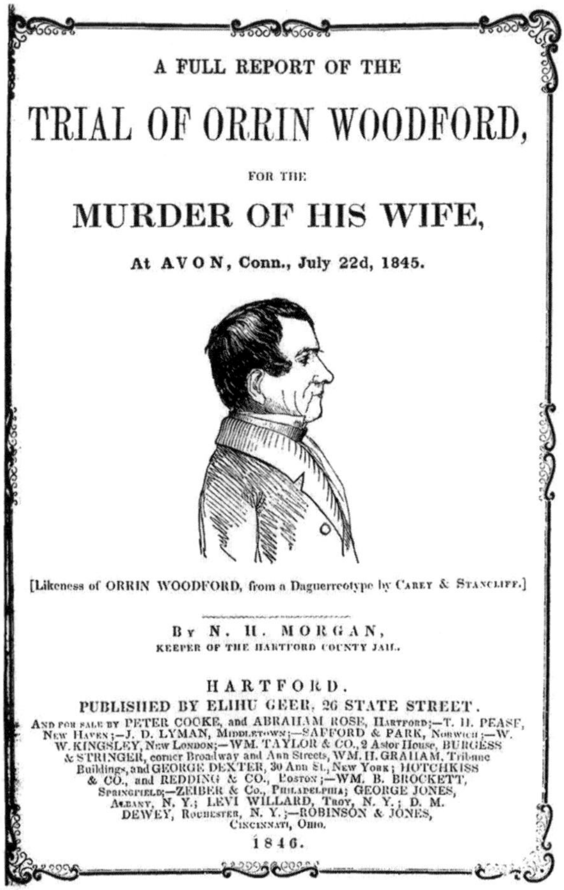

A FULL REPORT OF THE

TRIAL OF ORRIN WOODFORD,

FOR THE

MURDER OF HIS WIFE,

At AVON, Conn., July 22d, 1845.

[Likeness of ORRIN WOODFORD, from a Daguerreotype by Carey & Stancliff.]

By N. H. MORGAN,
KEEPER OF THE HARTFORD COUNTY JAIL.

HARTFORD.
PUBLISHED BY ELIHU GEER, 26 STATE STREET.
And for sale by PETER COOKE, and ABRAHAM ROSE, Hartford;—T. H. PEASE, New Haven;—J. D. LYMAN, Middletown;—SAFFORD & PARK, Norwich;—W. W. KINGSLEY, New London;—WM. TAYLOR & CO., 2 Astor House, BURGESS & STRINGER, corner Broadway and Ann Streets, WM. H. GRAHAM, Tribune Buildings, and GEORGE DEXTER, 30 Ann St., New York; HOTCHKISS & CO., and REDDING & CO., Boston;—WM. B. BROCKETT, Springfield;—ZEIBER & Co., Philadelphia; GEORGE JONES, Albany, N. Y.; LEVI WILLARD, Troy, N. Y.; D. M. DEWEY, Rochester, N. Y.;—ROBINSON & JONES, Cincinnati, Ohio.
1846.

Orrin Woodford. *From* A Full Report of the Trial of Orrin Woodford, *by N.H. Morgan.*

Orrin Woodford was the grandson of one of Huckleberry Hill's original landowners, John Woodford Jr., who owned and operated an inn on Whortleberry Hill Road in the late eighteenth century. By 1830, Orrin had married Diana Derrin, a descendant of a family that first settled in the Northington section of Farmington in the early 1700s. When they were first married, Orrin and Diana were living in the Satan's Kingdom area of New Hartford, and while there, Diana gave birth to their only child, Dan. Now with a family, Orrin and Diana wanted to find a new home and, in 1831, bought a house and farmland on present-day Huckleberry Hill Road near its intersection with Chevas Road. Orrin owned one of the best landholdings on the hill, with close proximity to Hawley Brook and the Farmington River to the west and access to Lovelytown to the east. Orrin and Diana raised their son, Dan, on the farm, and in 1845, when they were both forty-seven years old, they appeared to be a contented family, respected members of their church congregation. Active in politics, Orrin had been appointed as a delegate to the Whig Party state convention in 1842.

But Orrin was prone to excessive drinking, particularly hard cider, and when he drank, he began to envision things that were untrue. One day he carried an axe, hammer and chisel up the stairs of his house, saying he was going to dig for gold and silver. Jealous of his wife, Orrin hallucinated about Diana "entertaining"[36] groups of men from Collinsville in his absence who, he claimed, would wait for her in the currant bushes outside the house. When Orrin told Diana he was going to cut down the bushes, she said, "Cut them down then,"[37] knowing she was entirely innocent of the allegations.

Orrin was also physically abusive—the beating Diana took from him in mid-June left a mark over her eye "as big as a hen's egg," and she bore the bruises of repeated assaults.[38] While neighbors said that Orrin was usually well-mannered and acted rationally, he often became belligerent when drunk. He also inflicted psychological torture on Diana, with verbal abuse and false accusations. On a number of occasions, he tried to convince her that she was planning to poison his tea or liquor, later admitting to his son, Dan, that he "did it to plague her."[39] And in another instance, in 1844, when a kitten Diana liked ran under a cow that Orrin was milking and caused the cow to kick, Orrin killed the kitten and then threatened to do to Diana what he did to the cat.

On July 22, 1845, six weeks after the incident that left Diana Derrin Woodford badly beaten and needing care from her neighbor Sarah, Orrin planned to spend much of the day using his scythe and cradle to gather up oats. He had started out in the fields at nine o'clock in the morning, but in the middle of a heat wave, it wasn't long before the rising temperature and humidity became oppressive. As he often did, Orrin consumed eight to ten cups of hard cider in the morning and a similar amount in the afternoon. In the late morning, he told his thirteen-year-old son, Dan, to split wood and fix a fence. When done with the task, Dan dutifully returned the axe by the fireboard along the back wall of the kitchen.

Escaping the heat, around midafternoon, Orrin, Diana and Dan met in the house for dinner. After they finished eating, Orrin went across the road to sharpen his scythe at the grindstone, then put the scythe back in the cradle and said he would return to the fields. But it was still stifling hot out, and Orrin changed his mind.

Then about 4:30 p.m., when he and Diana were sitting in the "keeping" room at the front of the house, suddenly, the peace of the afternoon was shattered. Orrin once again began accusing Diana of infractions she did not commit. When she told him it was all in his imagination, Orrin slammed his fist on the table and raised his voice in anger, repeating the false accusations. Worried, Diana complained her head was aching from the bruises he had inflicted before. Orrin then told her he would make the next bruises deep, and he continued to impugn Diana for the next half hour.

At about five o'clock, Orrin instructed Dan to leave the house and drive the family's cattle away to watering. As Dan walked down the road toward Hawley Brook, worried about his mother, he turned back to see a distraught Diana sitting in the window. Half an hour later, when Dan was on his way back from Hawley Brook, he was about one hundred feet from the home when he heard two or three heavy blows coming from the house that sounded like an axe or hammer struck against a wall. Indeed, Orrin had violently attacked Diana again.

As Dan approached the house, his father, Orrin, walked outside to the front gate with blood splattered on his hat and pantaloons. Orrin calmly stated that he thought he may have just killed Diana, telling the boy, "[I] must be hung."[40] Dan was struck with horror and started toward the house. Realizing the consequences of what he had just done, Orrin offered Dan one hundred dollars to convince him that he did not need to go into the house.

Knowing he needed to do something, Dan then told his father he was going to head up to neighbor Nancy Hawley's house to get help. Orrin told him not to, but Dan insisted, knowing the situation was urgent. When he got to the Hawley homestead, Nancy told him to go next door to the Walkers. There he met Sarah Walker, who had aided Diana six weeks earlier. Trembling with fear, Dan collapsed on the steps of Sarah's home, telling her what had happened. With no one else in her house who could help, Sarah headed over to Hannah Woodruff's, as she knew Hannah's two adult sons were there.

On hearing the news, Hannah's sons, Martin and Daniel, rushed to Orrin's house as fast as they could. When they got there, Orrin told them he was a "dead man" and would "give up."[41] Pushing his way past Orrin, Martin walked into the kitchen, and there in the corner, by a table and basket of clean clothes, was Diana, lying on her back on the floor in a pool of blood. She was gasping but still alive, and Martin frantically told Dan to fetch a doctor.

When Nancy Hawley, Sarah Walker and Hannah Woodruff came to the house moments later, the three confronted Orrin, and Sarah scolded him for breaking his promise not to abuse Diana again. Orrin replied, "Mrs. Walker, when I done that I was as insane as a man could be."[42] Hannah Woodruff was perturbed by Orrin's reaction, telling him, "You need not try to make me think you are insane; you are no more insane than I am; if you are, cider and rum has made it.[43]

After entering the house, the three women along with the Woodruff brothers brought Diana to the bedroom. A short time later, Orrin walked back in and asked, "Is this Diana?" Sarah responded, "You know it is," to which Orrin replied, "I am sure it is not Diana," then turned and left the house.[44] Just fifteen minutes after she was placed in bed, Diana breathed her last breath.

A few minutes after Orrin was told his wife was dead, he turned to his neighbor Edward Cowles and told him, "Diana isn't dead, she is in the house well enough."[45] Despite originally confessing to his son and to the Woodruff brothers, Orrin now claimed he knew nothing of what had happened.

Running with haste, two doctors from Collinsville, including Samuel Brown, arrived on the scene along with about one hundred residents from Whortleberry Hill, Unionville and Collinsville. Dr. Brown found several grisly wounds on Diana's body, including one large one on the left side of her head that looked like it was caused by the blow from the head of an axe and a four-and-a-half-inch-long gash in her stomach. The doctor noted Orrin's anxious state and later testified that he couldn't tell if Orrin's apparent insanity that evening was real or feigned. As the town sheriff could not be found for several hours, neighborhood residents held Orrin captive with ropes, restraining him all that night. The next day, Orrin was arrested and brought to jail, where he was held pending a trial.

Three months later, in October 1845, Orrin Woodford was indicted for the murder of his wife, Diana Derrin Woodford, and he pleaded not guilty by reason of insanity. The insanity defense first arose as a legal concept in England in 1843, and the trial of Orrin Woodford would be one of the first cases to test the defense in the United States.

Dan Woodford, later in life. *From the* Hartford Courant.

At the trial, which took place in February 1846, some testified that they had seen Orrin drinking hard cider on the day he killed Diana and that his actions were nothing more than a drunken rage. However, Dr. John S. Butler, superintendent of the Retreat for the Insane in Hartford, concluded that Orrin "beating his wife to make her acknowledge guilt is evidence of insanity." In his remarks, Dr. Butler claimed that Orrin suffered from mania and hallucinations and that "insanity often induces…a craving for liquor and tobacco." He further argued that Orrin suffered from "monomania," meaning that while he appeared rational most of the time, he was obsessed with one topic—in this case, a specific delusion about his wife being unfaithful. Dr. Butler concluded that Orrin's history of hallucinations showed that he was, in fact, insane. As to insanity, Butler claimed, "I never knew it feigned."[46]

While Dr. Butler was convinced of Orrin's insanity, the prosecutor, T.C. Perkins, asserted that Orrin had full possession of his senses, as evident from his confession just after the murder. He also cited the testimony from Sarah Walker that Diana herself found Orrin dangerous only when he was drinking too much. Perkins reminded the jury that Orrin Woodford told Sarah Walker he had frequently abused his wife and asked Diana "not to expose his faults."[47] Was not this evidence that Orrin was fully aware of his actions?

As the trial concluded on Wednesday, February 4, 1846, the judge instructed the jury that if they found the defendant was insane at the time of the killing, they could not convict him of murder. After deliberating for three hours, the jury was unable to agree on a conviction of murder. Instead, they came back with a verdict of manslaughter, and Orrin Woodford was sentenced to ten years in prison.

Many people were not satisfied with the verdict, believing Orrin should have been hanged for the crime, and others argued that capital punishment laws made juries reluctant to reach guilty verdicts. Still others thought the verdict was a reasonable compromise. All agreed the jury had been presented with an unusual case. As it turned out, the verdict ensured that

Orrin Woodford would not see freedom again. He died in prison on March 26, 1855, about a year shy of serving his full ten-year term.

Fifty-six years after Diana's murder, the Woodford house on Huckleberry Hill Road was bought by William "Fritz" Schumann and his wife, Matilda, who would turn the home into a summer boardinghouse that welcomed guests on vacation from New York City. They offered their visitors authentic German cuisine and access down to the Farmington River for fishing and swimming. Few, if any, knew of the home's notorious past, and in the 1930s, Schumann's boardinghouse, once the scene of a grisly murder, was rumored to be a nudist colony.

6

THOSE RECURRING NIGHTMARES

Orson Woodford

Forty-year-old Whortleberry Hill farmer Orson Woodford, cousin of Orrin Woodford, looked forward to the day as he awoke on the morning of Sunday, April 22, 1855. Sunday was a welcome break from the everyday routine of planting crops, tending to his orchards and sawing timbers. But Orson was feeling unsettled as he sat down to eat breakfast that morning. The night before, his sleep was interrupted by the most frightening dream he ever had. In the nightmare, vivid and harrowing, Orson had a vision of being badly hurt by his circular saw.

Orson Woodford lived along Whortleberry Hill Road near the intersection of present-day Huckleberry Hill and Verville Roads. Built in 1784, his home was one of the houses constructed by Orson's grandfather John Woodford Jr.

Perhaps Orson brushed off the nightmare on that Sunday morning as he and his wife, Cornelia, looked forward to the Sabbath, resting before a busy week ahead. As the weather had warmed up after a cold winter, he knew that April was a good time to work outside with his circular saw cutting wood. Still waiting for the last frost so he could plant his crops, Orson was likely planning to saw lumber from timbers, and he resolved to get to that work in the coming week.

After he went to bed on Sunday night, however, he had the same haunting nightmare and became more troubled when he awoke on Monday morning. So vivid was the dream, he mentioned it to his wife, Cornelia. As he went to bed on the evening of Monday, April 23, Orson hoped the nightmare would not return. But return it did, and when he arose the next morning on April 24, he said to Cornelia, "I had the same ugly dream last night."[48] And then Orson Woodford headed outside to cut wood, possibly with his son William, who was fourteen at the time.

Common in the mid-nineteenth century, the circular saw that Orson used was powered by a horse that walked on a treadmill. The forward motion of the horse powered the turning of the arbor or shaft located at the head of the treadmill, and on the other end of the arbor, the circular saw was affixed by a bolt, or arbor nut. Horse-powered tools could be used for many jobs, such as grinding corn or grain and for pumping water for irrigation from a nearby stream or pond. On this day, Orson planned to use his horse-powered saw to cut timber. As he got to work on the morning of April 24, 1855, Orson led his bay horse onto the wood-slatted platform of the treadmill. When he disengaged the brake, his horse began to walk, giving power to the saw. He then laid down logs on a rail and began feeding them into the path of his circular saw.

Whether his nightmares caused Orson to check on the working condition of his circular saw on that Tuesday morning is not known, but later in the morning, the unthinkable happened. As Orson was feeding logs into the circular saw, the shaft that turned the blade suddenly broke free from its

Horse-powered saw. *Sam Moore of Farm Collector.*

housing, flying into Orson's right arm. In an instant, the blade struck near the elbow, almost severing his forearm.

He no doubt screamed and called for either William or his wife, Cornelia, to help. Presumably, a tourniquet was applied to stop the bleeding, and Orson was brought to lie down. While efforts were made to try to comfort him, unfortunately, the wound would prove fatal, though it would take twelve agonizing hours before he passed away.

One of the causes of a catastrophic failure of a circular saw is the loosening of the blade due to misalignment or damage to the blade, a loose arbor nut, worn arbor bearings or damage to the arbor itself. As either Orson or a witness explained right after the accident, "The saw caught in a crooked stick and was torn with the shaft from its fastenings."[49] A piece of wood or stick may have jammed against the shaft, causing it to break, projecting the spinning blade into Orson's arm and resulting in catastrophic injury.

The tragedy was hard on the family. Cornelia and her daughter Ellen ended up moving to New Britain, Connecticut, and Cornelia later remarried. Before he turned twenty, Cornelia's son William moved to Montgomery, Alabama, and later enlisted in the Confederate army in 1863 at age twenty-two. The probate record of Orson's estate listed the real estate and personal possessions typical for a farmer of the day: his eighty-five-acre farm, two bay horses, a plow and house furnishings. Then, at the end of the estate inventory, was a solemn reminder of the tragedy—cords of lumber and "part of" a sawing and threshing machine.[50]

PART III

SLAVERY, ABOLITION AND THE CIVIL WAR

7

A MATTER OF CONSCIENCE

David Bartlett Takes a Stand

In July 1850, twenty-two-year-old David W. Bartlett was incredulous about the reprimand he was facing from the West Avon Congregational Church. Given his church's refusal to take an unequivocal stance against slavery, all he had asked for was to withdraw his membership. His church, however, refused to let him leave on his own terms, insisting that "by repentance & confession"[51] he admit the error of his ways.

Well before David made his request for withdrawal in May 1850, he had become an abolitionist and decided he could no longer tolerate a church that tacitly accepted the institution of slavery. What infuriated him most of all was that one of the members at West Avon, Shubael Tillotson, was an enslaver, an insult to all that David thought his church should represent.

David W. Bartlett. *Bartlett Family Collection.*

While he knew in his heart that withdrawing his church membership was the right thing to do, it was certainly an audacious request. The son of Reverend John Bartlett and his wife, Jane, David and his siblings were expected to attend church regularly. His father had recently stepped down as pastor of the West Avon Congregational Church, and the family continued to worship every Sunday, listening to the sermons of John Bartlett's appointed successor, the Reverend Joel Grant.

Nonetheless, David was resolute in his convictions. He could not look past the fact that the very same church that taught him to love his neighbor as himself refused to condemn slavery. To David Bartlett, not only was slavery wrong and must be proscribed, but also more actions were needed to stop the practice. So he resolved to leave the church of his upbringing. In May 1850, David sent a letter to Reverend Grant explaining why he wanted to withdraw, stating succinctly that the church leadership "had not acted as he thought they ought concerning slavery."[52] As he would soon find out, however, David was going up against an institution that excelled at disciplining its members.

Born in 1828, David Bartlett moved to West Avon at age seven when his father, John, became pastor of the West Avon Congregational Church. Reverend John Bartlett, a graduate of Yale College, was known to be "brilliant in conversation" and "few excelled him in the art of telling a story in a terse, witty and vivid manner."[53] David clearly inherited the same attributes. After attending the Avon Academy next to the Avon Congregational Church, David took an interest in writing and began contributing to local newspapers while still a teenager.

Then, between 1845 and 1846, when David was just seventeen or eighteen years old, a man named Elihu Burritt from New Britain, Connecticut, took notice of his writing talent and asked David to come work with him in Worcester, Massachusetts. Burritt had just started a newspaper called the *Christian Citizen*, a publication devoted to the causes of abolition, temperance and world peace. David, who met Burritt through his older brother John, jumped at the opportunity. Elihu, known as the "Learned Blacksmith," was a pacifist, and soon after David joined the *Christian Citizen*, Burritt traveled to England, where he formed an international society known as the League of Universal Brotherhood. Elihu's society was devoted to "the abolition of all institutions and customs which do not recognize and respect the image of God and a human brother in every man, of whatever clime, color, or condition of humanity."[54]

While Burritt was lecturing in Europe, David Bartlett decided to start up his own publication in Connecticut with help from a reform-minded minister named William Burleigh. In September 1847, at age nineteen, he

Elihu Burritt. *From* Elihu Burritt: A Memorial Volume, *by Charles A.M. Northen.*

became editor of a magazine in Hartford called *The Nonpareil, a Monthly Journal of Thoughts, Fancies, Facts and Opinions*. The magazine included poems, book reviews and other human-interest stories, and as editor of this publication, David gained valuable experience.

Elihu Burritt then wrote to David from England, asking him to join him there and serve as his private secretary. Excited by the offer, in the fall of 1847, David sailed with his cousin Rufus Reynolds to Europe, where he stayed for about one year supporting Burritt. Returning to Avon in the fall of 1848, David got a job as a journalist and was living in Avon in May 1850 when he made his request to Reverend Grant to withdraw his membership from the church.

At about the same time that David was working with Elihu Burritt, the abolitionist movement was gaining momentum, and churchgoers were among the most ardent in their opposition to slavery. Spurred, in part, by William Lloyd Garrison's publication of *The Liberator* and the formation of the American Anti-Slavery Society in 1833, many religious adherents in the North became strident abolitionists. This subjected them to attacks from angry mobs who claimed that antislavery advocates were undermining national unity. Despite the hostility they faced, many churchgoers in northern states increasingly believed that slavery in the South was inconsistent with their faith and incompatible with the nation's founding principle that all people are created equal and have the unalienable right to life, liberty and the pursuit of happiness. In 1848, three months before David left to work for Burritt in London, the State of Connecticut passed "An Act to prevent Slavery" that prohibited any people from being held in slavery in the state, including bringing any enslaved people to "be left, or sold."[55]

Reverend Joel Grant's congregation was divided on the cause of abolition. Just as fervent as antislavery parishioners were in wanting the church to

Reverend Joel Grant. *Courtesy of American Antiquarian Society.*

speak out against the practice of slavery, another faction of his congregation did not want him to take such a strong pro-abolition stance.

Undoubtedly, Grant pondered carefully what to do about David Bartlett's request to withdraw, especially since he was the son of the church's former minister. After contemplating his options, Joel Grant decided that he and Deacon Carlos Day would meet with David and offer to recommend him to another church that did not have any enslavers among its members, such as the Avon Congregational Church in East Avon. That same year, Grant had given David's mother, Jane, and younger sister, Julia, permission to transfer to the East Avon church given their own objection to the West Avon church's stance on Shubael Tillotson. David, however, continued to insist on withdrawal. When he met with Reverend Grant and Deacon Day on July 5, 1850, he made it clear that he had no interest in transferring to another church. In response, the church membership passed a resolution admonishing David:

> *Whereas David W. Bartlett a member of this Church has signified to us his withdrawal from us avowedly because the church takes no action with respect to that which he judges a matter of discipline & whereas he declares that in making such a withdrawal he has no intention to connect himself with any branch of the Church of Christ....Resolved that such an act is powerless to dissolve the natural relation between him and us; & consequently, he is still under our watch & care & is still subject to our discipline precisely as are all members who violate the rules of Church obligation....*
>
> *Resolved therefore that David W. Bartlett be, & he hereby is, suspended from the privileges of church membership until by repentance & confession he shall give us warrant to restore him to them, or until we shall have reason to take further steps in a course of discipline.*[56]

Since its inception as the Second Ecclesiastical Society of Farmington in 1751, the West Avon Congregational Church had routinely disciplined members who did not show up for church on Sundays, and Grant was determined that David would not be treated any differently.

Suspended from membership and ostracized by his church community, twenty-two-year-old David Bartlett took a job as a foreign correspondent for American newspapers in England, with his cousin Rufus Reynolds joining him once again. They set sail for Liverpool and then took a train to London, where David spent the next year in the capital city, visiting not only "abodes of wealth and splendor" but also "the haunts of the poor and down-trodden."[57]

One day, David and Rufus ventured into the eastern part of the city, an area called the Spitalfields, where David was horrified at the abject poverty he witnessed: obnoxious smells, crowded dwellings, prostitution, frequent robberies and constant hunger. His "blood ran cold" at the sight of the "horrible wretchedness." He noted that the vast difference in living conditions of the wealthy and the poor in London was "a great gulf almost like that between heaven and hell."[58]

His trip to the Spitalfields reinforced his view about the need to uplift the human race. As David summed it up, "Everything which tends to raise the civil position of the *whole* people of any country, adds to the comfort, sobriety and religious fervor of that people, and everything that tends to depress the masses in their civil rights, adds to their woe, vice and wretchedness. Give to a body of men their civil rights, and you will add to their dignity of character, and they will strive earnestly to be worthy of their position."[59] David's experience in Europe had instilled in him a determination to fight for the oppressed.

His time in London only reinforced his conviction to withdraw his membership from the West Avon Congregational Church, and when he returned to Avon in the summer of 1851, he refused to attend Sunday worship. Through the autumn of that year, Deacon Day made several visits to David's home, imploring him to confess his sins and reminding him of his obligation to attend church. When David told the deacon he was not attending due to his suspension, Carlos Day reported back to Grant that David would "not attend public worship at all alleging as a reason that he was under censure by this church."[60]

Disappointed with David's response, in January 1852, Reverend Grant persuaded the church membership to pass a resolution requiring Bartlett to appear at the next regular meeting of the church, scheduled for February 13. David refused to appear, however, and did not comply with a summons to attend subsequent meetings on March 2 and April 30. Not surprisingly,

David did not heed any of the requests, with Grant later remarking that any time the church sent a letter to him on the matter, David "would destroy it without giving it a perusal."[61]

Grant was adamant that Bartlett's antislavery sentiment was no reason for failing to attend church, stating, "For two years, or nearly that time, you have been entirely separated (according to your own avowal) from this church [and] you have not sought union with another though both in this country and in Europe there are many which accord with you in the particulars respecting which you complain of this church." But David remained defiant, believing the church had "no more control over [me] than the State of South Carolina."[62]

With David refusing to appear as requested, a motion was made by Deacon Day at the April 30 meeting to excommunicate David Bartlett. Thirteen male members voted to excommunicate. Just one, Isaac Baldwin, who lived at the northern end of present-day West Avon Road, voted nay. Enslaver Shubael Tillotson abstained.

The distinction between excommunication and withdrawal was important to Reverend Grant, as the church viewed excommunication as another step in demanding that the sinner recognize their error and repent so they could once again receive communion. Anyone excommunicated at the time faced harsh judgment from members of the community. The West Avon church was not going to let David Bartlett go away quietly, and in the end, his resolve to stand up for what he knew was right had cost him the censorship of his church.

With his ties to the Congregational Church severed, David went on to do what he could to support the cause of abolition. Shortly thereafter, in December 1852, he and his younger brother Henry purchased the *Hartford Republican* newspaper, an antislavery, free-soil paper that later merged with the *Hartford Evening Press*. David was named editor in chief of the *Evening Press* and, in 1854, began serving in Washington, D.C., as a correspondent for the *New York Independent*, another pro-abolition newspaper. In September 1854, David married Julia Painter of Milford, Connecticut, and he and Julia would end up being together for fifty-eight years, raising a family of four children.

Affected by the depravity of the underprivileged he had witnessed, David Bartlett admired the reformers of his day, writing a book in 1855 called *Modern Agitators: or, Pen Portraits of Living American Reformers*. Through his descriptions of these social reformers, David gave a clear picture of his own thoughts on slavery and abolition. Of William Lloyd Garrison, he said, "The same devotion to human liberty which Garrison…manifested,

David W. Bartlett. *From the* Springfield Republican.

when displayed by the actors in the drama of the American revolution, caused a thrill of animation the world over; but when evinced on behalf of the down-trodden African, it assumes the name of fanaticism. We have no more doubt that fifty years hence the name of Garrison will be revered by the American nation, than we have of the ultimate overthrow of human slavery in this country."[63]

In discussing Frederick Douglass, Bartlett noted his strong intellect and brilliant oration, adding that Douglass was proof that Black people could "rise to an equality with the whites."[64] This put David well ahead of his time, as many white Americans did not think Black people could ever live in equal standing with whites.

In 1857, Bartlett was invited by Dr. Gamaliel Bailey to become assistant editor of the *National Era*, an abolitionist newspaper in Washington, D.C. Published in a jurisdiction where slavery was still legal, the *National Era* was the only free-soil newspaper in the nation's capital and was often subject to harassment for denouncing slavery. When Gamaliel Bailey died in 1859, David left the *National Era* and began serving as Washington, D.C. correspondent for the *New York Evening Post* and the *Springfield Republican.* In 1860, he was one of the few pro-abolition correspondents remaining in the nation's capital. David's time in Washington, D.C., put him on the front lines of the abolitionist movement and soon near the front lines of a war.

After reporting on the Civil War and later supporting his brother's business back in Avon, he continued as a journalist for the *Springfield Republican*, going by the pen name "Van."[65] Then in 1875, at the suggestion of a family member, David left journalism to serve as American secretary of the Chinese Legation, or embassy, in Washington, D.C. David Bartlett's story is remarkable. A man of conviction, he bravely defied the conventional wisdom of his elders.

8

AN INGLORIOUS COMPROMISE

Reverend Wright's Dilemma

Just six months after David Bartlett was excommunicated, Reverend Joel Grant decided it was time for a change. He had once served in the ministry in Illinois, and on October 3, 1852, he informed his West Avon congregation that he had accepted a call to serve as pastor of a Congregational church in Lockport, Illinois, thirty-five miles southwest of Chicago. In February 1853, two months after Joel Grant and his wife, Abigail, left for Illinois, a council of area ministers was convened, and all agreed that Reverend William S. Wright would be a suitable replacement as pastor of the West Avon church. Originally from Wethersfield, Connecticut, Wright would eventually serve as minister in South Glastonbury, but in 1853, the West Avon congregation was grateful to install him as their preacher.

On joining the church, Reverend Wright heard of the rancor caused by David Bartlett's attempt to withdraw his membership a year earlier, and he clearly hoped to instill harmony in the church once again. But with antislavery sentiment continuing to increase, in April 1854, a group of twenty-one parishioners from First Church of Christ, Congregational, in Farmington under Reverend Noah Porter sent a letter to the West Avon church demanding that they excommunicate enslaver Shubael Tillotson. In their letter, the Farmington parishioners insisted that Reverend Wright "take the prescribed steps of Christian Discipline" in order "that so great a reproach may be taken from the Christian name."[66]

When Reverend Wright did not respond, the Farmington church members then asked their pastor, Reverend Noah Porter, to send a letter on behalf of the Farmington church with the same request. Porter was facing the same divisiveness in his church that Reverend Grant, and now Reverend Wright, was dealing with in West Avon. Half of his parishioners were adamant that slavery was inconsistent with the teachings of Christ, and the other half insisted that no professed Christian, including a law-abiding enslaver, should be denied the taking of communion.

In August 1854, Porter sent a letter to his former colleague in West Avon, retired Reverend John Bartlett, that repeated the arguments made by Farmington church members in April. Tillotson, Porter asserted, "avowedly justifies the system of slavery as it is established by the laws of the Southern…states," while such an institution is clearly "contrary to the principles of the Gospel—particularly the great law of the Redeemer's kingdom 'Thou shalt love thy neighbor as thyself.'" Noah Porter was strident on the evils of slavery, adding that "we are especially bound as Christians to have no fellowship" with the "crying sins of our land." Pointedly appealing to the West Avon church, he asserted, "We cannot doubt that in this, you are of the same mind & the same judgement, with us." However, Porter gave West Avon some wriggle room. He recognized that "there may be some…peculiar cases in which a person may for a time & in some modified sense, sustain the relation of a slave-holder, consistently with the christian profession."[67] Porter was nonetheless clear in his letter to John Bartlett: in his view, Reverend Wright was duty bound to perform an examination of the Tillotson case and respond.

Only a year into William Wright's ministry, the reverend found himself in a very uncomfortable position. The issue of slavery could not be put to rest.

In the early 1820s, looking for adventure and a way to earn money, four sons of Elias Tillotson, a farmer on Lovely Street in Avon, banded together to form a partnership selling shelf clocks. The brothers—Giles, Shubael, Oliver and Romanta—made their way across both northern and southern states, traveling as far west as Ohio and as far south as Mississippi and Louisiana. Then in 1825, on behalf of all four brothers, Shubael Tillotson acquired a half interest in a cotton plantation that was a couple of miles from the Mississippi River in New River, Louisiana, near the town of Donaldsville in Ascension Parish. The Tillotson brothers would come to own the plantation outright by May 1827 and, evidently, were not troubled by one unseemly fact about the operation—it made its money on slave labor.

Around 1828, the plantation changed crops from cotton to sugar, and after Giles and Oliver stopped participating, the partnership was renamed S.&R. Tillotson. The operation grew such that, by 1860, the plantation had 134 enslaved people. Enslaved laborers working on the sugar plantations faced hardship throughout the year. Sugar was grown in Louisiana's southernmost parishes, and the workers spent long hours planting, weeding, harvesting and grinding the raw sugarcane and then packing the crystallized sugar into wooden barrels known as hogsheads. In 1845 alone, S.&R. Tillotson produced 350 hogsheads of sugar, equivalent to over 22,000 gallons of sugar in liquid form.

Even compared to the ordinarily harsh conditions of southern slavery, sugar plantations were particularly dangerous, with enslaved workers suffering from cane knife lacerations, milling accidents and boiler explosions. After the Civil War, one former enslaved man of a Louisiana sugar plantation recalled, "It was a rare thing if a man lived from more than ten to twelve years of those who worked at the mill."[68] Because sugar was a particularly profitable crop, however, the Tillotson brothers were not about to give it up, whatever their misgivings might have been about the "peculiar institution."

While the Tillotsons were growing their plantation in Louisiana, the abolitionist movement was gaining strength in the North. Abolitionist members of the Farmington church had been outraged by slavery ever since hosting Mende Africans who commandeered the *Amistad* in 1841 to avoid being sold into slavery. The Mende had been detained in Connecticut while standing trial for mutiny and piracy, and when they were finally acquitted of the charges against them, abolitionists in Farmington offered to house them until they could return home to Africa. Thirty of the thirty-eight surviving Africans arrived in Farmington on March 18, 1841, and stayed with town residents for eight months.

Hosting the survivors of the *Amistad* did much to change perceptions of Black people in Farmington and surrounding towns and strengthened the abolitionist cause. Reverend Noah Porter and his wife housed a Mende girl named Margru, which no doubt reinforced Porter's views about the evils of slavery. Margru would later attend Oberlin College and become a mission schoolteacher in Sierra Leone. Antislavery sentiment was emboldened after the Fugitive Slave Act of 1850, which held northerners liable if they did not return fugitive slaves to their owners in the South. This infuriated abolitionists in the North and strengthened their resolve to fight for the end of slavery. Many of the fugitive enslaved people who arrived in Connecticut after 1850 passed through Farmington, which was then considered the "Grand Central Station"[69] of the Underground Railroad in the state. Some of these fugitives continued north into Massachusetts, passing through Avon.

Despite the strong pro-abolitionist sentiment among many in the congregation, the membership of the Farmington church was divided on the issue of slavery. When on February 10, 1842, the antislavery faction of the church adopted a resolution to ban enslavers from worship, a sizeable minority of the congregation believed that those parishioners who voted for the resolution were being "holier than thou"[70] and had no right to judge the Christian character of other adherents to the faith. Over the next eleven years, Farmington church members who opposed banning enslavers from attending church tried unsuccessfully to rescind the resolution and, in January 1853, filed a formal protest.

During the summer, Shubael and Romanta Tillotson would come back to Avon to escape the heat of Louisiana and grow tobacco at the family farm on Lovely Street. Many citizens of Avon and Farmington were indignant about that, however, because Shubael and Romanta didn't just bring themselves—they brought some of their enslaved workers.

Despite objection from his abolitionist parishioners, in February 1853, Reverend Noah Porter gave a sermon where he disagreed with those church members who wanted to excommunicate enslavers and deny them from taking communion. Among other Bible passages, the pastor cited Paul's Epistle to the Corinthians, where he said: "By one Spirit we are all baptized into one body, whether we be Jews or Gentiles, whether we be bond or free; and have all been made to drink into the one Spirit."[71] While Porter would make it clear that he viewed slavery to be "a stupendous wrong,"[72] citing this verse likely rankled the antislavery faction of his congregation, as it was one of many biblical verses that had been used over centuries to justify slavery.

In arguing that slaveholding was not a sin worthy of excommunication, Porter struggled to make a convincing argument, especially since he acknowledged, as the Congregational Convention at Albany, New York, had done in 1852, that slavery is a "gross violation of the most sacred rights of man, is utterly inconsistent with the law of God and is totally irreconcilable with the spirit and principles of the Gospel."[73]

Reverend Porter then argued that slaveholding *as a system* was a sin but those connected with it were not necessarily sinners, asserting that it was not right "to cast out a brother only because he sustains"[74] a relationship to slavery. He then dug a deeper hole for himself, making the argument that the "humanity of their masters"[75] should be taken into account. With seemingly conflicting statements throughout the sermon, Porter tried to thread the needle. Essentially, the message he gave to his congregation was that they should denounce slavery but embrace the enslaver.

Sensing, perhaps, that his arguments were not compelling, at the end of the sermon, Reverend Noah Porter made one last plea. He noted that "there are still other churches in various stages of progress toward a similar separation from slavery. By degrees, prejudices are softened, errors are corrected, and better feelings diffused through the community around these churches. While the Society may not be accomplishing all it would wish for the removal of this great evil, it is doing much."[76] In other words, like the nation had done for its first eighty years of existence, Reverend Porter hoped to kick the can down the road.

During the summer of 1854, Reverend Wright must have spent considerable time pondering how to respond to the Farmington church's demand to excommunicate Shubael Tillotson. It was complicated given the divisions within his own church. Congregational ministers of the era had to tread carefully on the question of slavery. When Reverend Jarius Burt of the First Congregational Church in Canton Center, Connecticut, spoke too strongly in favor of abolition, some of his parishioners tried to force him to resign. When Burt died suddenly in January 1857, his detractors thanked God for their deliverance.

Among Wright's parishioners in West Avon were at least four men who were members of the Connecticut Anti-Slavery Society, founded in 1838: Gideon Goodrich, Elizur Porter, Romanta Porter and Edgar Woodford. Undoubtedly, these four, as well as other abolitionist members of the church, would have been deeply troubled by member Shubael Tillotson being an enslaver. On the other side of the coin, Shubael was part of the church family, and slavery was legal in the South. Shubael had been a faithful member of the West Avon church since 1831, and in August 1853, less than a year before Farmington parishioners sent their letter, his daughter Genevieve was baptized in the church.

After church members in Farmington sent their letter to Reverend Wright in April 1854, the issue was tabled for several months as the West Avon Congregational Church was consumed with a scandal. During that spring, a thirty-four-year-old married parishioner named Franklin Woodford was accused of committing adultery with a twenty-two-year-old single woman named Phebe Woodford, possibly a cousin or niece. After months of pressuring Franklin to confess, in September 1854, Franklin finally admitted that he had "transgressed the laws of christian chastity,"[77] and with his confession, Franklin and Phebe were allowed to remain in the congregation. The scandal, however, was a distraction to the membership, and as a result, they did not address the question of Shubael Tillotson until September.

Finally, after the Sunday service on September 17, 1854, the letter from the Farmington church regarding Shubael Tillotson was discussed, and a resolution was adopted for Reverend Wright to "make enquiries of Mr. Tillotson with a view to an examination into the case."[78] Whether or not Reverend Wright actually sent a letter to Shubael Tillotson in the fall of 1854 is not known, but when Shubael died in November of that year, the issue resolved itself.

Shubael and Romanta Tillotson did not exactly fit the mold of the archetypal southern plantation owner, although they were certainly complicit in the practice of slavery. Despite spending much of his time in Louisiana, Shubael had served in the Connecticut State House of Representatives, elected as a Whig in 1847, a year before Whig Party candidate Zachary Taylor was elected U.S. president. While the Whig Party was not officially antislavery, abolitionists preferred the party over the staunchly proslavery Democratic Party, and many of Shubael's constituents were abolitionists.

After Shubael died in November 1854, his widow, Betsey Ann, and their four children spent less time at the Louisiana plantation and more time at their home in Avon. When the Civil War broke out in 1861, Betsey demanded that her brother-in-law Romanta make "an early adjustment of their affairs"[79] so she could get a distribution from Shubael's share of the business. But in the summer of 1862, the Civil War began to negatively affect the plantation, constraining Romanta's ability to settle with Betsey. In August 1862, Union army steamers made their way upstream to seek control of the Mississippi River, fighting a battle in Donaldsonville, Louisiana, near the Tillotson plantation and putting all of Ascension Parish in great agitation. With the Louisiana countryside impoverished by the war, the plantation was raided, either by civilians or the Confederate army, further draining resources of the business. Finally, in the spring of 1864, Betsey Ann left with her family to go back to Avon and received a modest distribution from Romanta in September of that year. Shortly thereafter, the plantation faced an obstacle it could not overcome—when all enslaved people were emancipated by Abraham Lincoln, the plantation was no longer profitable, and the land was subsequently sold off.

Although Reverend Wright was able to conveniently sidestep the dilemma over the question of slavery in 1854, shortly thereafter, led by parishioner Edgar Woodford, his congregation would be forced to revisit the issue yet again.

9

A HIGHER LAW OF LOVE

Edgar Woodford's Resolve

For Edgar Woodford, the request he made to his fellow church members in 1855 was incontrovertible. The dispute over an enslaver taking communion may have gone away with Shubael Tillotson's death, but the imperative for the West Avon Congregational Church to take an unequivocal stand against slavery had not. All Edgar asked for was that the church recognize it should take all Christian means necessary to oppose slavery, "with a view to securing harmonious action."[80] That, however, was too much for the majority of his church brethren in 1855, when he first brought his motion to the floor. Undeterred, Edgar knew the struggle would not end until slavery was banished from the nation. Like David Bartlett before him, he was a fervent abolitionist, but while David wanted nothing to do with an ecclesiastical society that allowed an enslaver to take communion, Edgar Woodford decided he would try to effect change by working within the church, and he considered his failed motion merely a temporary setback.

Ambitious and highly principled, Edgar was a sixth-generation descendant of Thomas Woodford, who came with Thomas Hooker's company to Hartford in 1636. When he was nineteen, Edgar married Mary Elizabeth Kellogg, daughter of Avon Congregational Church's first pastor, the Reverend Bela Kellogg. He joined Mary's brother, Bela Crocker Kellogg, in becoming a member of the Anti-Slavery Society and resolved to do everything he could

Edgar Woodford. *Courtesy of John Banks.*

to move the country toward abolition. To provide for himself and his family, he taught himself civil engineering and surveying and, in his mid-twenties, helped create several maps depicting New England. A skilled draftsman, he became county surveyor and created one of the first maps of Hartford County in 1855.

Early in 1855, when he was thirty years old and serving as clerk of the West Avon Congregational Church, Edgar Woodford decided that it was time once and for all to have the church make a definitive declaration against the practice of slavery.

At a church membership meeting in January 1855, Edgar presented a resolution to condemn slavery. As it was still a contentious issue, his motion was postponed until March and then tabled again until June. At a meeting on June 30, it became clear to Edgar that his motion was facing strong opposition, with several members claiming his draft resolution was unclear or unnecessary. Once again, the motion was tabled, and Edgar was instructed to rewrite his proposal. Undeterred, Edgar came back on August 24, 1855, with a new resolution that was put to a vote:

> *Resolved. That we do believe American Slavery to be inconsistent with the spirit of the Gospel which includes love to our neighbor & requires that we do unto others as we would that they should do unto us…and furthermore commands that we have no fellowship with the unfruitful works of darkness but rather reprove them.*
>
> *And be it further Resolved that as individuals and as a Church we will aim to discountenance & oppose this baleful system by all appropriate & Christian means in our power.*[81]

Indicative of the division in the church over the question of abolition at the time, the resolution failed narrowly, by a men-only vote of eight opposed to six in favor.

Edgar did not despair long, however. In February 1856, a group of antislavery advocates in New Haven called a meeting to organize a team to travel to Kansas, and on March 7, Edgar was elected as a director of the contingent that came to be known as the Connecticut Kansas Colony.[82] Two years earlier, Congress had passed the Kansas-Nebraska Act, which gave both territories the right to decide whether they would permit slavery when they were admitted to the Union as states. In November 1854, aided by a flood of proslavery Missourians who crossed over the border to vote illegally, Kansas territory voted for a proslavery candidate as its delegate to Congress.

Northerners refused to accept the outcome of the referendum as legitimate and set up a government of their own in Lawrence, Kansas. After outbreaks of violence occurred between pro- and antislavery forces in late 1855 and early 1856, many "Free Staters" from New England and other northern states decided they needed to move to Kansas to help counter the proslavery sentiment. After the meeting in New Haven in March 1856, fifty-seven men, four women and two children from across Connecticut, including Edgar Woodford, headed out to Kansas on March 31. The trip took about two weeks, with the group first traveling by train to Jefferson City, Missouri, and then by wagon to Lawrence and other towns in eastern Kansas.

About a month after their arrival, on May 21, 1856, a proslavery mob ransacked the town of Lawrence, destroying printing presses and looting homes and stores, prompting abolitionist John Brown and four of his sons to kill five men at a site about fifty miles south of Lawrence in retaliation. News of the violence spread throughout the nation and the future of Kansas hung in the balance. It is not known if Edgar was in Lawrence at the time of the bloodshed, but within a few months, he returned to Connecticut and remained there until January 1857, when he encouraged more abolitionists to join him in Kansas. Among them was his younger brother Oswald. Before agreeing to move to Kansas, Oswald Woodford, an ordained minister, was serving as principal of the Cherokee Male Seminary in the Oklahoma Territory. The seminary had been established after the Trail of Tears, the forced removal of Cherokees from their ancestral homes in the southeastern United States. Committed to abolition himself, Oswald agreed to move with his family to Kansas, serving as a home missionary in a town called Grasshopper Falls.

When the Kansas territory's proslavery Lecompton Constitution was blocked from ratification by the U.S. Congress in February 1858, Edgar moved back to his family in Avon, once again attending services at the West Avon church. While his motions to denounce slavery failed to gain support of the membership in 1855, Edgar was determined to try again. Much had happened in the meantime. In addition to the developments in Kansas, in

1857, the Supreme Court handed down the Dred Scott decision, denying Scott's right to sue for his freedom and declaring that Congress had no authority to ban slavery from a federal territory. So, in May 1858, Edgar thought the time was ripe to bring a new resolution to the church membership:

> *Resolved—That we regard the involuntary enslavement of one portion of the human race by another as a violation of the law of love and, therefore, a sin against which the Church of God should everywhere bear distinct testimony and from the complicity with which she should by all means keep herself.*[83]

This time, Edgar's motion passed unanimously. Regardless of what the constitution said about slavery, Edgar knew that the church and the nation needed to adhere to a higher law of love.

And at the same time, the country was heading toward war. When the Civil War began in the spring of 1861, President Abraham Lincoln made it clear that the objective of the war was to preserve the Union, not to free enslaved people. That may have been the reason Edgar Woodford did not enlist in the Union army in 1861, despite being captain of the local militia in Avon. Over the next fifteen months, however, Lincoln's views about slavery would evolve. In July 1862, the president presented a draft of an Emancipation Proclamation to his cabinet as he waited for a Union victory on the battlefield.

Then in August 1862, as it became increasingly evident that Lincoln intended to emancipate the enslaved, Edgar Woodford decided to join the war, enlisting as a private in Company K of the Seventh Connecticut Regiment, led by his friend, Lieutenant Colonel Joseph Roswell Hawley. Before the war, Hawley served as editor of the *Hartford Evening Press* after he took over the job from David Bartlett. Known as a staunch abolitionist, Hawley was regarded as the first man from Connecticut to volunteer for the Union army. In the summer of 1862, he was serving as a lieutenant colonel of the Seventh Connecticut and would eventually rise to the level of brevet major general.

Joseph Roswell Hawley. *Brady-Handy Collection.*

On the Sunday before he left for the war in late August 1862, Edgar Woodford was pensive as he attended the morning and afternoon services at the West Avon Congregational Church with his wife, Mary, and his three children: fifteen-year-old Mary, thirteen-year-old Edgar Jr. and eleven-year-old Anna. Two days later, he said goodbye to his family, first heading to Hartford and then traveling by train to New Haven. When he left New Haven on September 1 en route to Hilton Head, South Carolina, Lieutenant Colonel Hawley invited Edgar to join him in his stateroom on the steamship *Ben De Ford*.

As part of Union General Winfield Scott's Anaconda plan, which included a blockade of Southern ports, the *Ben De Ford* was directed to scour the Atlantic coastline to force Confederate batteries out of their strongholds. While en route, Edgar was assigned the duties of a quartermaster, responsible for distributing supplies and provisions. When they reached Florida, the ship turned up the St. John's River toward Jacksonville, and Edgar, suffering from the heat, contracted a fever, likely typhoid fever, which was running rampant in 1862.

On the afternoon of October 1, a party sent from the *Ben De Ford* to dislodge Confederate troops from a battery came under withering fire from the enemy. The battle continued all through October 3 until finally the Confederates evacuated their fort on St. John's Bluff. On the river, returning Union troops struggled to get back on board the *Ben De Ford*, having to climb up a swinging rope ladder. While it was not his duty as quartermaster, despite his illness, Edgar Woodford pitched in to help haul men up the side of the ship.

When helping the sailors get back on board, it became evident that Edgar was seriously ill, and he soon collapsed, bedridden. All that evening and over the next two days, doctors on board cared for Edgar, but his condition continued to worsen. He passed away on the morning of October 6, 1862, with Lieutenant Colonel Joseph Hawley at his bedside. Hawley's own summation of the cause of death was "congestion fever," also known as "camp fever."[84] When Mary Woodford heard of her husband's demise, her face turned ashen, the loss overwhelming.

Edgar Woodford lived a "noble and precious life"[85] and, for the cause of abolishing slavery, made the ultimate sacrifice. After the war, in 1867, Joseph Hawley went on to buy the *Hartford Courant*, which he merged with the *Hartford Evening Press*. Known after the war for leading Civil War commemorations in the years to come, Hawley would never forget the sacrifice that Edgar Woodford and other soldiers made in support of their country.

10

FIGHTING FOR EMANCIPATION

Leverett Holden and Harrison Woodford

On April 4, 1865, Private Leverett Holden stood with other soldiers of the Twenty-Ninth Connecticut Regiment on the banks of the James River looking across at the just vacated city of Richmond, Virginia, when a boat passed by, pulled by twelve sailors. Acknowledging the crowds of emancipated people who shouted out and clapped their hands, President Abraham Lincoln waved to the onlookers. One Black woman, seeing the president and his entourage, exclaimed, "Glory to God. Give Him the praise for his goodness," yelling with such fervor that her voice gave out. As Isaac Hill of the Twenty-Ninth Connecticut said in speaking of Lincoln's arrival, "No triumphal march of a conqueror could have equaled in moral sublimity the humble manner in which he entered Richmond."[86]

Five days later, General Robert E. Lee surrendered at Appomattox Courthouse and the Civil War was over. The Northern states went to war in 1861 intent on preserving the Union and bringing the Southern states to account for their act of treason. But in September 1862, when Abraham Lincoln announced his intention to emancipate Blacks living in the rebellious states, it added a new objective to the war. The goal of ending slavery meant everything to the approximately 4.5 million Black people living in the country at the time, nearly 4 million of them enslaved. Leverett Holden of Avon and other men in Connecticut who joined the Connecticut Twenty-Ninth Colored Infantry Regiment understood clearly what was at stake when they enlisted in late 1863 and early 1864. But while the Emancipation Proclamation crystallized for them a clear moral objective of the war, for many white Union soldiers, fueled by racism, the announcement weakened their impetus for fighting.

On Christmas Day 1862, white soldier Harrison Woodford of Avon, four months into his three-year enlistment in the Sixteenth Connecticut Regiment, wrote home that the motivation to support the Union was waning in the army. "It is hard work to get the men into a fight. There is a great lack of patriotism in the army and I must say for myself that I cannot see from the present aspect of things what all this loss of life is for."[87] Harrison said it wasn't just the hardship of fighting that was demoralizing to the regiment. Although a Northerner, he resented both antislavery advocates and Black people, effectively blaming them for the predicament he was in. With the Emancipation Proclamation set to take effect just a week later on January 1, 1863, Harrison wrote, "The soldiers do dam [*sic*] the abolitionists & [n——] the worst kind." Black soldiers, he said, "are riding around on horses and have their baggage carried and we poor fellows can trudge along with our loads on our backs."[88] Other soldiers in Harrison's company reflected the same prejudice, demoralized by the "idea of fighting for negro emancipation."[89]

Leverett Holden and Harrison Woodford had many things in common. They were farmers from Avon who lived within a couple of miles of each other and shared a common enemy. On enlisting, both were devoted to the cause of the Union. As an inducement to enlist, Leverett and Harrison each received bounties for joining their respective regiments, and both faced combat soon after being deployed. But while each of them was expected, if necessary, to make the ultimate sacrifice on the battlefield, their life experiences before and after the war were worlds apart. The Civil War forced the nation to address the injustices of racism for the first time in earnest, and the conflict brought out the strongest of emotions in Leverett and Harrison.

On August 6, 1862, twenty-one-year-old Harrison Woodford was one of four Woodford cousins from Avon who enlisted in Company I of the Sixteenth Connecticut Regiment. Raised on a farm, he enthusiastically joined the army to fight for the cause of preserving the Union. With the Northern army having suffered a string of defeats, more manpower was needed, and new recruits were rushed into battle in the summer of 1862.

Harrison was mustered at Camp Williams in Hartford on Sunday, August 24, and after being issued their gear, the newly minted soldiers groaned under the weight of their knapsacks as they readied to depart. They soon left for New Haven, where they boarded a steamer to take them to the front.

It was not long before Harrison Woodford had an abrupt awakening to the horrors of war. While staying in barracks in Washington, D.C., on August 28, he could hear cannon fire at the Second Battle of Bull Run thirty-five miles away. Two days later, Harrison saw Union General George McClellan returning to the city after a demoralizing defeat, with a mile-long train of the dead and dying returning from the battlefield. As one fellow soldier of the Sixteenth Connecticut put it, "As we gazed upon these blood-bespattered men, worn down with fatigue, our hitherto exuberant spirits became completely subdued and in almost dead silence we passed by the wagonloads of mangled humanity."[90]

Having received little training since their enlistment and woefully unprepared, the Sixteenth Connecticut was thrust into battle at Sharpsburg, Virginia, reporting to Colonel Francis Beach, who, in turn, was under the command of Union General Ambrose Burnside. As the sun rose on Wednesday, September 17, 1862, a Confederate force four miles long on the west side of Antietam Creek began to fire cannon shot at Union troops. Laying low in a cornfield under continual fire, some of the Sixteenth Connecticut soldiers felt faint or "sick"[91] and retreated to the rear. As the regiment clambered up the hill on the other side of the creek to another cornfield, the unit came under withering fire. One soldier remembered being "as scared as a hunted rabbit,"[92] but the recently formed regiment held its position.

Unbeknownst to them, however, Confederate General A.P. Hill was leading his brigade toward the Sixteenth Connecticut from the opposite side of the cornfield and soon fired on Harrison's regiment at close range. Robert Kellogg, one of the soldiers of the Sixteenth Connecticut, remembered "it was a hail storm....Our men fell on every side."[93] It was not long before the regiment's ranks broke, with the men fleeing the cornfield. Realizing he was outnumbered, Union General Burnside ordered his troops, including the Sixteenth Connecticut, to fall back to Antietam Creek to defend Burnside Bridge. Finally, under a relentless Confederate assault, Burnside was forced to retreat.

A stinging defeat for the Union army, the Battle of Antietam was the single bloodiest day of the Civil War. Of the 940 men of the Sixteenth

Connecticut who went into battle that day, 56 were killed, 184 were wounded and 192 were captured or declared missing. The scene of human suffering was almost beyond comprehension. Surgeons attended to the wounded over the next two days, filling two cartloads with amputated legs, feet, arms and hands. Remarkably, when writing home, Harrison Woodford made no mention of the Battle of Antietam other than commenting that a friend from Avon, Corporal Henry Evans, was killed in battle.

After Harrison participated in another crushing Union defeat at the Battle of Fredericksburg, Virginia, on December 13, 1862, he wrote his 1862 Christmas Day letter with his morale at a new low. Pessimistic about where the war was headed, he told his friends at home, "We may fight forever and then another way will have to be devised to settle it."[94]

Fortunately for the Sixteenth Connecticut, after Antietam and Fredericksburg, the regiment settled into extended periods of garrison duty, avoiding the front lines. Harrison was grateful to a point, but when boredom settled in, the regiment was once again itching for action.

By November 1863, the Sixteenth Connecticut found itself near Portsmouth, Virginia, where the men passed the days repairing breastworks, and Harrison got word that the army was offering bounties to entice at least five hundred more men to volunteer. Now disillusioned by fifteen months of war, Harrison informed his mother that no amount of bounty could entice him to join again, telling her, "Knowing what I now know about war it wouldn't be no temptation."[95]

In January 1864, as the Sixteenth Regiment was sailing through Pamlico Sound en route to guard Union forts in Plymouth, North Carolina, recently recruited Leverett Holden of Avon was training in New Haven, Connecticut, with other members of the Twenty-Ninth Connecticut Regiment.

Born in Vernon, Connecticut, and one of the few Black residents of Avon, thirty-eight-year-old Leverett Holden was working as a farmer when he, along with nine hundred other Black men from the state, volunteered for the Twenty-Ninth Connecticut Regiment in late 1863. In 1850, before he moved to Avon, twenty-six-year-old Leverett was working for the family of Elisha Wadsworth at their home in Hartford on the corner of Prospect Street and Albany Avenue. By 1854, he had moved to Avon to work as a farm laborer, quickly earning a reputation for being trustworthy, good-natured and hardworking, and he continued to live in town through the first three years of the Civil War.

At about the same time that Harrison Woodford was telling his mother that men would be crazy to enlist merely to receive a bounty, in late November 1863, Leverett Holden learned that the Connecticut General Assembly had finally agreed to the formation of a Black regiment and that large bounties were being offered.

While free Black men were certainly motivated to fight for the cause of ending slavery, the importance of the bounties could not be overlooked. Provided he enlisted by January 5, 1864, the State of Connecticut promised Leverett a $300 bounty, more than a year's pay for an unskilled laborer. In addition, the state offered him another $10 for every four months served as well as a monthly stipend to supplement that paid by the Federal government. On top of the state's bounty, the Federal government promised $300, and Hartford County offered another $75. The bounties were likely strongly appealing to Leverett.

The fact that he could even enlist to fight for his country was remarkable, as the formation of a Black regiment in Connecticut in late 1863 was highly controversial. There was strong resistance in the state, driven by racist feelings that Black men could not fight on par with white soldiers. Though a relative handful of Black men had served in white regiments earlier in the war, they were deemed unfit for the battlefield and were often assigned noncombat duties, serving as cooks, laborers and teamsters.

Connecticut Governor William Buckingham, a strong supporter of President Lincoln, had a very different view of the role Black people should play in society. In a message to the Connecticut General Assembly, he expounded that slavery must be exterminated and that "every man, whether high or low, rich or poor…of whatever tribe or race or nation…be protected in all the inalienable rights which God has given him."[96]

In November 1863, Governor Buckingham succeeded in calling a special session of the General Assembly to approve the formation of Black regiments. Some legislators squabbled over how to fund the regiments, but many of them made it clear that their real reason for opposing the bill was because they objected to the "arming of negroes."[97]

Conveying a racist fear of Black people all too common at the time, House Leader William Eaton, a Democrat opposed to the war, called Black men "both cowardly and ferocious" and said, "You will let loose upon every household south of the Mason and Dixon's line a band of ferocious men who will spread lust and rapine all over that land." Eaton was appalled that

Governor William Buckingham. *From* The Life of William A. Buckingham, *by Reverend Samuel G., D.D. Buckingham.*

Frederick Douglass, 1856. *National Portrait Gallery.*

the General Assembly would even consider sending "uncivilized" men to battle, arguing the war should be conducted "in a white man's way."[98] Despite the objections to enlisting a Black regiment, thanks to Governor Buckingham's support, the bill passed 120 to 71.

Eaton was one of many who expressed the view that nothing had changed since the Founding Fathers adopted the U.S. Constitution, arguing that citizens should accept a Southern state's right to practice slavery, "ignoring the moral view of the question, regarding only its political character."[99] But the moral view of the question was certainly top of mind for Leverett and other Black men as they considered whether to enlist. In response to the appeal for new recruits, and eager to receive the offered bounties, Leverett Holden joined the Twenty-Ninth Connecticut Infantry Regiment on December 15, 1863, training at what is now Criscuolo Park in New Haven.

Since Black men were not permitted to lead the troops, it took two months to find white officers willing to head the regiment. In the meantime, on January 29, 1864, the Twenty-Ninth Connecticut was visited by the formerly enslaved famed orator Frederick Douglass. Douglass had implored President Lincoln to allow Black men to fight as early as 1861, believing that, by participating in battle, Black men could show "by our own right arms that we are worthy to be freemen."[100]

Douglass told Leverett and the Twenty-Ninth Connecticut, "You are pioneers of the liberty of your race. With the United States cap on your head, the United States eagle on your belt, the United States musket on your shoulder, not all the powers of darkness can prevent you from becoming American citizens. And not for yourselves alone are you marshaled—you are pioneers—on you depends the destiny of four millions of the colored race in this country. If you rise and flourish, we shall rise and flourish. If you win freedom and citizenship, we shall share your freedom and citizenship."[101]

Colonel William Burr Wooster. *From* General History of the Burr Family, *by Charles Burr Todd.*

Finally, in early March, Colonel William B. Wooster from Derby, Connecticut, agreed to lead the regiment, and the Twenty-Ninth was ready to depart for Annapolis. As the men were about to leave New Haven on March 8, 1864, mothers, wives and sisters stood weeping for their sons, husbands and brothers.

After they reached Annapolis, the Twenty-Ninth Connecticut headed down to the coastline of South Carolina and soon learned that they would only be paid $7 per month, less than what was promised and less than the $13 per month white privates in the military earned. Adding insult to injury, of the bounties they were told they would receive, only the state bounty was paid.

Leverett and his comrades had little recourse even though now they were being told by their officers that they were expected to fight as bravely as the white troops. Black regiments faced hostility not just from the Confederate

The Twenty-Ninth Connecticut (Colored) Infantry Regiment. *Library of Congress.*

army but from many Northerners as well. When the Fifty-Fourth Massachusetts Colored Regiment lost nearly half its men trying to take Fort Wagner in Charleston, South Carolina, in July 1863, Connecticut Democrats accused Republican newspapers of waging a propaganda campaign, railing against "flaming accounts of 'negro bravery.'"[102]

On April 16, 1864, the Twenty-Ninth Connecticut arrived in Beaufort, South Carolina, where the men set up camp awaiting further orders. That very day, four hundred miles to the north, Harrison Woodford learned, ominously, that the Confederates had just finished construction of a casemate ironclad ram that was up the Roanoke River from where he was stationed in Plymouth, North Carolina.

Situated on the south bank of the Roanoke River, near Albemarle Sound, Plymouth was strategically important to both sides in the war and by early 1864 was serving as a supply depot for the Union army. The Sixteenth Connecticut arrived there in January as part of a force of only 1,600 men to defend the garrison along with four Union gunboats that patrolled the river to protect the town's fortifications.

Once again, showing his deep-seated prejudice, Harrison wrote to his mother from Plymouth stating, "This is a great place for deserters & refugees & [n——] to come in. The way they manage it, our fellows will go up the rivers in boats & they will come down to the shore & come aboard." Referring to the escaping enslaved people, Harrison continued, "There was a great many more lying around in the swamps that wanted to come in. They are a generally ragged & rough looking set & they look very destitute."[103] Among his unit, Harrison was hardly alone in his disdain for Black soldiers.

From January through March 1864, the men of the Sixteenth Connecticut spent most of their time on picket duty and manning the forts, and few saw any chance for combat. Another Hartford County regiment, the Fourteenth Connecticut, resented what they viewed as "that nice, white gloved duty,"[104] the Sixteenth Connecticut enjoyed far from the front lines. By mid-April, however, the soldiers guarding the forts at Plymouth had begun to hear rumors the Confederates might be planning an attack. In the spring of 1864, Union forces were spread too thin to defend all the forts captured along the North Carolina coast, leaving Plymouth vulnerable. Writing to his father on April 16, Harrison mentioned there was a "great deal of talk about a RAM the Rebs have got up the river."[105] That "RAM" was none other than the CSS *Albemarle*, an ironclad steam-powered ship launched in April 1864 that was considered nearly invincible. Rebel citizens in the area told Union soldiers the CSS *Albemarle* "would make kindling wood of our gunboats,"[106] and just one day after Harrison sent his letter, the quietude the Sixteenth Connecticut had experienced for the previous sixteen months came to a shattering end.

With a battle beginning on Sunday, April 17, Confederate General Robert Hoke commanded a force to retake Plymouth that outnumbered Union troops by at least four to one. On Monday the eighteenth, the Sixteenth Connecticut and other Union troops were pushed back into their forts when seven thousand Confederate soldiers descended on the town and fired on the Union fortifications. Harrison Woodford and the rest of the Sixteenth retreated into Fort Williams, one of three Union forts at the center of the Union breastworks. Though outnumbered, Harrison's regiment made use of their own twelve-pound brass howitzers to answer the Confederate assault. The attack was unrelenting, however, and continued until midnight, pausing only briefly before resuming at dawn the next day.

Matters worsened considerably in the early morning hours of the nineteenth when General Hoke ordered the CSS *Albemarle* to float down the Roanoke. Aided by heavy rains that had swollen the river, the ironclad easily crossed over chains and other obstructions placed by the Union army, and soon the Sixteenth Connecticut was facing constant bombardment from the ram.

The siege of the Union forts continued for the rest of April 19, and after nearly one hundred men in the Sixteenth Connecticut were killed or wounded, it became evident to the survivors that they "would either be killed or go to Libby,"[107] the nickname given to the notorious Confederate prison. By the morning of Wednesday, April 20, 1864, the situation was clearly hopeless, and finally, at about 9:00 a.m., Union General Henry Wessells hoisted the white flag. Nearly all of the 430 survivors of the Sixteenth Connecticut were taken prisoner, including Harrison Woodford.

General Wessells had tried to condition his surrender on General Hoke agreeing to treat Black soldiers and white North Carolinians fighting for the Union as prisoners of war, but Hoke refused. Prison was not an option for them. One private in the Sixteenth Connecticut observed that "they showed the negroes no mercy but shot them down in cold blood."[108]

Harrison Woodford and the other captured men of the Sixteenth Connecticut were forced to march with little food or sleep and were then packed into trains, forty-two men to a boxcar, en route to Andersonville, a Confederate prison eleven miles northwest of Americus, Georgia. When they arrived, they saw 12,000 other captured Union soldiers, many emaciated, crammed into twenty-six acres with no trees or shelter to protect them from the elements. As Oliver Gates, another Sixteenth Connecticut soldier, noted on arriving at the prison, "If any sight would make a man's heart sink,"[109] the inside of Andersonville would. A fellow private in the Sixteenth Connecticut, George Champlin, said of the prison on the day of his arrival, "It is a dirty filthy place. A large number die here daily. Twenty one died today."[110] By late June, Champlin was describing the constant toll of death as being like the "falling leaves"[111] of autumn. Over the duration of the war, 41,000 Union soldiers were crowded into the Andersonville stockade and nearly 13,000 of them perished, including about 160 of the 430 imprisoned from the Sixteenth Connecticut Regiment.

Throughout his captivity, Harrison heard rumors of a pending prisoner exchange, such as one promising a release on July 4, 1864. When that day passed and other rumored exchanges did not occur, the prisoners became despondent, many giving up all hope and even the will to live.

Months passed without any progress as the North adopted a policy of not agreeing to prisoner exchanges unless the South promised to repatriate Black soldiers. The new policy on exchanges came about after Confederate General Nathan Bedford Forrest refused to treat captured Black soldiers as prisoners of war at the Battle of Fort Pillow in Tennessee on April 12, 1864, executing nearly three hundred of them. Further dampening the hope of a prisoner exchange, Union General Ulysses S. Grant thought it was in the North's strategic interest not to let a dwindling Confederate army replenish its troops with released prisoners.

Word that the U.S. government insisted on Black soldiers being included in prisoner exchanges angered members of the Sixteenth Connecticut Regiment and other soldiers being held at Andersonville. Sergeant Oliver Gates of the Sixteenth said he was "sorry" the Union "ever armed a [n——] as a Soldier for I think if she had not, prisoners would have received proper care and the exchange would have been continued....The idea that the prisoner is patriotic enough to say that he is willing to stay here a Prisoner until the [n——] is recognized as a Soldier as subject of exchange equal with the white man is entirely false." Gates said of his white prisoners, "They all seem to hate the [n——] with a perfect hatred."[112] Weeks of captivity turned into months, and the surviving members of the Sixteenth Connecticut despaired as summer turned to autumn.

While Harrison was longing for his release under the hot summer sun of Georgia, Leverett Holden and the Twenty-Ninth Connecticut had been given orders to participate in General Ulysses S. Grant's siege of Petersburg, Virginia, a move taken by Grant to disrupt a key supply route for the Confederacy. In one of their first engagements of the war, on September 2, 1864, the Twenty-Ninth "found the whole brigade engaged in front of the enemy"[113] and, after five hours of fighting, drove the Rebels back inside their fortifications close to Richmond. Remarkably, the Twenty-Ninth suffered no fatalities.

Soon after he fought outside Petersburg in early September, Leverett began to feel unwell, eventually becoming so sick that on September 27, he had to be transported to a hospital in Alexandria, Virginia, run by the Union army's Tenth Corps to treat Black soldiers. Other members of the regiment, including Colonel William Wooster, contracted fevers at the same time. While Leverett was miserable with a fever and facing an uncertain recovery, the timing of his illness was fortuitous. Just two days after Leverett was sent to the hospital, the Twenty-Ninth Connecticut began a series of battles lasting a month that would prove to be the regiment's biggest test of the war.

In the Battle of Chaffin's Farm along the James River, the Twenty-Ninth fought gallantly, and the Union army won the day as Confederate troops were forced back to their fort. With their courageous fighting during the battle, the Twenty-Ninth Connecticut and other Black regiments proved to the nation that they were every bit as capable and brave as their white counterparts. As Black chaplain Alexander Newton of the Twenty-Ninth Regiment put it, "The colored troops were the first to enter the field and the last to fall back."[114]

To inspire his men to keep fighting despite taking heavy losses, one Black regiment commander told his troops, "Remember Fort Pillow,"[115] referring to the Confederate massacre of captured Black soldiers five months earlier in Tennessee. Ironically, the very event that changed the Union's policy on the treatment of captured Black soldiers, drastically reducing Harrison

Woodford's chance of release from prison, served as an inspiration for Black troops in battle.

Fortunately for Leverett, he missed all the action at Chaffin's Farm and two subsequent battles, remaining in his hospital bed until he recovered in November. While Leverett was regaining his health in Virginia, Harrison Woodford was enduring his seventh month of captivity seven hundred miles to the south, and hope of survival was fading fast.

As the calendar turned to November, Harrison had become a mere skeleton of a man, unable to walk without a crutch. Believing he was close to death, he was resigned to his fate when, mercifully, he got word that he and his fellow prisoners would be paroled. After arriving in Annapolis, Maryland, on December 17, he wrote to his family with the wonderful news that "through the marvelous goodness of an allwise God," he was still alive and out of the hands of the Confederates. Harrison Woodford barely survived his imprisonment. He thanked God who "snatched me…from the jaws of death," adding that "a few weeks more I think would have decided my fate."[116] Harrison told his family that of the seven Woodfords from Avon to have enlisted in the Sixteenth Connecticut, only he and his cousins Wallace and Edward were still alive. Wallace, however, suffered even worse from his imprisonment at Andersonville, and just days after returning to Avon, he died in the arms of his family.

After the war, the fortunes of Harrison and Leverett diverged considerably. Harrison returned to life as a farmer in Avon, married a woman named Minnie Case and raised a family, including three children. Earning the respect of his peers, he went on to serve in town government and was a delegate to the Republican Party convention from the first district in Connecticut. Remembered as an "honored and influential citizen, held in high regard by his fellow townsmen,"[117] Harrison was, for a time, the treasurer of the West Avon Congregational Church and served on the Board of the Avon Creamery before passing away at age sixty-two from heart failure.

Leverett, on the other hand, returned to life as an outsider in a white man's world. Soldiers of the Twenty-Ninth Connecticut, like the Fifty-Fourth Massachusetts before them, were led to believe there would be benefits given to them after their service, but the promises went largely unfulfilled. After the Twenty-Ninth Regiment returned to Connecticut in

November 1865, the state legislature passed a law barring Black people from voting, one of the benefits that Governor Buckingham thought he would be granting the returning soldiers. At a parade held for the Twenty-Ninth Connecticut outside the Old State House in Hartford on November 24, 1865, the governor apologized, stating that "Connecticut now denies you privileges it grants to others, for no other apparent reason than because God has made you to differ in complexion."[118] A Union victory may have freed the enslaved, but Black men would not enjoy the same rights as white men.

Leverett returned to life as a farm laborer in Avon, and not long after the war ended, he was living with a woman named Martha Williams. In addition to working as a farmhand, "Lev,"[119] as he was known, did odd jobs around town, including one time cleaning the chimney at Avon Congregational Church and another time cutting and stacking wood for a family. When Leverett enlisted at age thirty-eight, he had already outlived the average lifespan of a Black man of the era. Just twelve years after he mustered out of the army, he died at age fifty-two, buried in an unknown grave in Avon.

It is not known whether Harrison Woodford ever reconciled with the notion that he fought so valiantly for emancipation or even if he knew Leverett Holden personally. The end of the Civil War did not bring an end to racial division, but it marked a new beginning in Black people's struggle for social justice.

From the town of Avon, at least ninety men served in the Civil War, more than the town's quota. At least twenty-seven paid the ultimate sacrifice, either killed in battle or succumbing to disease. Another thirteen soldiers were wounded and survived, and many others were medically discharged. Including Harrison Woodford, a total of fifteen servicemen from Avon spent time in Confederate prisons, of whom seven died either during their internment or shortly thereafter. The community of the West Avon Congregational Church was hit particularly hard. Of the twenty-five residents of West Avon who enlisted in the Union army, thirteen did not come home, including Edgar Woodford, Harrison Woodford's uncle Robert and two of his cousins, Wallace and Sheldon, as well as Henry Evans, who died at the Battle of Antietam.

PART IV

THE TOWERS OF AVON

11

DANIEL WADSWORTH'S MONTE VIDEO

At the dawn of the nineteenth century, standing on the ridge of Talcott Mountain looking west across the Farmington River Valley below, thirty-four-year-old Daniel Wadsworth admired the view from an idyllic spot that would become his and his wife Faith's summer home. Having studied architecture in his youth and having consulted with his wife's uncle, the renowned painter John Trumbull, Daniel created a grand design for his country estate. Years earlier, his father, Jeremiah, had encouraged him to see the beauty of the Metacomet Range and to build a summer residence there, and now he resolved to fulfill that dream.

Daniel Wadsworth by Thomas Sully, 1807. *Courtesy of Wadsworth Atheneum Museum of Art.*

Daniel marveled at the views in all directions. Looking west across the valley, he saw the Farmington River, straight and clear as a canal in some places and then meandering north in graceful bends, bisecting a vast acreage of farmland with country homes dotted along its path. To the north, he could see as far as Mount Holyoke and Mount Tom in Massachusetts, and to the south, down to Sleeping Giant Mountain in Meriden. Looking east lay the broad valley of the Connecticut River and the church steeples of the city of Hartford. Not long after that first visit to Talcott Mountain,

Daniel Wadsworth decided to use his wealth to become a patron of the arts. Treasuring the natural beauty of the countryside, he supported painters who depicted landscapes in romanticized grandeur, displaying the potential greatness of America. And soon he and Faith would have their own idealized mountain paradise in what became Avon, a summer home they decided to call Monte Video.

Daniel inherited his wealth from his father, Colonel Jeremiah Wadsworth, and from an early age, Daniel's upbringing shaped his life and his love of the arts. Jeremiah first became affluent as a merchant and then greatly enhanced his finances during his time serving as commissary-general for the French army in North America during the American Revolutionary War.

After serving as deputy quartermaster for the Continental army during the early part of the American Revolution, in September 1780, the Marquis de Lafayette recommended to French Commander Rochambeau that Jeremiah Wadsworth would serve as an excellent quartermaster to supply the French troops in North America, and Rochambeau agreed. However, in what would likely be regarded as self-dealing today, Jeremiah and a man named John Carter formed a company that entered into an exclusive agreement with Rochambeau to supply the French army with provisions. From that arrangement, Wadsworth profited handsomely, accumulating much of the wealth that his son Daniel would inherit.

When Jeremiah traveled to Paris to conduct business in 1783, he took his twelve-year-old son, Daniel, with him. Daniel had injured his right eye after a fall at age two and his left eye when he was eleven, and Jeremiah hoped that a physician in France could help his son. While there, Daniel learned a bit of French and saw sights of splendor, visiting the court of Louis XVI and Marie Antoinette. In September 1783, Daniel and his father saw Joseph and Étienne Montgolfier send a sheep, a rooster and a duck aloft in a hot air balloon over the Palace of Versailles in the presence of the king and were excited by the prospect that humans could "travel in the skies with great ease and rapidity."[120] After visiting France, Jeremiah and Daniel spent time in London, where the boy attended school, and, while there, John Trumbull painted a portrait of Daniel with his father.

His time in Europe exposed Daniel to arts and literature and opened his eyes to the possibility of enriching the arts in America. In his youth, he studied architecture and painting, and while he never mastered either discipline, his exposure to the subjects gave him an even deeper appreciation of the arts.

In June 1794, when Daniel was twenty-two, he married Faith Trumbull of Hartford, niece of the painter John Trumbull and daughter

Jeremiah Wadsworth and his son Daniel by John Trumbull, 1784. *Courtesy of Wadsworth Atheneum Museum of Art.*

of Jonathan Trumbull Jr. A good friend of Jeremiah's, Jonathan Trumbull Jr. was serving at the time in the U.S. House of Representatives. The marriage of Daniel and Faith joined together two of the most powerful and prosperous families in Hartford.

Faith Trumbull (later, Faith Wadsworth), by John Trumbull, 1791. *Yale University Art Gallery.*

Almost certainly with encouragement and help from his father, when Daniel was in his twenties, he was engaged in a business that traded for rum and molasses in the West Indies. But when Daniel inherited his father's fortune in 1804, becoming the wealthiest resident of Hartford, he stopped working in the business. Although he was of the social elite, citizens of Hartford regarded him with admiration. A bit of an eccentric, he often wore an artist's cap and a cloak at home and, when traveling around town, wore capes of various lengths and colors, often wearing several layers. He suffered from ill health, and because of that, during winters, he placed a foot stove in his oversized yellow carriage with a stove pipe sticking out the side of it to exhaust the fumes. One observer quipped that his carriage resembled a "steamboat on wheels."[121]

Over the years, much of the correspondence between Faith and Daniel concerned the status of their well-being and how bad weather contributed to their ill health. In 1811, when Faith was just forty-two years old, she complained to a friend about the health issues she was experiencing, concerned about aches and pains she associated with "old age."[122] One of delicate health himself, Daniel was described as "fragile, stooped and shy"[123] and was said to have been a hypochondriac throughout his life. His constant concern for his health likely stemmed from the loss of his sister Harriett to consumption in 1793. He had traveled with her to Bermuda in the fall of 1792 hoping she would recover in the warmer weather, but she perished six months after their arrival.

Despite his eccentricities, one reason Daniel was respected by the people of Hartford was due to the efforts he made to aid the poor. His father, Jeremiah, had been described as "kind and benevolent; always the protector of the widow and fatherless and the helper of the distressed,"[124] and Daniel carried the same mindset. In heavy snowstorms, Daniel delivered food on a sleigh throughout the poorer neighborhoods of Hartford. In 1833, he founded the Hartford Orphan Asylum, which eventually merged into the organization now known as the Village for Families and Children. In 1819, he was one of the organizers of what became the American School for the Deaf and, in 1824, helped establish the Retreat for the Insane, now incorporated as part of the Institute for Living in Hartford.

Before Daniel married Faith Trumbull in 1794, Jeremiah Wadsworth showed his son the beauty of Talcott Mountain in what is now Avon and its unsurpassed views of both the Connecticut and Farmington River Valleys. That trip to the Metacomet Range when Daniel was a young adult inspired him to embrace and promote the enduring beauty of the American continent. Later, when his father was still alive, he embarked on a plan to build his "mountain paradise"[125] atop the Metacomet ridge.

Daniel's love for the arts, nurtured in his youth, was strengthened by his connection to Faith's uncle John Trumbull, who produced many portraits of the country's founding fathers as well as iconic scenes of the Revolutionary War. Even before Daniel's marriage to Faith, the Wadsworths were well acquainted with the Trumbull family. As early as 1785, when he was twenty-nine and struggling to make ends meet, John Trumbull received financial support from Jeremiah. Today, Trumbull is considered to be the "patriot artist,"[126] celebrated for his series depicting the Revolutionary War, including the four large history paintings hanging in the U.S. Capitol rotunda, and he was one of the first American artists to try his hand at painting landscapes. There wasn't much of an art market in America until the late nineteenth century, so Daniel,

John Trumbull, self-portrait, circa 1802. *Yale University Art Gallery.*

and his father, Jeremiah, before him, were among the earliest patrons of American artists.

Starting around 1799, Daniel became a frequent traveler, visiting mountain ranges throughout the Appalachians, from the White Mountains in New Hampshire down to the Shenandoah Valley of Virginia. In time, Daniel would amass a vast art collection focused on landscape paintings inspired by these scenes, including John Trumbull's *Niagara Falls from Below the Great Cascade on the British Side*, one of his earliest from 1808.

To realize his father's dream of a summer retreat on Talcott Mountain, in 1805, Daniel began the process of acquiring fifty separate parcels amounting to 250 acres, including a piece of land he bought from John Trumbull. But his frail health often interrupted his plans. On August 25, 1805, when he was at home in Hartford and Faith was away at the Trumbull family home in Lebanon, Connecticut, Daniel wrote to her that he was "only walking very gingerly in the shade to the houses of our neighbors… this temperance of caution more that I thought I'd get strength to visit the Mountain and give orders with as much as was going on."[127]

Approximately one hundred laborers were employed to construct the house and grounds, and the project took several years to complete. As work progressed, Reverend Rufus Hawley and other community members took part in a barn raising at the site in October 1806. Finally, in 1809, Daniel and Faith's summer home at Monte Video was completed. A vanguard of his time, Daniel asked that the house be built in the neo-Gothic style, the first such home in Connecticut. He consulted with John Trumbull on the architectural designs for the house, and Trumbull visited the villa at Monte Video as it neared its completion in March 1809. The "mansion house at the mountain,"[128] as it was referred to in the estate inventory after Daniel's passing, had three parlors, artfully furnished, an organ and eight bedrooms to entertain guests.

In addition to the elegant home, the plans for the estate included a hexagonal viewing tower made of wood, fifty-five feet tall and sixteen feet in diameter with a spiral staircase of eighty steps on the inside. The tower was completed in 1810, and in his desire to serve his community, Daniel decided to do something quite unexpected—he opened the tower to the public every day but Sundays and the Fourth of July. When completed, the Monte Video estate was a sight to behold, replete with extravagant gardens, gravel walkways and velvety lawns that led down to a lake filled with "crystal"[129] clear water, now known as Hoe Pond. Reverend Rufus Hawley and his wife, Elizabeth, once again were invited to Monte Video

The Wadsworths' Gothic Revival home at Monte Video. *Courtesy of Friends of Heublein Tower.*

in September 1812, this time to visit Daniel and Faith in their new home at the mountain estate.

In the early years of Monte Video, Faith enthusiastically invited family and acquaintances to visit her summer residence, asking a friend in August 1814 to "ride up before the season changes,"[130] and the Wadsworths hosted guests there for nearly four decades. In September 1811, while staying at their summer home, Faith wrote to her brother-in-law Benjamin Silliman, a scholar of chemistry and the natural sciences, excitedly informing him that she had witnessed a magnificent comet in the night sky. "I was up long enough to believe the direction it was taking was toward the West… and we made an observation with the telescope." Faith reported she had "never…seen any comet to be compared to this…I beg you will inform me whether I have made a discovery or not."[131] Visible in the northern sky, the Great Comet of 1811, which will not pass by earth for another 2,800 years, streamed brilliantly across the heavens that year, peaking in September and October.

Daniel's lookout at Monte Video was the first viewing tower in the country opened to the public and soon became a popular destination for tourists and visitors. Faith, however, was less than enthused. In time, thousands of people from Hartford and other nearby towns came to the Wadsworths' mountain estate to stroll the grounds and enjoy a picnic on the lawn, and Faith complained of feeling like a prisoner in her own home. On Saturday, September 1, 1821, Faith's niece Maria Silliman was visiting Monte Video and observed "there were 24 waggons [*sic*], 73 people, 2 chaises and 5 teams."[132] The crowds only increased in the ensuing years, and in 1839, Faith wrote, "It seems some time as if all [of Monte Video's] beauties were devoured by strangers."[133] Despite the hordes of visitors, Daniel held firm that the tower and grounds remain open to the public, and they did so the entire time the Wadsworths owned Monte Video.

Benjamin Silliman, by John Trumbull, 1825. *National Portrait Gallery*.

In addition to building Monte Video, Daniel used his fortune to sponsor emerging artists of his time, including Thomas Cole, Frederic Edwin Church and Thomas Sully. In 1825, John Trumbull recognized the talent of Thomas Cole when he passed by a frame shop window in New York City displaying Cole's work, and Trumbull introduced Cole to Wadsworth that same year. Daniel immediately became a patron of Cole, who was living in an unheated attic at the time and was tremendously grateful for Daniel's financial support.

When shown Cole's landscape painting of New York's Kaaterskill Falls in 1826, Daniel marveled at the grandeur of how Thomas depicted the scene. The purpose of creating an idealized view of the world through art was perhaps best expressed by John Trumbull's mentor in England, Benjamin West, who said a painting must present the image "in a way to excite awe & veneration" and that the viewer's "feelings must be roused & His mind enflamed by a scene great & extraordinary. A mere matter of fact will never produce this effect."[134]

Commonly known as the founder of the Hudson River School, Thomas Cole became a good friend of Daniel's, with the painter visiting Monte Video on several occasions. Cole greatly admired the beautiful scenery and spectacular flower gardens, reminiscing to Daniel of "the many happy hours I spent at…Monte Video—also those rambles—those sunsets I enjoyed with you [which] have never faded in my mind."[135]

When visiting Avon Mountain in 1828, Thomas Cole captured the sublimity of Monte Video on canvas. Commissioned by Daniel, Thomas painted *View of Monte Video, the Seat of Daniel Wadsworth*, presenting a romanticized view of the landscape looking south from the tower showing the Gothic-style villa the Wadsworths built next to the lake. Today, Cole's painting of Monte Video remains an enduring depiction of Daniel's dream that opened the American landscape to the public.

In time, Daniel would become a patron to other artists of the Hudson River School. Coinciding with the opening of the Erie Canal in the 1820s, which gave Americans access to the West, the paintings of the Hudson River School encouraged citizens to travel to see the natural beauty of their new country. Daniel was at the forefront of that movement. Later in life, in 1848, he helped launch the career of Hartford's own Frederic Edwin Church, introducing him to Thomas Cole, who gave Frederic the chance to live and study in Catskill, New York.

When the Wadsworth Tower on Avon Mountain blew over in a windstorm in 1839, Daniel built a new wooden tower secured by cables

View of Monte Video, the seat of Daniel Wadsworth, Esq., by Thomas Cole, 1828. *Courtesy of Wadsworth Atheneum Museum of Art.*

that was ten feet taller than the first and once again encouraged the public to visit the grounds.

In 1841, he donated the land that had been his father's home in Hartford to create the art gallery that would become the Wadsworth Atheneum and raised funds for its construction. The museum was opened to the public in 1844, and pursuant to his will, Daniel left many of his paintings to the Atheneum, including "A view of my farm called Monte Video on the mountain in Avon, Connecticut…done by Thomas Cole, artist."[136]

As Hartford poet Lydia Sigourney put it after the museum opened, the Atheneum embodied Daniel's lifelong aspiration to "elevate national character"[137] through the arts. His commitment to expanding the public's admiration of its young country cemented Daniel Wadsworth's place in American history as a key figure who helped "to establish an American cultural heritage."[138] Daniel and Faith's summer home in Avon played an important role in that journey.

After Faith passed away in 1846, Daniel spent most of his time at the Wadsworth home in Hartford until he died there in 1848. And with Daniel's passing, residents of the Hartford area were left wondering whether they would still be able to take their summer excursions to the Avon tower.

12

FROM THE EDGE TO THE LEDGE

David and Clarissa Collins

As her one hundredth birthday celebration came to a close on January 1, 1914, Clarissa Ely Collins was sad to see the crowd slowly disperse from her home on Hillhouse Avenue in New Haven. No longer able to walk, she had been confined to her bedroom for the past six months and had to be carried down to the first floor to welcome her guests. And yet, her mind was still sharp, her memory excellent, and she was not going to miss this day. It was a joyous gathering with a magnificent display of flowers. There to celebrate with her were her family and friends, some of whom she had not seen in years, and Clarissa undoubtedly recounted the blessings of a life fully lived. She had experienced many joys in her life, and, among her most cherished memories, Clarissa was especially fond of the time that she spent with her family at Monte Video.

Monte Video had become such a popular weekend destination that within just a few weeks after Daniel Wadsworth died in July 1848, residents of the Hartford area began to wonder what would happen to the mountain estate and the tower. In September 1848, the property went up for sale in an estate auction. The winning bid went to David Chittenden Collins, one of the founders of the Collins Company in Canton, Connecticut, with the sale closing in April 1849. Clarissa, the daughter of William and Clarissa Ely of

Hartford, married David Collins in 1832, and the two moved into their main home on Farmington Avenue in Hartford on a site that would later become the home office building of the Aetna Life Insurance Company.

David was the son of Alexander Collins and Elizabeth Watkinson of Middletown, Connecticut. When Alexander died unexpectedly on a trip to Vermont in 1815, twelve-year-old David Collins went to work in Hartford for his uncle David Watkinson. While employed at his uncle's business in the early 1820s, David Collins learned how to make axes and decided to open his own blacksmith shop in Hartford that forged and tempered edge tools by hand using iron supplied by his uncle's warehouse. He then learned from Charles Morgan, a skilled blacksmith from Somers, Connecticut, that there was a market need for a company that could make a high-quality ready-made axe.

In 1826, David convinced his brother Samuel, or "Sam," and his cousin, William Wells, that the time was ripe to open a business manufacturing edge tools based on the axes designed by Charles Morgan. Ever the optimist, David Collins was described by his brother, Sam, as "too sanguine to be cautious,"[139] and a business was born. The partners bought a five-acre parcel of land and an old gristmill along the Farmington River in the south section of Canton that would come to be known as Collinsville. As the story is told, David Collins himself felled trees with an axe to clear the land for the new factory, and the three partners each contributed $15,000 to start the business.

Two years after the Collins Company was formed, the introduction of a trip hammer significantly increased production, enabling each worker to forge and temper eight axes per day. In just five years, by 1831, the company had grown to two hundred employees and produced 200,000 axes per year.

In the early years, the company made a hard bargain with its workers. Often, they made employees work overtime, including evenings, with the understanding that the company would not require "more than an average of twelve hours labor per day through the year."[140] In 1832, facing a disgruntled workforce, the company reduced daily hours to ten. Given the long hours, the company provided housing near the factory—though, if an employee did not adhere to any terms of their contract, the company could charge them back rent.

In the mid-1830s, Elisha Root, whom Sam Collins described as a "mechanical genius,"[141] developed a machine that could form a piece of wrought iron directly into the shape of an axe without the need for a trip hammer. This improvement, along with other Root patents, further increased the capacity of the plant, and the Collins Company became the preeminent manufacturer of edge tools in the world. By 1861, the company had become highly profitable, and the Collins brothers built a model company town in Collinsville. Eventually, competitors took market share, but the firm continued to manufacture edge tools until 1966.

Many of the immigrants working at the Collins Company were Germans who ended up settling in an area on Huckleberry Hill Road in Avon about a mile from the factory. Near the intersection of Huckleberry Hill Road with present-day Verville Road, this section of town came to be known as "Little Germany."[142] Like with many "company towns" that were created across America during the industrial age, the Collins Company had significant influence over how its employees lived their lives. Sam Collins, a supporter of the temperance movement, did not allow the sale or consumption of alcoholic beverages in Collinsville. Accordingly, an entrepreneur living just over the border on New Road in Avon opened a saloon catering to Collins Company employees looking to imbibe.

About a year after buying Monte Video, David and Clarissa decided that they, like the Wadsworths, would allow people to visit the tower, and the public rejoiced at the news. The Collins family split their time between their homes in Hartford, New Haven and Avon, and over the next thirteen years, they welcomed many family members and friends to enjoy the scenery at their Avon summer estate.

When David and Clarissa bought Monte Video in 1849, they had four daughters and would soon welcome a son, Charley, in March 1850. As a well-to-do family, the Collinses had a servant and a cook at Monte Video and brought in tutors for their children. The couple enjoyed a strong bond, writing often to each other when either was away, with David splitting his time between Collinsville and the company's office in New York City. When he was traveling, Clarissa pined for her husband to return. She was nevertheless supportive of the long hours he spent working, writing to him, "I am anxious to have you attend to your business affairs as far as health will admit."[143] David complained of rheumatism, and given the prevalence of infectious diseases of the era, the two often expressed concern for their health and that of the children.

Beginning in 1849, the Collinses spent their summers at Monte Video, arriving in late June and staying through mid-September, and invited family and friends to join them. One particularly close friend of Clarissa's was Mary Sigourney, daughter of Hartford's famed poet Lydia Sigourney, and Mary once knitted white woolen stockings for the Collinses' daughter Marian. The Collins family enjoyed their time at Monte Video each summer, though occasionally they found it difficult to obtain fresh meat, coffee or other supplies from the general store in Avon.

The years passed peacefully, and then, during their thirteenth summer at Monte Video, on August 10, 1861, David Chittenden Collins died unexpectedly, when he was only fifty-five years old, leaving Clarissa a widow. After David's passing, Clarissa spent most of her time in Hartford or in New Haven, where she was raised, and was unsure of what to do with Monte Video. In the summer of 1864, however, an event took place that likely convinced her it would be unwise to keep the mountain estate.

On the humid evening of Tuesday, July 19, 1864, with the Civil War not yet settled, many residents in downtown Hartford were sitting outside, trying to stay cool as the temperature was still near eighty degrees well into the evening. Those living in higher elevations of the city could look west toward Talcott Mountain and see the fading twilight behind the crest of the mountain. Then suddenly, at around 9:20 p.m., residents saw an orange glow along the top of the ridge that, in just minutes, grew into an inferno. There could be no mistake. The Wadsworth Tower at Clarissa Collins's Monte Video estate was ablaze. Onlookers were amazed at the spectacle as residents rushed to higher ground to get a better view. The conflagration did not last long—by 10:00 p.m., the beloved tower had fallen.

Monte Video had become a favorite destination for a weekend excursion, and questions quickly turned to whether the tower would be rebuilt. But with her husband dead and her children all grown, Clarissa decided to sell her summer residence on the mountain. Two years after the fire, in July 1866, she sold Monte Video to a man named Dr. Henry L. Sheldon of the U.S. Navy. It soon became clear, however, that Dr. Sheldon had no interest in rebuilding the tower or allowing the public to stroll the grounds. Visits to a viewing tower in Avon, it seemed, had come to an end.

13

"OFF TO THE TOWER!"

Henry Bartlett's Dream

On a beautiful day with clear skies, the Reverend Joseph Twichell of the Asylum Hill Congregational Church in Hartford and Samuel Clemens (a.k.a. Mark Twain) were once again taking one of their long hikes to the Bartlett Tower on Talcott Mountain in Avon. As the two close friends often did, that day they took a steam train from Hartford to Bloomfield on the Connecticut Western Railroad, hiked approximately five miles from there to the tower and then hiked another eight miles back to Hartford via the Albany Turnpike through West Hartford.

As they got close to the tower on their way up from Bloomfield and crossed into Simsbury, the hiking trail intersected a gravel road that brought visitors traveling by horse and carriage to the tower from the Weatogue Gap. Arriving at the road, Twichell and Clemens came upon a carriage occupied by loquacious acquaintances of theirs from Hartford. They exchanged pleasantries, but the two friends were in no mood to have their fine walk spoiled by chatty conversation. So, when the traveling party in the carriage invited Twichell and Clemens to join them for a midafternoon lunch at Henry Bartlett's place on the mountain, Reverend Twichell politely declined, saying the two had just eaten a lunch they had brought with them.

But as Twichell and Clemens walked the rest of the way to the tower on their way to the "Royal View"[144] overlooking the Farmington River Valley, they realized they had just put themselves in a difficult predicament. The truth was that they had not eaten a thing and were, in fact, starving. When they arrived, they quickly found the proprietor, Henry Bartlett, and asked

Left: Reverend Joseph Twichell. *Yale University*.

Right: Samuel Clemens (Mark Twain). *A.F. Bradley*.

Opposite: Matthew "Henry" Bartlett. *From the* Hartford Courant.

if he could serve them dinner, with Clemens exclaiming, "I am hungry as a bear!"[145] They pleaded to be served anywhere other than the dining room—a cellar or attic, if need be, but Henry replied that he had neither a cellar nor an attic. When Twichell and Clemens pressed Bartlett again, Henry said he would be willing to allow the two to dine in his private sitting room and library on the second floor. After all, Henry regarded them as friends and two of his most faithful guests.

As the pair ate their dinner from the sitting room, they remarked to each other about the spectacular views, looking west across the Farmington River Valley, east to Hartford and north toward Mount Tom and Mount Holyoke. Reverend Twichell turned to his friend and said: "Clemens, this is fine! This is capital!!" Mark Twain couldn't let his friend feel completely satisfied without some ribbing, however, retorting, "Now, Joe, I suppose the language you used to those people in declining their invitation you would call duplicity, but I call it lying!"[146]

About the same time Dr. Sheldon bought Monte Video from Clarissa Collins in 1866, Matthew "Henry" Bartlett of Avon was standing on the summit of Mount Holyoke in Massachusetts enjoying the view from the Prospect House, a hotel owned by John and Frances French. While there, Henry was struck with an idea that would become his life's purpose. Although he avoided service in the military during the Civil War, the past five years had nonetheless been extremely challenging for Henry.

M. H. Bartlett.

At the start of the Civil War, he had moved to Washington, D.C., at the suggestion of his older brother David Bartlett, who was working as a correspondent there for the *Springfield Republican*. With his brother's help, Henry found employment in the U.S. Postal Service and then at the U.S. Treasury, but over the next two years, his health deteriorated. He began to experience chest pain, had difficulty breathing and was spitting up blood. It was clearly a respiratory illness, likely either pneumonia or tuberculosis, and as Henry's condition worsened, many of his friends and coworkers did not expect him to survive. Unable to continue working, Henry decided to return to Avon, Connecticut, to get fresh air, a common prescription for respiratory illness at the time.

Back in Avon, his condition stabilized a bit, and Henry bought himself a horse and carriage so he could take long excursions in the country that would expose him to the open air. Inspired by the Frenches' money-making enterprise at the top of Mount Holyoke, he resolved to rebuild the Wadsworth Tower on Avon Mountain where he could "breathe Talcott Mountain air"[147] and regain his health. He promptly contacted Dr. Sheldon to see if he could buy Monte Video. Henry's heart sank, however, when Dr. Sheldon demanded $18,000 for the estate, as he knew he would not be able to raise that kind of money.

Henry did not despair long, however. Having spent many a day in his youth hiking Avon Mountain, he knew that the ideal site for a tower was actually on a spot about a quarter-mile north and fifty feet higher than the location of the previous Wadsworth towers. After spending hours researching and contacting landowners, Henry was able to secure a thirty-acre parcel on the ridge, on a slice of Avon near where the towns of Avon, Simsbury and Bloomfield meet. But when Dr. Sheldon refused to sell Henry the right to access the parcel via the existing road from the Albany Turnpike, Henry faced another obstacle. Undeterred, he then went about securing additional parcels to the north so that people could access his planned tower via the Weatogue Gap in Simsbury (present-day Route 185).

Partnering with his nephew Charles Kellogg, grandson of Avon Congregational Church's first minister, Bela Kellogg, Henry built his tower and summer house in 1867 "with the idea of charging people to visit,"[148]

Above: The Bartlett Tower, Avon. *Courtesy of Friends of Heublein Tower.*

Opposite, top: Henry Bartlett's summer residence. *Courtesy of Friends of Heublein Tower.*

Opposite, bottom: Dance floor next to Bartlett's tower. *Courtesy of Friends of Heublein Tower.*

opening it on July 4 of that year. At a height of about fifty-five feet and located on the ridge about forty yards south of where the pavilion stands today, the tower stairs had four landings with windows and benches, leading up to a viewing platform at the top.

Henry charged visitors fifty cents to hike to the top of the tower and welcomed them to picnic on the grounds. North of his tower, just over the town line in Simsbury, he constructed a summer house where his guests could buy a meal or refreshments. He named his summer home on the mountain King Philip House[149] given the legend of the Wampanoag sachem Metacom, derisively nicknamed "King Philip" by the colonists. According to the legend, in March 1676, as warriors burned the town of Simsbury during King Philip's War, Metacom was said to have watched from a cave just below the "Royal View."[150] Henry offered his visitors amenities, including croquet, swings and a picnic area as well as a restaurant, piano and dance floor. Guests could stay overnight for $1.50, meals included, and day visitors could buy a lunch, including a "plate"[151] of ice cream, for less than a dollar. In the year the tower opened, thirty-two thousand people visited Bartlett's mountain resort.

While guests praised the tower and the beautiful views, they let Henry know that his carriage road up to the Royal View was too steep, as many people who hike the trail today from the parking lot of Talcott Mountain State Park can attest. So, to provide easier access to the tower from the south, Henry reached out to his wealthier brother David to see if he would be willing to buy Monte Video from Dr. Sheldon. David, who was living in Washington, D.C., at the time, agreed, and in the fall of 1867, he purchased the mountain estate, giving his brother Henry rights to access the new tower from the Albany Turnpike. With access secured from both the north and the south, Henry built a road connecting the two routes. With two ways to approach the tower, he hoped it would encourage more residents from Hartford and surrounding towns to come to Talcott Mountain each year to enjoy the views.

After earning enough money, Henry Bartlett purchased Monte Video from his brother David in 1872 and then sold it a year later to a man named Henry Judd, who gave Henry continued access to the tower from the Albany Turnpike. For the next two decades, Bartlett's tower became a favorite destination, from young couples courting their affection for one another to socialites taking a pleasure trip from Hartford.

Samuel Clemens met Joseph Twichell in 1867 when attending a social gathering of the Asylum Hill Congregational Church in Hartford, where Twichell served as pastor. Clemens had just returned from a five-month journey to Europe, Egypt and the Holy Land that inspired him to write a humorous account of his travels called *The Innocents Abroad*, his first big literary and financial success. Clemens and Twichell hit it off at once and became lifelong friends. After Samuel Clemens married Olivia Langdon in 1870, the young couple initially lived in Buffalo, New York. Then, in 1871, they moved to Hartford and built a home at Nook Farm, where Twain would write his best-known books, including *The Adventures of Tom Sawyer* and *Adventures of Huckleberry Finn*. With Samuel Clemens now in Hartford, he and Joseph Twichell began enjoying long walks together, even attempting to walk to Boston on one occasion. In 1877, Twichell and Clemens traveled together to Bermuda and a year later visited Germany and Switzerland, which inspired Mark Twain to write *A Tramp Abroad*.

The two would often hike to the Bartlett Tower with their good friend Charles Dudley Warner, who was coeditor of the *Hartford Courant* with Joseph Hawley. Warner was one of the literary figures who lived at Nook Farm, an area along the Park River in Hartford that was home to intellectuals, writers and social reformers, including Samuel Clemens and Harriet Beecher Stowe.

Samuel Clemens almost always visited the tower by hiking there, but one day in October 1877, he came by carriage to show his wife, Olivia, and their two young daughters the views from the tower. During this visit, to show his appreciation to Henry Bartlett, Clemens brought a half dozen of his books, autographed. In the copy Henry received of *The Innocents Abroad*, Twain wrote on the flyleaf:

> *To Mr. Bartlett, who has robbed the historical command "Away with him to the tower!" of all its terrors—this, With grateful acknowledgements of*
> *Mark Twain*
> *Hartford, Oct. 1877*[152]

The Bartlett Tower had become a beloved destination for summer excursions. Henry had survived serious illness and found his remedy in the breathtaking and breath-giving scenery of the Talcott Mountain Ridge, and he was happy to share it with the public. While the mountain resort was not as profitable as Henry envisioned, he met many of his lifelong friends there and was pleased that it had become a landmark for visitors to enjoy.

Then in October 1888, when the fall foliage was in full display, a businessman from New York, accompanied by two women, was visiting the summer house and tower when he introduced himself to Henry. Bartlett proudly showed him around and brought him up to the top of the tower to see the views. The man, who evidently must have never visited the Alps, was amazed at the scenery to the point of claiming he had not seen anything like it in Europe. He then asked Henry if he would be willing to sell his property. Bartlett replied: "I don't think I do. I have lived here twenty-two years and I guess I will spend the rest of my days here."[153] Not satisfied with the answer, the businessman made it clear he was willing to pay top dollar. He wanted the "whole mountain top"[154] and Henry's help in getting it.

14

A MOUNTAIN OF A GIFT

The Robert Hoe Affair

Two years after Robert Hoe III died in September 1909, the executors of his estate had given up any hope of a quick and smooth settlement of his financial affairs. What had initially seemed like spurious claims from people trying to contend for a piece of Hoe's fortune had turned into tales of intrigue and scandal. Among them, a woman named Cornelia Roberts was asserting that Robert Hoe had effectively deeded her his Monte Video summer residence in Avon, Connecticut. The allegation seemed absurd. How could Hoe have conveyed Monte Video with no mention of that in his will? Also highly unusual was that the will did not list Robert's wife, Olivia Hoe, as a beneficiary. Rather, most of the financial assets were to be distributed among Robert and Olivia's children and grandchildren, with his extraordinary collection of rare books and fine art to be sold at auction.

By any measure, Robert Hoe III had a remarkable career. His firm, R. Hoe & Company, had grown to be one of the premier manufacturers of printing presses in the world, with plants in New York City and London. Yes, he had been given the opportunity to assume the business from his father, but by his own industry, Robert had successfully grown the business even more over the years. R. Hoe & Co. was the first to provide newspapers with the ability to print in color and the first to develop the octuple press, which greatly increased the hourly production rate of newspapers and periodicals, enabling publishers to keep their costs down.

Beyond his professional achievements, Robert and his family had risen to be at or near the highest level of New York society. He owned multiple properties, both commercial and personal. Among them were his main home on East Thirty-Sixth Street in Manhattan, a country estate in Westchester County and a summer residence on Talcott Mountain in Avon, Connecticut, the famed Monte Video. He was an avid collector of paintings, drawings, porcelain, furniture and other artifacts. An art critic of the time said that "as a collector, Mr. Hoe was simply omnivorous."[155] While many wealthy individuals specialized in a single area of interest, Robert Hoe had a veritable museum in his house—a "collection of collections"[156] as one writer called it. Given his interest in the history of printing, he amassed an impressive accumulation of rare books, including highly prized volumes that dated to the fifteenth century, back to the beginning of printing itself. Respected by his colleagues, wealthy beyond all measure and firmly cast into society's upper echelon, Robert Hoe III had it all.

Robert Hoe III, circa 1880. *Courtesy of Friends of Heublein Tower.*

In 1805, Robert Hoe I, along with his brothers-in-law Peter and Matthew Smith, started Smith, Hoe & Company to manufacture printing presses in New York City. Renamed R. Hoe & Co. in 1822, the business was taken over by sons Richard and Robert Hoe Jr. and became known for its state-of-the-art presses. By 1856, the company's machines could print ten to fifteen thousand sheets of newspaper per hour, and as a result, R. Hoe & Co. played a large part in enabling the rapid expansion of newspapers in the nineteenth century. Robert Hoe III assumed control of the business in 1886, and by the turn of the twentieth century, the company had become highly profitable with a factory on Grand Street in lower Manhattan that employed 2,500 workers and another plant in London that employed 800.

With his successful business and family background, Robert possessed a "deep streak of elitism"[157] and clearly viewed himself as being above the working class. When two workers painted Hoe's private apartment and asked how he liked the job, he fired them for "daring to address him in the factory yard."[158] And when another employee got on the same elevator Hoe was using, Robert dismissed him as well.

Robert Hoe made every effort in his life to position himself and his family at the highest level of New York society. While not technically part of Ward McAllister's "Four Hundred"[159] of high-society individuals living in New York during the Gilded Age, the Hoes nonetheless lived a life of luxury and mingled with New York's elite. When in New York City, Robert and Olivia Hoe and their eight children lived on East Thirty-Sixth Street in Manhattan in the highly prestigious Murray Hill section of the city. The home was magnificently furnished with a chandelier lighting a foyer that led to a dramatic winding staircase. Adorning the walls were several paintings by European masters, including Rembrandt's *Young Girl Holding out a Medal on a Chain*. To help run the household, Robert and Olivia had thirteen servants and a governess for the children. While Robert and Olivia allowed their younger children to eat with the family at the midday meal, in the evening, the children were prohibited, as dinners were always formal, in "full dress."[160]

A trustee of the Metropolitan Museum of Art in New York, Robert considered himself among the cultured class of society and supported opening the museum on Sundays, as he believed it would "elevate the condition of the laboring classes."[161]

At first, Henry Bartlett resisted Robert Hoe's overtures for the Talcott Mountain land, but the price Hoe offered was too attractive to turn down. Robert made it clear, however, that the deal would only be consummated if Henry could work with the neighboring landowners such that Hoe could buy all of the parcels along the ridge, amounting to some 520 acres. Robert Hoe was a private individual, and he wanted a private mountain retreat. Because Henry had sold Monte Video to Henry Judd in 1873, and a man named Ethan Ely of Longmeadow, Massachusetts, owned land just north of Bartlett's tower, Henry had to arrange a multiple-party transaction to meet Robert Hoe's demands.

In February 1889, a deal was reached whereby Ely and Judd first sold their parcels to Henry Bartlett, and then Henry, in turn, sold the 520 acres, including his tower, to Robert Hoe. Henry still wanted to offer a viewing tower to the public, however, so he used the sale proceeds to build another tower in 1890. His new tower was on the Metacomet Ridge seven miles to the north, just south of Tariffville in Simsbury, a short walk from the train station there.

True to his word about wanting privacy, Robert Hoe did not want the public coming to visit Bartlett's first tower in Avon. After he was unable to discourage visitors from trespassing on his property, in May 1893, he decided to tear down both the tower and the summer house that Henry had built. Shortly thereafter, Robert decided he wanted even more land to secure his privacy at Monte Video, buying up seven additional parcels in 1894, including one from Chester Woodford of Nod Road in Avon.

It is not clear how much time the Hoe family actually spent at Monte Video. Given they had other homes in New York City, Westchester County and the Adirondacks at the time, they may not have made it up to Talcott Mountain all that often. When Robert did visit, it may have been without his wife, Olivia. As early as 1890, shortly after then fifty-one-year-old Robert Hoe acquired Monte Video, a twenty-eight-year-old single woman named Cornelia Whitehead of New York came to visit the mountain estate. How she and Robert Hoe came to know each other is uncertain, but it would become evident that Robert must have been quite fond of Cornelia.

Cornelia Whitehead grew up in Brooklyn, New York, the second of five children to Henry Whitehead and his wife, Charlotte. In November 1910, a little over a year after Robert Hoe passed away, fifty-two-year-old Cornelia Whitehead married her thirty-eight-year-old first cousin, a lawyer named Owen Roberts, who was a veteran of the Spanish-American War and worked as a trader on the floor of the New York Stock Exchange. Now, as Cornelia Roberts, she told the executors of Hoe's estate that Robert Hoe had deeded her Monte Video by way of two separate parcels, one conveyed on June 17, 1890, and the other on March 16, 1894. The idea that Robert Hoe would convey all of Monte Video to a non-family member, and to do that beginning just sixteen months after acquiring it, seemed impossible to believe.

Near the end of his life, Robert himself clearly did not believe he had given title to Cornelia. Seven months before he died, in February 1909, he signed a lease giving her the privilege of living at Monte Video for twenty-one years, renewable for another five years, after which it would revert to the Hoe family. But even the lease transaction was eyebrow raising to the executors managing Hoe's estate—for what would have prompted Hoe to do that? After Cornelia Whitehead Roberts died in a sanitarium in July 1912, the two key witnesses to the nature of the relationship were both dead.

In addition to Cornelia's assertion that she owned Monte Video, the executors had to deal with a claim by another woman from Kentucky named Margaret Johnson Brown, who alleged that Robert had conveyed to her shares in the Metropolitan Trust Company, a New York bank. They soon learned that, beginning in 1905, when he was sixty-six years old, Robert began a relationship with Margaret. Thirty-two years old and married at the time, Margaret Brown was the daughter of Hoe's superintendent of his plant in London. Robert made promises to Margaret in appreciation for her affection, and despite objections from Hoe's executors, a court awarded her $260,000 from the estate for the value of the common stock Robert gave her.

In 1914, Hoe's executors sued the estate of Cornelia Whitehead Roberts to contest Owen Roberts's claim of ownership of Monte Video and its 520 acres, arguing that the lease was invalid and that Cornelia had fraudulently filed deeds of title with the Town of Avon land records office. Hoe's executors had a point: Cornelia did not file those documents with the Town of Avon until November 1909, two months after Hoe's death. As with Margaret, the executors contended that Cornelia Whitehead had duped Robert through a "meretricious"[162] relationship, implying the two were having an affair. They further asserted that Cornelia had given no real consideration for the property and that Hoe had never actually delivered the deeds to her.

The manner in which the deeds were filed with the town clerk in Avon was, in fact, highly irregular. Cornelia was able to get an employee in the county clerk's office in New York to testify that Robert Hoe executed the instruments conveying title to Cornelia back in 1890 and 1894, asserting that he recognized the handwriting of the notary public who validated the documents. On that basis, Avon's town clerk at the time, Oliver Bishop, certified the recording of the deeds in Cornelia's name. Resolution of the legal dispute between Hoe's executors and Cornelia Roberts's estate was complicated by the fact that Cornelia's will named several beneficiaries, including her mother, sister and niece, all of whom went by the name of Charlotte. Moreover, in her will, Cornelia granted New York lawyer Lewis Cass Ledyard Jr., who was presumably her personal attorney, the right to live at Monte Video during his lifetime.

While Cornelia and Owen were married for only twenty months before she died in July 1912, the marriage may not have been a happy one. In her will, which she prepared six months after marrying Owen, her husband was left with only "porcelain vases and figurines,"[163] with most of her estate bequeathed to her mother and sister, along with her niece who was named as residuary legatee. Under Connecticut statutes, however, a surviving spouse has the right to elect a "statutory share" equal to one-third the value of the estate, so Owen quickly probated Cornelia's will in Avon. When Cornelia's niece Charlotte, a resident of New Jersey, found out, she sued in Hartford Superior Court, claiming the will should have been probated in New York, arguing that 20 Broad Street in Manhattan was her aunt's principal address. But the Hartford Superior Court, in its original ruling and on appeal, concluded that Cornelia's primary home was, indeed, Monte Video.

How Cornelia's estate was ultimately adjudicated is unclear. In the end, Owen likely settled out of court with Lewis Cass Ledyard Jr. and the assorted Charlottes, as he ended up with all of Monte Video.

After Cornelia died, Owen married a woman named Florence Wadley, and they had one child, a daughter named Katherine, or "Kit."[164] Born in 1918, Katherine would end up inheriting Monte Video and owning it until 1986. In 1939, when she was working as a twenty-year-old model with the Powers Agency in New York City, Kit met forty-four-year-old aviator Eugene "Gene" Vidal, who was rumored to have previously been the lover of Amelia Earhart. When she and Gene married in December of that year, Katherine Roberts became the stepmother to author Gore Vidal, who was the only son of Gene and his first wife, Nina Gore.

Owen Roberts would turn out to have something in common with Robert Hoe, as he became an art collector for the rest of his life. In 1924, Owen sold his membership in the New York Stock Exchange and moved to Beijing, China, with his wife, Florence, and daughter, Katherine, where they spent the next five years. While there, he and Florence amassed one of the largest collections of Chinese porcelain and art in the world, lending some pieces to the Metropolitan Museum of Art.

Robert Hoe III, circa 1895. *Courtesy of Friends of Heublein Tower.*

Arguably the greatest testament to Robert Hoe's wealth and place in society was his collection of art and rare books. Robert was a true bibliophile with a deep appreciation for the history of printing and admiration for those who were the first to print books in England, particularly William Caxton and Wynken de Worde.

In addition to rare books, Hoe collected many rare manuscripts, including one about King Henry V, dating to around 1670, as well as extremely rare English poems dating back to a time before the first printing press. In addition to owning a Gutenberg Bible printed on vellum, one of only four in existence, Hoe owned a copy of a Latin dictionary called *The Catholicon*, the only other work known to have been printed by Johannes Gutenberg. His collection also included a Bible written in calligraphy around the thirteenth century that contained St. Jerome's Latin version of the scriptures. It is no wonder that Robert Hoe treasured his ancient Bibles and the works of Gutenberg and England's first printers. Hoe fancied himself like them—an innovator who believed he had done as much as they had to develop the art of printing. Art collectors of the time noted that Robert's assemblage of books included "all the great masterpieces of English literature."[165] All told, it was an extraordinary collection. A catalogue of Hoe's books and manuscripts written by English authors before the year 1700 "took up six volumes."[166]

Robert's home on East Thirty-Sixth Street in Manhattan was so stuffed with books and artifacts that a visitor described it as "a cluttered arsenal of the history of book-making. From basement to attic, volumes were packed like sardines, two-deep, in bookcases piled upon bookcases."[167]

Among his rare books, Robert's most prized possession was Sir Thomas Malory's *Le Morte D'Arthur* published in 1485 by England's first printer, William Caxton. The book, which tells the tale of King Arthur and the Knights of the Round Table, is considered by many to be the first true English novel, and Robert Hoe III owned the only near perfect copy of it in existence. The book was so valuable that financier J.P. Morgan, a prodigious collector of rare books himself, once offered Robert all thirty-six Caxtons in his possession in exchange for it. Many regarded Robert's library of rare books as, "beyond all question, the finest this country has ever contained."[168]

In settling the estate of Robert Hoe, seven surviving children and grandchildren were given an interest in shares of R. Hoe & Company. Including the value of the business, real estate properties and proceeds from the sale of the rare books and artwork at auction, Hoe's estate was valued at about $8 million, or over $250 million in today's dollars. Although Robert Hoe had rebuffed J.P. Morgan's offer to buy *Le Morte D'Arthur* years earlier, when Hoe's rare books were auctioned off in the spring of 1911, Morgan finally secured the book he treasured above all others, paying what was then an eye-popping sum of $42,800.

Hoe's wife, Olivia, was not named in the will, but under New York law in existence prior to 1930, she would have received a dower interest, or about one-third, of the value of her husband's real estate in New York, including their homes in Manhattan, Westchester County and Upper St. Regis Lake in the Adirondacks.

Olivia Phelps James Hoe. *Courtesy of Friends of Heublein Tower.*

From 1805 to 1909, the eastern edge of Avon along the crest of Talcott Mountain attracted men who had big ambitions and left their impression on the town. After the era of the Avon towers, a German immigrant named Gilbert Heublein, who ran a successful business selling premixed cocktails, decided to build a Bavarian-style "castle on the mountain"[169] for his wife, Louise. Completed in 1914, the six-story tower located just over the town line in Simsbury included a ballroom on the top floor that today serves as an observation deck to those visiting Talcott Mountain State Park.

Many people who visit Gilbert Heublein's tower in Simsbury today believe it is the only tower to have stood on the ridge. But Heublein was inspired to build for the same reasons that Daniel Wadsworth and Henry Bartlett built their towers and for the same reason that David Collins and Robert Hoe III wanted to own Wadsworth's Monte Video. To this day, the mountain beckons people to visit the traprock ridge so rich in history and exceptional in its beauty.

PART V

PLACES OF DOOM

15

THE FUSE IS LIT

The Climax Fuse Factory Fire

On Friday, September 15, 1905, under sunny skies, the sixty-three workers at the Climax Fuse factory in Avon were ready to eat their lunch, a respite from the hard labor. On that Friday, the weather was beautiful; partly cloudy skies in the morning had given way to sunshine, and the temperature rose to the low sixties. As it was still warm enough to eat outside, the workers could get out of the gritty air of the factory. Life was not easy for employees at the plant; they had to work at least ten hours a day, six days a week, with most workers paid $1.00 to $1.50 a day depending on their experience level. The company preferred younger workers for the factory, as they could pay them less than older workers, with about half of the employees under the age of twenty-six. And the Climax Fuse factory heavily recruited women because they were paid less than men.

The Avon plant was run by a forty-seven-year-old man named Frank Hadsell who had worked on and off for Climax Fuse since 1884, when he took a job there as a nightwatchman and later became a foreman. Still bitter from the loss of his wife, Mary Bowen, or "Mate"[170] as he called her, twelve years earlier, Frank poured himself into his work.

As plant superintendent, Frank managed the day-to-day operations, including personnel decisions. His peer, forty-nine-year-old John Andrews, was superintendent of the mechanical department and was responsible for maintaining the machines that ran the factory. John Andrews started working at the Avon fuse factory when he was thirteen years old and loved building and maintaining machines, eventually becoming the plant's "master

Frank Hadsell with family members, 1911. *Clint B. Hadsell Collection.*

mechanic."[171] Always interested in new technology, he became one of the first Avon residents to buy a car.

Business had been increasing steadily for Climax Fuse since the 1890s, and Frank had been busy trying to find more workers to supply the factory. Many were immigrants or the children of immigrants, and Frank made trips to Ellis Island to fill the demand for labor. Employees who were new to the company likely heard of the dangers of working in a fuse factory, but they needed a job and were grateful to have one.

In the nineteenth century, the safety fuse was a critical invention that enabled the construction of the railroads and the exploration of mines. Prior to the fuse's invention in the 1830s, blasting away rock was an extremely dangerous proposition, as construction workers and miners would fill wooden tubes, straws or goose quills with black powder and hope they could get out of the way in time. With nothing to slow progression of the flame through the tubes or quills, the blast would often occur immediately after ignition, and many workers were killed as a result.

In 1831, William Bickford of England invented a method of encasing black powder in twisted yarn, producing a fuse that would burn slowly enough to give workers time before the blast ignited. The production of safety fuse in the United States was started by a company in Simsbury that eventually became Ensign-Bickford. While the jobs of miners and construction workers got a lot safer due to the invention, the process to manufacture the fuse entailed a significant risk of accidental explosions or fire as the black powder and varnish used in production were highly flammable.

As a competitor to the operation in Simsbury, in 1852, Avon farmer Romeo Andrews, grandfather of John Andrews, started up his own fuse production facility in Avon. Faced with cash flow problems, however, Romeo's business ran intermittently for eighteen years before ceasing operations in 1871. Then another investor, Franklin M. Alford, also of Avon, resumed operations in "a rather haphazard way,"[172] and just two years later, in 1873, the business came to an abrupt, and explosive, end. Sparks from a coal stove ignited yarn and powder dust floating in the air, resulting in a blast that caused the death of an employee and the destruction of the factory.

Then in 1880, Romeo Andrews's son Albert, John Andrews's uncle, started up another safety fuse manufacturing plant on the same site, but the factory suffered the same fate as Frank Alford's. On June 25, 1883, when a kettle of tar boiled over, it ignited a store of black powder, causing an explosion that destroyed the whole facility, and the future of the company was in jeopardy. Despite the disaster, in 1884, Albert Andrews gained the financial backing of a man named Harry Chapman of the Metallic Cap Company in New Jersey. Seeing the synergies between fuse production and his own business of manufacturing blasting caps, Harry was enthusiastic about rebuilding and investing in the operation. The new business in Avon became the Climax Fuse Company, with Albert Andrews as its first president.

Between 1884 and 1892, Climax Fuse was highly successful and grew rapidly. Then in 1892, Harry Chapman struck up a friendship with Ralph Ensign, his competitor in Simsbury, resulting in Ensign-Bickford & Co. acquiring a half interest in Climax Fuse.

At the most basic level, safety fuse at the time was produced by pouring black powder into a line of rope (or jute yarn) as the line was being braided. Yarn was then spun in the opposite direction around the fuse (called "countering") to prevent the jute yarn from untwisting. The fuse was then varnished with tar or asphalt to make it waterproof, as many customers needed fuses that could be used in mines or other places where the fuse would be exposed to water. Miners and construction workers could be confident that they would have time to safely get away after igniting the blasting cap as the safety fuse produced by Climax Fuse at the time had a burn rate of about three feet per minute.

Most of the sixty-three employees at the factory on Friday, September 15, 1905, worked in the main building of the plant and were about evenly distributed on two floors. On the second floor, a man named Otto Prowe was the foreman of the area responsible for producing cloth tape and spinning the yarn. Typically, when young women and teenage girls joined the company, they were assigned to the cloth cutting and yarn spinning room under Otto. Unlike all other employees who were paid a daily wage, yarn spinners were paid on a piecework basis, just six-tenths of a cent per yard spun. Those who

Climax Fuse women employees. *Clint B. Hadsell Collection.*

Coilers at Climax Fuse, 1900. *Clint B. Hadsell Collection.*

were willing to work extra-long hours and could spin as much as 1,300 yards per week earned as much as employees who were paid a daily wage.

On September 15, 1905, the spinning and countering room consisted of ten young women and girls, all but one under the age of twenty-five. The group included Molly McCarthy, the sixteen-year-old cousin of six McCarthy siblings who worked at the plant, and her twenty-four-year-old friend Julia Sullivan, who joined Climax Fuse just two days earlier, as well as twenty-one-year-old Maggie Connors and the recently married eighteen-year-old Claire Wilde. Also among the yarn spinners was eighteen-year-old Nora Ryan; twenty-year-old Nellie Canfield, whose brother and father worked at the plant; and a twenty-three-year-old Polish immigrant named Mary Litzkowicz whom Frank Hadsell thought of as a "good, willing, quiet worker."[173] Rounding out the department were the teenage sisters Diana and Florence LeGeyt and one mother, twenty-six-year-old Minnie Tucker from Granby, who had a five-year-old son.

Also on the second floor was the coiling department, headed up by Clint Hadsell, Frank Hadsell's brother, where the fuse was coiled into barrels to prepare the product for shipment. Clint's group included several young men, among them Horrace Morron, Michael McCarthy and Michael's younger brother Timothy.

On the first floor was one of the plant's most experienced employees, Jimmie Joyce. As the overseer of the finishing department, he ran the taping machines that encased the jute yarn and was responsible for waterproofing the safety fuse in a bath of asphalt. Jimmie had about ten workers in his area, including the most tenured employees at the plant, Charlie Dimock, brother-in-law of Otto Prowe; Mary Ann Burke; and two of the other McCarthy brothers, Dick and Simon. Right around the corner from the finishing department on the first floor was Mary Ann's husband, William Burke, who headed up inspection. In William's area, employees ran their fingers along the length of the fuse looking for imperfections like a section with insufficient powder or evidence of knots that could indicate a weakness in the strand.

As a safety measure, the company kept its store of black powder away from the first floor. Despite this mandate, powder was nonetheless present in the finishing room. Before waterproofing, small grains of remnant powder could be found along the fuse, and those grains either collected in sawdust on the floor or ended up floating in the air. And a plant filled with asphalt, powder and sawdust was a recipe for disaster.

On that sunny September day, each of the employees had a story to tell, many about trying to make it in America as part of an immigrant family.

Yarn spinner Nora Ryan lived with her older sister Mary Ann Burke and brother-in-law William. Just two years earlier, the three of them had been living in Bristol, Connecticut, when they decided to make the move to Avon to work at Climax Fuse. In addition to Nora, the Burke household included William and Mary Ann's two children, a twelve-year-old son and a ten-year-old daughter. Like many of the other employees eating their lunch that day, William, Mary Ann and Nora likely talked about their plans for the coming Sunday, their one day off.

Jimmie Joyce, foreman of the finishing room, was a veteran of Climax Fuse, and his wife, Anne, had been a jute yarn spooler at the factory until she left in 1904. In September 1905, Anne was seven months pregnant with their first child, and the Joyces were looking forward to raising a family. On Jimmie's team, forty-one-year-old Patrick "Patsy"[174] Loughman; his

John Andrews (*seated second from left*) and Jimmie Joyce (*seated with dog*). *Andrews Family Collection.*

wife, Lillian; and their three daughters had recently moved to the area, and another employee, James Wallace, was the thirty-year-old son of Irish immigrants who supported his wife, Mary, and their three children back in Springfield, Massachusetts. Also on Jimmie's team was Michael Canfield, age fifty, the father of six children, including son Michael Jr. and daughter Nellie, both of whom worked at the plant.

The children of Irish immigrants, there were a total of seven McCarthys working at the factory. In addition to nineteen-year-old Simon, fifteen-year-old Timothy and eighteen-year-old twins Michael and Dick, there was twenty-two-year-old Patrick and an older sister Mary, along with their fifteen-year-old cousin Molly, who spun yarn. The McCarthys were well known in town as being a musical family, forming their own brass band. Common for that era, all the McCarthys had started their employment with Climax Fuse as children, having to drop out of grammar school so they could support the family. Their father, John McCarthy, had passed away five years earlier, leaving their mother, Mary, a widow, and they had no other option but to work at the factory to make ends meet.

All told, at least one-third of the Climax Fuse employees on that September day were the children of immigrants, most of them Irish, but some of central European descent. Although the work was demanding and the days were long, employees at the plant looked forward to a brighter future.

Early in the afternoon of September 15, after their lunch break was over, all the employees returned to their stations for the afternoon shift. The belt-driven spinning machines started up, and everyone got back to work. The air in the factory was still filled with fine particles of black powder and yarn lint from the morning session, but the workers had learned to live with the conditions. Yes, employees were aware of the plant's history, but those explosions had been in the distant past. There were newer machines now, and the new buildings constructed by the company a few years earlier had sprinkler systems installed that would extinguish a blaze if there ever was a fire.

Jimmie Joyce returned to his post as foreman in the finishing room on the first floor, and one of the first tasks that he had to solve was to clear hardened asphalt from a hole in the frame of the reel from which the fuse was drawn to soak in the liquid asphalt below. After waterproofing a line of fuse, Jimmie found that once again the hole in the reel frame had been clogged with asphalt. And as he had done countless times before, he took a red-hot iron poker and applied it to the inside of the hole to melt out the asphalt. The hot iron once again did the trick, as he successfully cleared the asphalt from the frame. But unbeknownst to Jimmie, as he went to draw another fuse through the still "red-hot reel"[175] for waterproofing, the next line of fuse to be treated was inadequately covered with yarn and tape. Then Jimmie Joyce turned the crank on the reel.

In the early afternoon, Dr. Edward W. Kellogg, grandson of Avon Congregational Church's first pastor, was standing on the lawn of his summer residence on West Main Street directly opposite the Climax Fuse factory. Though he lived most of the year in Hartford, Edward inherited his childhood home in Avon from his father, Bela Crocker Kellogg, and loved to spend time there. With the weather still warm in mid-September, it had been a quiet day as he relaxed, enjoying the outdoors in the waning days of summer. Suddenly, at about 1:40 p.m., Edward heard a muffled explosion. It didn't seem like much at first, but just seconds later, to his horror, Dr. Kellogg saw a wall of flame race through the first floor of the main factory building and then smoke billowing up through the second floor. A shower of stone and brick was followed by the terrified screams of employees trapped inside.

Just moments after the initial explosion, sheets of flame shot out in all directions and black smoke quickly filled both floors of the building, making it virtually impossible for employees to know which way to run. People trapped inside the building shrieked in agony, with many unable to find an exit. In no time, the fire leaped around the corner from Jimmie Joyce's finishing room to William Burke's inspection area, then swept up the broad staircase and elevator to the second floor where workers were spooling yarn and tape.

Superintendent Frank Hadsell was sitting in his office next to the factory floor when he heard the blast. He rushed to the finishing room on the first floor but could not enter due to the flames and smoke. Frank then went outside to see if he could get to the second floor, where he saw workers "tumbling out"[176] of the door on the west side of the building, some with their clothes on fire. Yarn spinner Maggie Connors appeared with her hair ablaze, which Frank promptly extinguished. Like Maggie, many of the young women in the yarn spinning room were overcome by the hot gas and smoke, which seared their lungs. Those who could raced to any exit they could find.

In the coiling shop on the second floor, Horrace Morron, age twenty-two, and one of the McCarthy twins, Michael, were sitting on stools when the fire erupted. Seconds later, a "heavy wind"[177] of flame and smoke blasted up the stairway and poured into the second floor where the two were sitting. Horrace jumped up and screamed for Michael to follow him to the window, but a moment later, a second blast separated them. Horrace managed to find the window and jump, landing twenty feet below unscathed, but Michael had been blown from the building by the force of the second blast and was severely burned.

For a number of employees on the first floor, passage through the main exit of the building was blocked, and some of the survivors climbed through windows to escape. Some of the victims perished when a wall of the building fell on them as they tried to make their way out, at which point they were engulfed in flames.

Jimmie Joyce and others standing nearby the explosion on the first floor died almost instantly, including James Wallace, Minnie Tucker and twin Dick McCarthy. As the flames consumed the first floor, their bodies were reduced to ashes. William Burke from inspection had attempted to flee through a window, but his way was blocked and he also perished.

In addition to Horrace Morron, other employees were able to get out of the building safely before being overcome by smoke or fire. Will Hadsell, superintendent Frank Hadsell's youngest brother, narrowly escaped. As he was standing on the second floor, flames shot up through the elevator shaft next to him. Staggered, he nearly lost consciousness but then saw the faint outline of a window, stumbled around some boxes on the floor and jumped out of the building.

Simon and Patrick, the two oldest McCarthy brothers, miraculously survived the explosion despite the force of the blast ejecting them from the windows. Simon, working in the finishing department on the first floor, was found outside the building, unconscious and lying on a "mortar bed."[178] When he came to, they found him unhurt. Patrick was working on the second floor when he was suddenly blown out of a window as well. Incredibly, he landed forty feet away in a pond fed by Nod Brook and was relatively unscathed.

Many of the injured who could escape were still scalding as Dr. Kellogg approached to see what he could do to help. Bursting onto the lawn from the burning building, the injured raised their hands above their heads because their burns were so painful. Kellogg rushed back to get ointment to apply to the injuries of the surviving victims, but several of the men and women who emerged were so severely burned their skin was "hanging in strips."[179]

Soon, others came to provide aid, including Dr. John C. Tanner of Avon, who began triaging the wounded. Seeing the severity of the injuries, he had someone make a telephone call to get other physicians in the area to assist and was soon joined by ten others, including Dr. Ralph Cox of Collinsville.

Within a couple of hours after the blast, Dr. Tanner set up a makeshift hospital in his home in Avon and bandaged his patients as best he could until they could be transferred to Hartford. Some were covered practically head to toe in bandages. For two of the most severely burned, including Mary Litzkowicz, he elected to have them stay at his home, as he did not think they could tolerate being moved. So horrific were the burns of some of the people in his care that Dr. Tanner worried that survival might be worse than death—knowing full well that no human being could live with that extremity of burns and keep their sanity.

In the immediate aftermath of the fire, nearby residents quickly rushed to the scene, many of them friends and family members in panic, trying to find out if their loved ones survived. The community responded with all the support it could muster. As newspaper reporters interviewed survivors,

Climax Fuse factory on fire, 1905. *Clint B. Hadsell Collection.*

villagers assisted doctors and nurses in caring for those badly burned, some taking the less severely injured into their homes.

One of the surviving McCarthy brothers likely ran home to tell their mother what had happened. Mother Mary McCarthy was well aware of the dangers of Climax Fuse, having once worked in the coiling department herself. When informed of the tragedy, she learned that sons Simon and Patrick and her daughter Mary were all safe and relatively unhurt. But the news on the others was not good. Her fifteen-year-old son, Timothy, had incurred burns on both arms and was suffering terribly. In even worse shape was Michael, one of her twins, who had severe burns over much of his body. She was then told that her other twin Dick and her niece Molly were nowhere to be found. Later that evening, mother Mary was given the awful news that both had perished, incinerated by the flames. It became apparent that Timothy would recover, but despite Dr. Tanner's earlier hopeful prognosis, Michael was in grave condition. And less than forty-eight hours later, he perished, the doctors concluding Michael must have suffered injuries to internal organs.

Mother Mary McCarthy had endured extraordinary loss in her lifetime. She had borne twenty-one children with her husband, John, both Irish immigrants. Many of her children had died by disease or accident before the day of the Climax Fuse factory fire, and two days after the conflagration, as she

Twins Michael and Dick McCarthy. *From the* Hartford Courant.

mourned the loss of her twins, she had only six children remaining alive, including Simon, Patrick, daughter Mary and young Timothy.

On the Saturday and Sunday after the fire, people "by the hundreds"[180] came from all over the county to see the damage. Twenty-four hours after the blast, the factory was still a great heap of red-hot bricks and burning embers.

Among the survivors in critical condition after the fire were employees of the finishing department, including fathers Patsy Loughman and Michael Canfield along with Mary Ann Burke and Charlie Dimock. Also suffering third-degree burns were Nora Ryan, Mary Ann's sister, along with other yarn spinners Diana LeGeyt, Claire Wilde, and Mary Litzkowicz. All eight of the employees in critical condition had burns over most of their bodies, and by Tuesday, September 19, despite the efforts of Dr. Tanner and the other doctors who treated the injured, all had succumbed except Mary Litzkowicz, who was transferred to St. Francis Hospital in Hartford. There she languished for three more days, finally passing away on September 22.

Altogether, the fire resulted in sixteen dead and at least ten injured, with a number of the most seriously burned survivors taking months to recover, including Maggie Connors and Nellie Canfield. Of the ten young women and girls in Otto Prowe's yarn spinning department, seven perished, with the other three suffering severe burns. At least fifteen children lost their father or mother in the blaze, and there was an outpouring of grief as funerals were held over the following week.

As officials investigated the cause of the fire, they learned that the fatalities were higher than they should have been because the sprinkler system failed. The system was powered with the use of belts that worked by use of a pump, but the flames were so intense, the belts burned, making the sprinklers inoperable.

After the fire, factory superintendent Frank Hadsell tried to pin the blame directly on John Andrews, who was responsible for keeping the lathes and other equipment operating smoothly. Frank claimed that he had a conversation with Andrews about the danger of using the red-hot iron to clear the tar from the reel and that John agreed, telling Frank he would come up with a better alternative. Like Frank, John Andrews was away from the factory floor when the fire erupted and escaped injury.

For Ensign-Bickford, the property damage was a total loss. But the bigger loss was the tragic death of so many, with the lives of several survivors altered forever. Ensign-Bickford paid for the funeral expenses of all who perished and had life insurance on the deceased, but no amount of money could replace the loss of dear family members. Ira and Sarah LeGeyt had lost their oldest daughter, Diana, and for her tombstone chose words of comfort: "Budded on earth to bloom in heaven."[181]

Ruins of Climax Fuse fire, 1905. *Clint B. Hadsell Collection.*

While the loss of life was terrible, not long after the accident, Avon residents began to wonder whether the factory would be rebuilt. As Climax Fuse was by far the largest business in town, many people depended on it for their livelihoods. Town officials were relieved when, just four days after the fire, Ensign-Bickford announced it would rebuild the factory and resume operations as soon as possible.

Ensign-Bickford bought Climax Fuse outright in 1907 and continued to operate its plant in Avon for several decades. When detonating cords became an alternative to safety fuse for many applications beginning in the 1930s, production at the Avon plant declined, and the plant eventually closed in the 1960s. Since 1971, the rebuilt buildings of Climax Fuse have been used as office buildings for the Town of Avon and the police department.

Not only did Ensign-Bickford rebuild the factory, but it also erected single-family homes for its employees in Avon, including a number of houses along present-day Mountain View Avenue, Old Farms Road and Columbus Circle. About a dozen of the employees who were single continued to rent rooms at a boardinghouse next door, formerly known as the Chidsey house. But many workers refused to stay at the old Chidsey house when they learned of its notorious past. Indeed, twenty-five years earlier, the house had been the scene of a heinous crime.

16

A SUSPECT IN EARNEST

Avon's Double Murder

On Sunday morning, May 30, 1880, the Chidsey home on Albany Turnpike (West Main Street) in Avon looked peaceful and picturesque, a red two-story house with its windows shaded by lilacs and rose bushes in bloom. John Chidsey had died two and a half years earlier at age seventy-seven, and now the property was starting to look a bit worn. His widow, seventy-one-year-old Emily Soper Chidsey still lived in the house with her seventy-three-year-old sister, Maria Soper Avent, also a widow, but as the two were on in years, it was difficult to keep up the grounds. Nonetheless, the property was an idyllic spot. The back lawn led to a footbridge that crossed scenic Nod Brook, and beyond that, there was pastureland with two barns.

Just a few weeks earlier, Emily and Maria had decided the house needed a fresh coat of paint, and with the exterior recently finished, they had moved all the furniture away from the interior walls to enable workers to paint the inside of the house as well. The previous weekend, the men had finished the first coat of interior painting, and they were due to come back soon. In the meantime, however, the inside of the house was a mess.

By all accounts, Emily and Maria lived a quiet life and kept to themselves, rarely venturing far from home. Unfortunately for the two sisters, Sunday May 30 was anything but quiet.

Early that Sunday morning was peaceful in the village of Avon, with a seasonably cool start to the day under clear skies. At 7:00 a.m., a boy from the neighborhood was leading a cow to the Chidsey barns at the back of the property when he stopped to chat with Emily, and the two exchanged greetings. After that encounter, however, it was reported that no one saw or heard from the two sisters the rest of that morning or all afternoon.

With no sight of either sister all that day, in the early evening, at about 7:30 p.m., a neighbor across the street, Julia Reed, stopped by to check in on them. Not hearing a response but knowing the sisters must be at home, Julia pushed open the kitchen door and was utterly horrified by what she saw. There, on the kitchen floor, was Emily Chidsey face down, bludgeoned to death, with her head lying in a pool of blood. Shocked and frightened, Julia hurried from the home back across the street to get her husband, Luther, and to notify another neighbor, Henry Chidsey, who was Emily's brother-in-law.

When Luther and Henry entered the house, they pulled back a piece of rag carpet covering Emily's head and saw the impact of a severe blow, causing a massive loss of blood. Touching her cold hand, they reckoned Emily must have been killed many hours earlier. Knowing Maria was also in the house, the two walked upstairs and, finding no one in the bedroom, entered the adjacent sitting room, where they found a bloody axe leaning against the wall. Still no sign of Maria, they searched the attic, and there, to their horror, they discovered her corpse with a roughly torn piece of newspaper covering her head. Maria had also been struck by a heavy object, which they surmised must have been the flat iron, or tailor's goose, as it was called, that was on the top of a chest of drawers.

Tailor's goose.
Smithsonian Institution.

Word of the murders was sent to Hartford resident Julia Brewer, a sister of Emily and Maria, and police at the crime scene asked the Hartford Police Department to send an investigator at once. In response, recently retired detective Sidney Cowles hurried to the Chidsey home along with two doctors, R.W. Alcott and George Lewis. On arriving at the house, the doctors discovered that both women had fractured skulls, as it appeared the perpetrator struck each of them once with a crushing blow.

After identifying the bodies and the murder weapons, Cowles quickly turned his attention to finding a suspect and a motive. In talking with neighbors, no one at the time recalled seeing anyone along the road or in front of the house, so Cowles concluded the assailant must have approached the Chidsey home from the woods in the back where he could avoid detection. Searching the barnyard behind the house, he found the tracks of sharp-toed boots, not commonly worn by residents in town.

Walking back inside, the detective carefully assessed the condition of the premises. While the furniture was out of place due to the interior painting that was in progress, it otherwise showed no sign of damage or disturbance. Based on the doctor's testimony and the condition of the rooms, the detective concluded that the killing of both women must have been very quick. There was no sign of struggle. The women's clothing was not torn, and there was no evidence of blood splattered across the rooms. And the murderer, it appeared, made no attempt to hide his or her tracks; the axe and tailor's goose were left in full view. More baffling still was that the intruder made no attempt to steal anything of value from the house. The silver and more valuable pieces of furniture were plainly visible and left in place.

Thinking the killer might have had a financial motive, Cowles asked the neighbors what they knew about the sisters' finances. He approached a seventy-nine-year-old shoemaker named Phineas Gabriel, whose home had once served as a stop on the Underground Railroad. Phineas told the detective that he had assisted Emily with preparing her will in March and that Maria Avent had also written out her will that same month. Together, the sisters' assets were valued at around $10,000, or about $300,000 in today's dollars.

Phineas told Detective Cowles that when Emily drafted an update to her will in March, she intended to leave all her property to her sister, Maria Avent, if living, but sought to include a provision that their niece, twenty-five-year-old Florence Ridgeway, be allowed to live at the house whenever she wanted. And if Maria was not living at the time Emily passed away, she intended her estate to be distributed among other family members—her surviving sisters, nephews and nieces, including Florence Ridgeway.

Neighbors told Cowles, however, that Maria Avent disliked Florence immensely. Florence had lived with her aunt Maria when she was a child, and the two did not get along at all. Neighbors informed the detective that, from their perspective, Florence was a "bad character" who lived with a man named John Ridgeway on a "free love basis" during her "evil career."[182]

Thus, it was not surprising to learn that, in her own will, Maria stated that if Emily predeceased her, her property would go to all surviving sisters, nephews and nieces, *except* to her niece Florence Ridgeway. Because of her disdain for Florence, Maria had objected to Emily including the provision that allowed Florence to stay in the house anytime she wanted, and after much discussion, Emily agreed to remove that paragraph from her will.

Hearing about the dissension between Florence Ridgeway and Maria, Sidney Cowles concluded that if Florence was aware the two sisters had recently drafted wills, she might have incentive to come to the house with the aim of destroying the wills, particularly her aunt Maria's. His suspicion was raised further when he learned that Florence had visited Emily and Maria in April, just after the wills were drawn. And while incomplete drafts of the wills were found in the home, the signed wills were nowhere to be found.

Avon town residents passed a resolution offering a $1,000 reward for the arrest and conviction of the murderer, and when Detective Cowles left that day from the crime scene, he was highly confident he would bring the killer to justice. The case, he reasoned, should wrap up within a few days.

On Thursday, May 27, 1880, Dr. Abram M. Shew, superintendent of the Connecticut Hospital for the Insane in Middletown, Connecticut, was given alarming news by his staff. One of the hospital's patients, twenty-five-year-old Ernest Moses, had gone missing while working on the farm at the facility. Recognized as an expert in the treatment of mental illness, Shew had been superintendent of the hospital since it opened in 1868 and had taken measures to keep residents there safe. He embraced the idea that mental illness could be treated with humanity, and he was proud of the institution that he ran. But by 1880, the hospital had exceeded its capacity of 450 residents, and the overcrowded conditions increased the risk of patients leaving the premises without permission.

Connecticut General Hospital for the Insane. *Connecticut History.*

By the time the staff discovered Ernest Moses had escaped from the facility, they could not find him in the surrounding area. Suffering from mental illness, Ernest had been a vagrant for some time, and now he was on the run again.

A few days after the double murder, Detective Cowles tracked down Florence Ridgeway at her home in New York, and though he expected to get a quick confession, she refuted his hypothesis. Cowles started in on his line of questioning, asking Florence about where she was the day of the murders and about her relationship with her aunt Maria. Florence acknowledged that while she adored her aunt Emily, she disliked her other aunt due to poor treatment by Maria when she was a child. When Florence was able to prove that she was nowhere near Avon, Connecticut, on the day of the murders, Cowles came away satisfied that she was not the culprit. When asked who she thought might be behind the murders, Florence said she believed one of the unsavory characters who often came to the house for food likely entered the home with the aim of stealing money. She told Cowles that Maria kept money in the house and strangers may have become aware of that fact. Furthermore, she added, Maria often spoke ill of others and may have garnered enemies. When Cowles pressed Florence about the dispute her aunts had over whether to let her live in their home, she retorted, "No amount of money would induce me to remain in that dreadful house."[183] With his one lead failing to pan out, Cowles was back to square one. This murder was going to be very difficult to solve.

Just a couple of weeks after the crime, Constable Fred Farley of New Hartford found himself flummoxed about how to proceed with the Avon double murder. On June 22, 1880, after Sidney Cowles stepped aside, Justice of the Peace Chester Woodford of Avon directed a warrant to Farley asking him to pursue and arrest the perpetrator. Like Cowles, Farley initially struggled to make any sense of the murders and at the start made little progress.

With no apparent suspects or motive, the crime was baffling. But then Farley got a break. Thinking that, perhaps, the killer was someone suffering from mental illness, he inquired of the Connecticut Hospital for the Insane to see if they had any patients who were released or escaped back in May. As a matter of fact, they explained to Farley, a young man named Ernest Moses of New Hartford, Connecticut, escaped from the facility just three days before the murders and could not be found.

Farley promptly paid a visit to the New Hartford home of Ernest's parents, Harry and Caroline. As he suspected, their description of Ernest's behavior was disturbing to say the least. When he lived with his parents in New Hartford, Ernest often became violent, knocking his mother down to the floor on many occasions and threatening to kill her. He attacked his father, Harry, with a chain twice one day and threatened to kill him as well. Neighbors of the family in New Hartford told Farley that when Ernest got mad, he "would just as likely kill a person as not."[184]

Farley then learned more information that led him to conclude Ernest Moses was the likely culprit. Harry and Caroline said they had previously lived in West Hartford, and after they moved to New Hartford, Ernest would often travel back and forth between the two towns on the Albany Turnpike passing through Avon. Witnesses then came forward reporting that they believed a man matching Ernest's description had often stopped by to see Emily and Maria and they would feed him when he came to visit.

As he continued his investigation, Farley heard that, contrary to initial reports, a man with a blue shirt and dark pants was seen in the woods near the center of town on the day of the double murder. The detective then interviewed the engineer and conductor of the freight train that came through town in the early morning hours of Sunday, May 30, and they reported that a man matching Moses's description jumped off the train as it approached the station in Avon and headed across farmland toward the home of Emily Chidsey and Maria Avent.

Soon Farley was getting reports from people who had seen Ernest in the days and weeks after the double murder, informing him that Moses was in the vicinity of New Hartford, Barkhamsted and North Canton from June 1 to July 2. Perhaps fearing apprehension, Moses then left the state and was seen in the woods near North Adams, Massachusetts, on July 28. Now believing Ernest was the prime suspect, Farley printed up flyers with a description of Moses and sent them to police departments across the Northeast. Soon reports came in from neighboring states about possible sightings. But as the year 1880 came to a close, Ernest Moses was still on the run.

December 30, 1880, was a bitterly cold night in the "Dark Moon" section of Green Township in Sussex County, New Jersey. Farmer George Hibler was sitting in his home in the early evening after the day's work when he heard a knock. Opening the front door, George saw an unkempt and inadequately dressed young man standing there, shivering. Showing pity, George invited him in to warm up and gave him a bite to eat. Hibler tried to engage in conversation to learn about why this fellow was wandering about in such frigid temperatures, but he got little response. Eventually, his visitor began to open up, saying he had just walked from the old Yellow Frame Presbyterian Church about two miles away. Finally, after some time, the man revealed who he was, none other than Ernest Moses from New Hartford, Connecticut.

George let Ernest stay overnight, and the next day, New Year's Eve, Hibler brought him to the home of a neighbor, John Nugent, who had often worked to help the poor in Green Township. Ernest had been wearing only the woolen shirt, coat and pantaloons given to him by the hospital in Middletown and, on his feet, a thin pair of socks and boots. Nugent could see that Moses's feet were nearly frostbitten and did everything he could to make Ernest as comfortable as possible, later relating, "I never felt so sorry for any poor wretch in my life."[185] After consulting with the justice of the peace in town, Nugent brought Ernest where all homeless people were sent, to the Sussex County almshouse. But then a month later, without telling anyone, Ernest got up and left.

On February 27, 1881, a woman named Elizabeth Morris, who lived just down the road from the almshouse, made a gruesome discovery. Behind her home, in the woods, lying in the snow was the corpse of a man, frozen stiff. The tracks in the snow showed he had staggered in a dazed condition before setting himself down on a bed of leaves and twigs under a fallen tree, wearing only a shirt, pantaloons and boots. Ernest Moses was dead.

Farley heard from the police in Green Township that they had positively identified the deceased as Ernest Moses, and a day or two later, Ernest's father, Harry, made the sorrowful trip to New Jersey to bring his son's body home for burial.

Farley claimed he had "unquestionable proof"[186] that Ernest Moses was the murderer, but not all were convinced. Detective Robert Pinkerton, who was also investigating the case, disagreed with Farley's conclusion, stating "there is no legal proof whatever that Moses committed the crime."[187] After hearing Farley's accusations, friends and relatives of Ernest, including Harry and Caroline, refused to believe he committed the murders, contending he was at least fifty miles away from Avon on the day of the atrocity. Officially, the case would remain unsolved, but with the death of Ernest Moses, many were satisfied that the killer had been found and life returned to normal for all but the family members of the deceased.

Avon once again became a quiet village town where murders were unheard of until one day in March 1908. That murder bore little resemblance to the double murder of 1880, but it did have one peculiar similarity. It happened at the same house.

17

DOOMED AGAIN

The Murder House

On the first Friday of Lent in 1908, nineteen-year-old Bertha Dickman Lynch faced an impossible choice. In 1906, she married John Lynch, a neighbor eleven years her senior whom she met while working at the Climax Fuse plant. The first year or so of marriage was rocky, but when their daughter Mary was born in 1907, she trusted things would work out. Then serious trouble started when John lost his job in late 1907, and now, on a Friday morning in March 1908, she stood face to face with the intoxicated, angry man that her husband had become. Fearing that John would become violent, she ceded to his demand to take their ten-month-old daughter, Mary, away from her for the day. But inside, Bertha was seething. How dare he take Mary when Bertha was the only parent acting responsibly—the only one who could realistically care for the child? Furious with the injustice of the situation, she resolved that she was not going to be bullied any longer.

As the eighteen-year-old daughter of German immigrants Hugh and Catherine Dickman, Bertha had suffered the loss of her father but had the good fortune of living with many other people close to her age. When Hugh died in 1904, her mother, Catherine, or Carrie as she was known, moved the family from their home in Collinsville to Avon, where Carrie operated a boardinghouse for employees of Climax Fuse at the old Chidsey home. Despite its reputation after the murder of Emily Chidsey and Maria Avent, the boardinghouse was right next door to the plant, and Carrie took in single workers at the factory who needed a place to stay. Bertha started working at Climax Fuse when she was just sixteen years old, one of the lucky survivors of the deadly fire in September 1905. The old Chidsey home had been expanded and repainted white, and the house was just large enough to accommodate Carrie, her five children who were still living at home and about a dozen boarders.

Bertha Dickman Lynch. *From the* Hartford Courant.

Living just down the street from the boardinghouse was twenty-nine-year-old John Lynch. After John's father passed away years earlier, his mother, Nora, left the Lynch home in Bristol, Connecticut, and married an English immigrant named Charles Bailey. By 1900, John was living with his six younger half siblings in the Bailey home just one hundred yards from Carrie Dickman's boardinghouse.

Bertha met John in 1904 when the two were working at Climax Fuse, and they eventually fell in love. Since they wanted to be with each other, they put aside the potential conflict that could arise from one aspect of their relationship that was highly unusual for the time. He was Catholic and she was Protestant. For that reason, John's mother, Nora Bailey, and Bertha's mother, Carrie Dickman, strongly objected to the two getting married. Undeterred, John and Bertha decided to elope in 1906, marrying in Waterbury, Connecticut. Bertha left Climax Fuse in July of that year when John took a job working at the United States Rubber Company in Naugatuck, and the two started their life together. Yes, the fact that they were of different faiths was a potential thorn in the relationship, but John and Bertha figured they would work it out.

Upon getting married, Bertha and John lived at a boardinghouse in Naugatuck, and it did not take long before troubles arose in the marriage.

Needing to separate for a time, Bertha went to live in the Bristol home of John's brother, but not long after, John returned to reunite with Bertha.

By the autumn of 1906, Bertha learned she was pregnant, and in May 1907, when it was time to deliver the baby, she came back to her mother's boardinghouse in Avon, giving birth to Mary in an upstairs bedroom. For the first six months or so things went fairly smoothly back in Naugatuck, but then John was "thrown out of work at Christmastime,"[188] and the young family of three moved back to Avon to live in Carrie Dickman's boardinghouse.

Shortly after John and Bertha moved back to Avon, the underlying source of potential conflict in the marriage went from a simmer to a boil. While John was not regarded as a particularly devout Catholic by his church, he nonetheless wanted his daughter to be baptized into the Roman Catholic faith at St. Patrick's Church in Collinsville, but Bertha and Carrie strongly opposed. Having immigrated to the United States from Germany in 1884, the Dickmans attended St. Matthews, the German Lutheran Church in Collinsville, and Bertha insisted that Mary be baptized into the Protestant faith.

Not only did the young couple disagree on Mary's baptism, but John Lynch also found that living at his mother-in-law's house with all those boarders and Bertha's younger siblings had become intolerable. After Carrie asked her son-in-law to start paying rent, John approached Bertha about moving to the Bailey household down the street. But Bertha resisted, wanting to stay with her mother and her siblings. With the two at an impasse, on February 23, 1908, John left the boardinghouse and moved back in with the Baileys without Bertha. For the next ten days, he and Bertha shared custody of their ten-month-old daughter, but the arrangement was clearly untenable.

The Chidsey House, Where the Murder Was Done. Cross Shows Where Victim Fell.

Carrie Dickman's boardinghouse. *From the* Farmington Valley Herald.

While John had recently obtained a job as an outdoor laborer at the Climax Fuse plant, he had a day off on Friday, March 6, 1908, and that morning was determined to take Mary so he could ensure his daughter observed Lent. The night before, John had stayed with friends in Hartford, and after he arrived in Avon early on Friday morning, he had several drinks at the village tavern. Then, a little after 9:00 a.m., standing in a cold rain, he appeared at his mother-in-law's boardinghouse with the intent of taking his daughter with him. Seeing that her husband was adamant about taking Mary, Bertha reluctantly gave her consent, and John took the child in his arms and walked back to the Bailey home.

About an hour and a half later, however, around 10:30 a.m., he returned, telling Bertha he wanted some of the baby's clothes. Sensing that her husband was planning to keep Mary more than a few hours this time, Bertha refused to give John the clothes, telling him that she had earned the money herself to pay for them. The two got into a heated argument, and the young couple then headed upstairs to the very bedroom where Mary was born ten months earlier. On the first floor below were Bertha's mother, Carrie, and her brother Herman, who was home from school that day.

Not long after Bertha and John went upstairs, with the two still shouting at each other, a shot rang out and Bertha screamed. John had pulled out a .38-caliber revolver, pressed it against Bertha's chest and pulled the trigger. But while he intended to shoot her through the heart, the bullet entered just above, puncturing her left lung, and Bertha cried out in agony.

On hearing her daughter's terrified scream, Carrie Dickman rushed upstairs to find out what had happened. As she entered the room, she saw her daughter lying on the floor but still conscious, pleading with John: "Shoot me again! You have not completed your work; don't let me suffer, shoot again!"[189] John, however, had turned to see Carrie, and when he pointed the gun at her, she ran downstairs with John in pursuit. Frantically, Carrie and her son Herman ran out the front door together onto the snow-covered lawn to escape. While Herman was able to sprint well ahead and away from the house, Carrie slipped in the snow, allowing John time to catch up. When Carrie got back on her feet, John pressed the gun against her back and shot her, killing her instantly. After pausing and standing over his dead mother-in-law, he turned to see Herman near the woods, running toward the back of the house, and started after him, shouting, "You needn't run. You'll be the next!"[190] Realizing he would not be able to catch Herman, John turned and ran toward the Bailey house, making his way through the snow.

When he arrived back at the Baileys', John told his mother, Nora, what he had done, and she quickly ran over to the boardinghouse to see what she could do to help. When Nora got near the front door, she saw Carrie Dickman lying dead in the snow and turned to go into the house. Then, just as she crossed the threshold, she heard another shot ring out in the distance.

Moments earlier, back at the Bailey home, John Lynch had gone inside to see his daughter, Mary. He leaned over and kissed her on the forehead, knowing it would be the last time he would see her. As he went to leave the house, he was confronted by his stepbrother James Bailey, who attempted to take the gun away from him, but John abruptly pulled away. Leaving the house, John walked into the woods behind the home, pointed the barrel of the revolver at his heart and pulled the trigger. This time he did not miss his target, the bullet killing him instantly.

Meanwhile, back at the boardinghouse, not yet knowing her son had taken his own life, Nora Bailey headed upstairs, where she found Bertha prostrate on the floor. Bertha, still alert, recognized her mother-in-law and asked plaintively, "Why did John do it?"[191] Meanwhile, Bertha's brother Herman had run next door to Dr. Tanner's house, the same doctor who had treated the burn victims of the Climax Fuse factory fire two and a half years earlier. Tanner, and Dr. Ralph Cox of Collinsville, arrived on the scene. On assessing her condition, Cox expected Bertha would die within a few hours and, to ease her suffering, gave her morphine and some glycerin to alleviate her chest pain.

Over the next twenty-four hours, however, Bertha's condition stabilized, and Dr. Cox, along with a Dr. Boucher of Hartford, decided to remove the bullet, which had lodged itself below the shoulder blade. Rather than transporting Bertha to Hartford Hospital, the doctors performed the surgery at the house—and without anesthesia. Delirious and confused after the surgery, Bertha did not think she would live and was heard calling out for "John" and her "sweetheart."[192]

Despite the severity of her injuries and the initial prediction that she would not live, Bertha survived. Climax Fuse factory superintendent Sherman Eddy, Frank Hadsell's replacement, took up an employee collection so that a nurse could attend to Bertha during her recovery. Within a year after John Lynch's death, Bertha married a man named Robert Andrews Brown, who had joined Climax Fuse in 1906 and may have been living at the boardinghouse. Along with her daughter Mary, Bertha went on to have seven children with Robert and lived to the age of seventy-three.

At Carrie Dickman's funeral, the Reverend P. Molhorn of the St. Matthew German Lutheran Church in Collinsville warned against people of different creeds marrying. Rather than trying to find a compromise or switching to another religion that would be acceptable to both, John and Bertha held intractable views.

Soon after the murder-suicide of March 6, 1908, all of the tenants left the boardinghouse, with one aptly noting that "the place is doomed."[193] Despite its notorious history, new tenants, untroubled by the home's past, went to live at the "murder house"[194] until about 1922, after which it became a storehouse for Ensign-Bickford's Climax Fuse plant. Finally, in January 1928, the home was taken down when the town widened the Albany Turnpike. No one was sad to see it go. One newspaper headline summed up the demolition well: "'Murder House' Ghosts Made Homeless."[195]

PART VI

THE PRIVILEGED AND PROGRESSIVE

18

CAUGHT BETWEEN WORLDS

Yung Wing

In December 1880, at the height of his prosperity and success, Yung Wing, a naturalized American citizen from China, looked forward to many more years of educating Chinese youth in Connecticut. Two years earlier, he had been named a minister representing China at its legation, or embassy, in Washington, D.C., and decided the time was right for him and his wife, Mary Louise, to move their principal residence from her family home in Avon to a magnificent house on the corner of Prospect and Fern Streets in Hartford.

In 1871, he single-handedly convinced Viceroy Li Hongzhang to send thirty of China's best students each year to study abroad in the United States. The first Chinese national to graduate from an American university, Yung became convinced when he was a student at Yale College that China needed to adopt more of modern Western civilization, and he became determined to reform China through the education of its youth.

By the late 1870s, his Chinese Educational Mission on Collins Street in Hartford had become revered in the community and had grown to 120 students. But when Wu Zideng was appointed co-commissioner of the school in 1878, he was "shocked at the behavior of the boys who dared to look him in the face and were not inclined to say 'yes' to every word that came out of his mouth."[196] Wu was dismayed that the boys shunned their cultural traditions, even forgetting how to speak Chinese. After Wu Zideng reported his findings back to Beijing without informing Yung, his co-commissioner, Yung Wing's ambition to reform China, the country he loved, was in peril.

Born into a poor family in southern China, two miles west of the Portuguese settlement of Macau, Yung Wing began selling candy at age twelve to earn money after his father died and his prospects looked bleak. But he had the good fortune to attend a missionary school, first in Macau and then in Hong Kong, where he learned some English. The leader of the missionary school in Hong Kong was Reverend Samuel Brown of Massachusetts, and when Brown returned to the United States in 1847, he decided to bring a few of his students with him, including Yung Wing, so they could complete their education. When the students arrived in New York City, they stayed with David Ely Bartlett, Reverend Brown's brother-in-law and a cousin of Avon abolitionist David W. Bartlett.

After attending a preparatory school in Monson, Massachusetts, where Reverend Brown was raised, Yung became a Christian and enrolled at Yale in 1850. At college, he excelled at English composition, even winning first prize for one of his essays when he was a sophomore. Yung easily adapted to life in America, and after becoming a U.S. citizen and then graduating from Yale in 1854, he left for Hong Kong, aiming to take Reverend Brown's place at the missionary school there.

Yung Wing's ultimate goal, however, was to establish a Chinese educational mission in the United States, as he wanted Chinese youth to benefit from an American education as he had. He believed that for China to modernize, it needed to educate young men who could serve as intermediaries with Westerners. Over the next sixteen years, Yung worked in various jobs, starting as an apprentice to an attorney in Guangzhou, China, and then working as a translator for a Shanghai customs house before engaging in the trade of silk and tea.

Chinese officials distrusted Western influence given their experience with imperialists during the recent Opium Wars, and Yung had difficulty getting the Chinese government to embrace his idea for an educational mission. In 1870, however, he obtained the support of military commander Li Hongzhang, who thought the mission could help China "learn the technological secrets of the West."[197]

Contributing to Li's decision was the groundbreaking Burlingame Treaty of 1868, which, among other things, eased immigration between China and the United States and allowed students in China to attend schools in America. Following through on his promise, in 1871, Li secured funding to send thirty students abroad each year, most of them between

Yung Wing, 1878. *Sketch by Theodore Davis, from* Harper's Weekly.

the ages of twelve and sixteen. When Li Hongzhang finally approved setting up a Chinese educational mission in America, Yung Wing "walked back and forth in excitement and silently praised God."[198]

Years later, Yung remembered, "I was determined that the rising generation of China should enjoy the same educational advantages that I had; that through western education China might be regenerated, become enlightened and powerful,"[199] and now he had been given the opportunity. However, because Yung Wing had spent his formative years in the United States, Li did not trust that Yung was sufficiently Chinese, so he sent along a co-commissioner for the mission, a traditionalist named Chen Lan Pin. Chen's mandate was to ensure the boys continued to receive a classical Confucian education in addition to their Western schooling.

Soon after Yung Wing returned to Connecticut in 1871, Asylum Hill Congregational Church parishioner David Ely Bartlett, who first met Yung in 1847, invited him to attend church in Hartford to hear Reverend Joseph Twichell's sermon. When Twichell met Yung, he called him "the shyest person almost I ever met,"[200] and it took time for Yung to finally open up to the pastor. Given his own ambition to do missionary work, Twichell was intrigued by Yung's mandate to establish a school for Chinese boys and convinced him to locate what became known as the Chinese Educational Mission in Hartford. Twichell remarked, "I don't think I was ever more excited in my sympathies and admirations by anything of the kind in my life."[201] Yung took up residence right around the corner from Twichell's home on Woodland Avenue in Hartford and set out to find homes for the initial class of thirty boys.

He placed the students with families all through the Connecticut River Valley in both Connecticut and Western Massachusetts, where they attended public and private grammar schools and preparatory schools. The boys were required to study Chinese an hour a day and, every three months, attend classes at the Chinese Educational Mission in Hartford, originally established on Sumner Street. When the first class of pupils arrived in September 1872, David Ely and Fanny Bartlett agreed to host four students at their home in Hartford, and their family quickly made friends with the new arrivals. It helped that David was multilingual. A longtime teacher at the American School for the Deaf, he was first hired by Thomas Gallaudet when the school opened in 1828.

Also hosting a number of the Chinese was Dr. Edward Kellogg, who would later witness the Climax Fuse fire in 1905. A member of the Asylum Hill Church, Edward and his wife, Hilah, bought a home on Asylum Avenue in 1871 when he moved his homeopathy practice from Southington to Hartford and became a family physician to Samuel and Olivia Clemens. The Kellogg home and the American School for the Deaf were right next to each other, located on the present-day home office campus of the insurance company The Hartford.

First class of Chinese students, 1872. *From the* Springfield Republican.

Other Asylum Hill parishioners agreed to take students into their homes, and many pupils were placed with families in neighboring towns. Edward's father, Bela Crocker Kellogg, and his wife, Mary, housed two students in their Avon home on West Main Street despite having four of their own children still living with them, including twenty-one-year-old Jane "Jennie" and nineteen-year-old Mary Louise.

It did not take long before the Chinese boys adapted to American life, quickly picking up the English language and enjoying baseball games and other activities with their new friends. They were welcomed into the community, and each autumn, Twichell would bring the students on hikes up to Henry Bartlett's tower on Talcott Mountain.

When at the mission in Hartford, the Chinese students dreaded their afternoon schooling, where "no attempt was made to depart from the Orthodox Chinese method of instruction."[202] Each day, the boys had to study Chinese history and writing and were reminded how to make proper ceremonial obeisances to the emperor in Beijing. They looked forward to Sundays, when they could play and get "relief from the monotony of Chinese study."[203]

Co-commissioner Chen Lan Pin was disturbed when the students wanted to trade their silk gowns for Western clothes and became angry when a couple of the boys cut off their traditional single long braids of hair called "queues."[204] More concerning to Chen was that the students became accustomed to praying with their families at dinner and attending church services. While Reverend Twichell encouraged the boys' introduction to Christianity, he was well aware that Yung Wing had to make sure the students did not make any "formal public profession of their faith." However, Yung himself, a converted Christian, did not discourage the instruction.[205]

Chen tried to restrict the boys' freedom and keep them grounded in Confucianism, but his efforts were hopeless. One early participant in the program commented that once a student is given "free space to exercise its wings, off it flies to where natural instinct leads."[206] Yung was clearly annoyed with Chen's constraints on the boys, once telling Twichell, "I am quite anxious that American ideas…should prevail, not because I am hailed to Yankee notions, but because they are broad and sensible."[207]

Mary Louise Kellogg Yung, 1876. *Washington State University.*

In 1873, the Chinese government asked Yung Wing to return to China, requesting that he bring new Gatling guns for the arsenal. When forty-five-year-old Yung returned to Connecticut in early 1874, he confided in Reverend Twichell that he wanted to get married but believed that he was too Americanized to marry a Chinese woman and too Chinese to marry an American. Twichell disagreed on the second point. He suggested Yung court Dr. Edward Kellogg's sister Mary Louise, then twenty-three, who was tutoring two Chinese students staying with the Kellogg family in Avon. While her father, Bela, was a harness maker and the postmaster of Avon, the Kellogg family was not wealthy, and given Yung Wing's increasing prosperity, Bela encouraged Yung's pursuit of his daughter, telling the family, "It will set us all up" financially.[208] After a short courtship, Mary Louise and Yung were engaged.

In the summer of 1874, the Chinese government asked Yung to travel to Peru to investigate the working conditions of Chinese laborers. Back home in October 1874, the third class of Chinese students was soon to arrive, and with funding supplied by the Chinese government, Yung bought a Hartford building on Collins Street for $75,000 to house the larger number of boys.

When Mary Louise accepted Yung's proposal for marriage, the public reaction was strongly negative, as many thought a biracial union was utterly inappropriate. Twichell, however, was thrilled. Yung knew he was taking a risk marrying an American and had to obtain permission from the Chinese government. Interracial marriage was rare in the 1870s, and given societal attitudes, Mary Louise was courageous in her decision to marry Yung.

The wedding, which took place on February 24, 1875, in the Kellogg family home on West Main Street in Avon, was considered "a social sensation"[209] at the time. Braving treacherous conditions due to ice on

Albany Turnpike, Twichell and Yung traveled together in a carriage over Avon Mountain to get to the wedding. The ceremony, officiated by Reverend Twichell, was a blend of Chinese and American customs. Mary Louise wore a white crepe dress imported from China, elaborately trimmed with floss silk embroidery. While Yung wore a suit, two of the teachers from the mission, Yeh Shu Tung and Yung Yen Foo, attended in traditional Chinese gowns, and the contrast of their appearance with other guests was striking to Twichell. At the reception, both traditional Chinese and American food was served, after which Yung and his bride left on a train to New York City for a short honeymoon.

Despite approval from Beijing, Yung's marriage to Mary Louise Kellogg deepened the Chinese government's suspicion that Yung was committed to Western values and would fail to ensure his students would stay culturally Chinese.

After their marriage, Mary Louise helped her husband at the mission in Hartford and, when there, would visit with her older sister Jennie, who was teaching third- and fourth-year students at the American School for the Deaf. In 1876, pressured by the Chinese government, Yung Wing tried to get Chinese students admitted to the U.S. military academies but was denied. Yung knew the reason: "The race prejudice against the Chinese was so rampant and rank that not only my application for the students to gain entrance to Annapolis and West Point was treated with cold indifference and scornful hauteur, but the Burlingame Treaty of 1868 was…trampled underfoot…as though no such treaty had ever existed."[210]

When the Chinese government appointed Yung as a co-minister for Peru and Spain in March 1876, he had to spend more of his time in Washington, D.C. Meanwhile, Mary Louise stayed back in Avon awaiting the birth of their first child, a son named Morrison who was born in June of that year.

While the Yung family's principal residence was in Avon and they spent their summers there, they wintered between Hartford and Washington, D.C., depending on whether Yung was needed at the mission or at the Chinese Legation in the nation's capital. In the summer of 1878, Yung Wing convinced Mary Louise's uncle David W. Bartlett to become secretary of the legation, and David left his job as correspondent for the *Springfield Republican*. In the fall of 1878, Mary Louise was pregnant with their second child, Bartlett, when she traveled to Washington with her husband and two-year-old son, Morrison, and lamented that the family would not be in Avon for Thanksgiving.

Yung Wing, circa 1910. *Henry Holt & Co.*

When the Chinese government asked Chen Lan Pin, like Yung Wing, to spend more time at the legation in D.C., Chen appointed an "uncompromising Confucian"[211] named Wu Zideng to replace him as co-commissioner of the Chinese Educational Mission in Hartford. It soon became clear the change did not bode well for the school. Wu protested the students' Western clothing, their attendance at church and their participation in outdoor exercises and sports. Yung was constantly defending the students, recalling years later that Wu's "uncompromising conservatism…gnashes its teeth against all and every attempt put forth to reform the government or to improve the general condition of things in China."[212] The students detested their Chinese curriculum, looking on their time at the mission headquarters "as one of the evils of life which could not possibly be avoided."[213]

Worsening matters for Yung Wing was that by the late 1870s, fueled by racist sentiment, there was a backlash against Chinese immigrants in the West, leading to a ban of Chinese immigration in 1882. In the fall of 1878, David W. Bartlett warned Yung that he expected the U.S. government would amend the 1868 Burlingame treaty, weakening its protection for Chinese nationals living in the United States. Indeed, the rejection of Chinese nationals living in America was swift. When meeting with former U.S. President Ulysses S. Grant in 1879, Viceroy Li Hongzhang expressed "surprise and grief"[214] that Chinese students were not allowed to enroll in U.S. military academies, but Grant told him it was unlikely the U.S. government would reconsider.

Despite deteriorating conditions between Washington and Beijing, Yung Wing remained optimistic that things would work out with the educational mission, and in 1880, the Yungs decided to move from Avon, buying a home on Prospect Avenue in Hartford. Much of the time, however, Yung was needed in Washington, D.C., where he and his family enjoyed the privileges of being part of the diplomatic corps. Mary Louise relished hosting visiting dignitaries, welcoming Joseph Twichell and author Charles Dudley Warner in April 1880, telling sister Jennie, "Think of poor little me attempting to entertain such celebrities."[215] She and her husband often attended state dinners, including one in the spring of 1881 where Mary Louise met President James Garfield, William Tecumseh Sherman and Connecticut's own Joseph Roswell Hawley.

Back in Hartford, the success of the Chinese Educational Mission could not be denied, as many of its students enrolled in college, several of them attending Yale. It soon became evident, however, that the Chinese government was losing its zeal for the mission.

Just when the Yungs bought their home on Prospect Avenue, the government in Beijing concluded their Chinese students were becoming too Americanized. When the United States stopped the flow of Chinese immigrants to America, China moved to shut down the school, arguing that the Chinese Educational Mission was "subversive of the principles and theories of Chinese culture."[216]

Hearing of Li Hongzhang's plans to close the mission, in late 1880, Reverend Twichell and Samuel Clemens asked former President Grant to intercede given his relationship with Li. However, the intervention only delayed the recall of the students by six months. When Twichell learned of the final decision to close the school, he wrote: "The Mission is doomed....The disappointment of all its friends is extreme. Poor Wing, it is heaviest of all upon him."[217] With great sorrow, in July 1881, Yung Wing informed one hundred boys and young men, about sixty of them in preparatory schools or colleges, that they had been ordered to go back to China. Forlornly, the students returned to their homeland in the fall, and when they arrived, they were treated poorly, as "they stuttered and paused for words,"[218] unable to communicate in a language they had largely forgotten.

After the Chinese Educational Mission in Hartford was withdrawn, Yung Wing was called to Washington to serve in his role as minister of the Chinese Legation. Less than a year later, in January 1882, Beijing asked him to travel to Shanghai, where Yung unsuccessfully tried to negotiate the return of the students to Connecticut. Mary Louise and the boys stayed behind in Avon, but then in early 1883, Yung learned that his wife had fallen seriously ill. He returned in the spring to find her gaunt and speaking in a low whisper and he feared the worst. Fortunately, soon after Yung arrived, she began to regain her health, telling her husband that her illness was brought on due to anxiety about him being away from the family.

In 1885, however, Mary Louise's condition deteriorated again, and the Yung family spent the summer in Southampton, Long Island, hoping the ocean air would improve her health. Feeling better, over the following winter, Mary Louise went with the children to Washington, D.C., as Yung was required to be at the Chinese Legation. Returning to their life in D.C., they attended dinners among the diplomatic corps of the city, and Mary Louise helped organize a performance by the Yale Glee Club. By late April or early May 1886, however, her condition suddenly worsened, and she died from a kidney ailment on May 29. Yung and his sons were devastated. Mary Kellogg, Mary Louise's mother, helped care for Morrison and Bartlett in Avon with Yung remembering how she "assisted me in my work and stood by me in my most trying hours."[219] Now Yung Wing would have to navigate his way forward without his beloved wife.

After Mary Louise's death, Yung and his sons lived in different boardinghouses in Hartford, kicked out of one of them due to racial prejudice. While Yung Wing's dream of educating Chinese youth in America had ended in 1881, his drive to help reform and modernize China had not. When war broke out between China and Japan in 1894, he traveled back to his country of birth to see what he could do to support the war effort. Morrison, then eighteen, was a student at Yale University, and Bartlett, then fifteen, went to live in the home of Reverend Twichell.

After the Sino-Japanese War ended, residents in the north of China were upset by the growing influence of Japan and Christian missionaries from the West. In 1900, the "Boxers"[220] rebelled, spreading violence to Beijing and other cities, resulting in the death of several thousand Chinese Christians and several hundred Christian missionaries. From the Boxer Rebellion, Empress Dowager Cixi, seeking to preserve Chinese traditional values and resist Western influences, imprisoned Emperor Guangxu and went after reformers, including Yung Wing. Though Yung was not aware of it at the time, the empress placed a $100,000 bounty on his head.

Knowing he was in danger, Yung escaped from Beijing, first to Shanghai and then to Hong Kong, seeking protection in the British territory. As Reverend Twichell later said of Yung, "He could not fail to encounter among his own people, prejudice, suspicion, hostility."[221] With the help of friends, he returned to Connecticut in June 1902, just in time to see his younger son Bartlett graduate from Yale.

When the Empress Dowager Cixi died in 1908, Yung believed it would precipitate the reform movement in China, and he proved to be right when, in 1911, revolutionaries in southern China successfully overthrew the Qing Dynasty, ending its 267-year rule. Driven by the prejudice he faced on both sides of the Pacific Ocean, Yung Wing died in poverty in Hartford in 1912. But he left an enduring legacy to all international students from Asia that followed. As he had when Mary Louise passed away, Reverend Twichell officiated Yung's funeral, and in his remarks he observed that Yung "carried China continually in his heart."[222]

19

THE FIERCELY INDEPENDENT FANNY WHITMAN

In 1822, when she was twenty-eight years old, Frances "Fanny" Whitman was faced with a dilemma that had vexed many young women for millennia.[223] Born to a prominent family in the town of Farmington, Fanny fell in love with a twenty-seven-year-old schoolteacher named Seth Tillotson. A cousin of enslaver Shubael, Seth was the son of farmer Ashbel Tillotson and Phebe Woodruff Tillotson, and he and Fanny wanted to marry against the wishes of Fanny's parents. As the Whitmans were a wealthy and highly respected family in town, Fanny's parents, Solomon and Mary Whitman, were very unhappy with her choice in Seth, whom they did not consider worthy of their daughter. The Whitman family in Farmington went back many generations; in 1736, Fanny's grandparents Solomon and Susannah Whitman acquired the home that is today known as the Stanley-Whitman house.

Fanny had been restless from a young age, once running away from home, and Seth had to court her twice before they finally married in January 1823. Slender and short of stature, she had dark hair with a red streak in the back she called her "bit of Scotch."[224] And she had spunk. Progressive for her time, Fanny had no intention of adhering to her parents' wishes and informed them that she and Seth were going to be married. Her father, Solomon, did not take it well. Considering his options, however, he gave Fanny a modest sum of money, a "setting out,"[225] and then informed her that she had been cut out of his will.

When Seth's brother Hezekiah drowned in March 1823, Seth and Fanny moved into Hezekiah's farm, which had been built by Seth's father,

Ashbel, in 1820. The farm, known then as the Pine Woods Farm, was along the west side of the Farmington River, encompassing much of the land of present-day Sub-Edge Farm along Tillotson Road.[226]

In 1825, the Farmington Canal Company began building the canal that followed a route from New Haven up to Massachusetts, right by Pine Woods Farm, and during construction, Seth and Fanny took in many of the laborers as boarders. Though slight in stature, Fanny was strong-willed, the kind of person who didn't hesitate to take matters into her own hands. One day she found an inebriated man on her porch and ordered him to leave. When he refused and tried to push his way into the house, a petite Fanny pushed him back, right off the porch.

When Avon became a separate town in 1830, the land surveyors initially drew the town line just south of Seth and Fanny's farmhouse, which would have placed them in Avon. While most of their farmland would be in Avon, Fanny wanted to continue to live in Farmington, where she attended church, and by force of will, she insisted that the surveyors move the town line north by about one hundred yards to make sure the house was in Farmington.

Although they were faithful churchgoers, the Tillotsons did not always adhere to the strictures of the church, and Seth Tillotson was as free-spirited as his wife. During the height of the temperance movement in 1844, he was reprimanded by the Congregational Church in Farmington for drinking apple brandy and providing alcohol to his employees on his farm—"a violation of the total abstention pledge" he had taken.[227] As a result, on May 16, 1844, he was suspended from taking communion for six months.

After the Farmington Canal closed in 1848 and was replaced by the railroad, remnants of the canal remained, and there was one particularly wide spot next to the aqueduct that crossed the Farmington River known as "the basin"[228] where the Tillotsons would water their cattle. Later in life, Seth suffered from rheumatoid arthritis, experiencing debilitating joint pain that left him bedridden at times. One winter day, while he was lying in bed, his sons Hez and John drove their cattle to the basin, which had been frozen over with ice. Suddenly, the cattle fell in, trapped in the icy water. When Seth learned of the accident, despite his condition, he draped himself in blankets and climbed aboard a cart pulled by an ox to lead the recovery effort. As he approached the canal, however, the ox lunged forward, pulling the cart, and Seth along with it, right into the frozen waterway. Alarmed, Hez and John quickly pulled their father out of the icy basin and brought him back to the house to dry him off and get him in bed. Fearing the worst, the brothers did not think their father would live through the night. But at five o'clock the next morning, Seth yelled up to his sons, "Boys!, Boys! Time to get up!"[229] and he was ready to start the day.

Spirited and lively throughout her life, Fanny Whitman Tillotson lived life to the fullest. Well into her seventies, she was determined to show the younger generations just how to dance the "Pigeon Wing" when she tripped on the carpet and fell, injuring her thigh.[230] A woman of strong mind and body, she overcame this adversity, going on to live until the age of ninety-six.

Seth and Fanny Tillotson's farm eventually passed through their son Hez to their grandson Edwin Ward Tillotson. Then, in 1925, when he was seventy-five years old, Edwin was approached by representatives for a woman who wanted to buy his land. Tired of maintaining the farm, and with no interest from his children in taking over the operation, Edwin listened to the offer. While it was a little unclear what exactly the buyer was planning to do with the property, she offered a price he could not refuse. Something about building a school for boys.

20

GOING OLD SCHOOL

Theodate Pope Riddle's Tribute

Over a decade in the making, in the late summer of 1927, Theodate Pope Riddle's preparatory school for boys in Avon had finally come to fruition. While many fathers of the upper class during the Gilded Age would have been furious if their daughter rejected their place in society, in time, Alfred Atmore Pope came to appreciate that Theodate was different. She was independently minded and wanted her own career, and it was Alfred who suggested to his daughter that she study architecture. After he died in 1913, Theodate made a firm decision to build a boys' school in his memory.

Not long after Alfred's passing, Theodate endured multiple tragedies and setbacks. She had survived the sinking of the RMS *Lusitania*, had overcome the grief of losing her cousin and close friend Elizabeth Brooks and suffered the devastating loss of Gordon Brockway, a four-year-old boy under her ward whom she cared for as a son. Theodate had persevered, and through it all, she was determined, no matter what the obstacles, to build her school.

Ten years after she conceived of the idea to build a school for boys, beginning in the spring of 1923, Theodate was confronted with unfriendly demands from Avon's town selectman and the nuisance of a "dance hall" on an adjacent property, both of which threatened her plans.[231] Though her nettlesome neighbors to the north were a cause for concern, she had dealt with more challenging circumstances than this in her life and Theodate was resolute. Her school for boys was going to be built to her specifications, and she would make sure that no one got in her way.

Alfred Atmore Pope, who earned his fortune in the iron and steel industry in Ohio, instilled in his daughter a love of the arts and the inspired design behind them. During his trips to Europe, Alfred greatly admired the new French impressionist paintings of Claude Monet, Edgar Degas and others, as well as works by American artists Mary Cassatt and James McNeill Whistler. He bought many of their paintings, with Cassatt and Whistler becoming friends of the family. Indeed, Mary Cassatt represented the type of friend Theodate cultivated—a strong, independent woman who broke with the social norms of the time.

Though she grew up in Ohio, Theodate Pope attended Miss Porter's School in Farmington and fell in love with the countryside of the Farmington River Valley. Born into wealth, she had no interest in becoming a housewife or a socialite. In 1889, one year after completing her studies at Miss Porter's School, Theodate traveled with her parents to Europe, visiting France, Italy, Spain and England. Journeying to Europe with the Popes was Harris Whittemore, the son of one of Alfred's business associates, and Harris would become Theodate's lifelong friend and fellow art collector. It was during this trip to Europe that she became interested in a career as an architect.

Theodate was confident and determined. With blue eyes and golden-bronze hair, her appearance was formidable and self-assured, and from her youth, she knew that she was not anything like most other girls her age. "When other girls at Miss Porter's School were planning dresses, I was drawing plans for buildings," she once said.[232]

Upon her return from Europe, she loathed the idea of being "introduced to society" at a debutante ball. Said Theodate, "I was sullen with rage and boredom most of the time, and my parents finally gave up trying to fit me into their social pattern."[233] Instead, she convinced her parents, Alfred and Ada, to let her rent a cottage on High Street in Farmington, near Miss Porter's School. She loved the town and later decided to buy the cottage along with its forty-two acres.

In 1898, with the intent of moving with Ada from Ohio to Connecticut, Alfred purchased a parcel of approximately 250 acres on the hillside overlooking the village of Farmington. Theodate had been working on conceptual plans for the home since 1889 and, with moxie and her father's consent, sent the plans to McKim, Mead and White, an architectural firm in New York City. In 1901, the Colonial-style house

Mary Hillard. *From* Mary Robbins Hillard, *by John T. Dallas*.

was constructed, complete with a sunken garden and a six-hole golf course. Now known as the Hill-Stead Museum, the home included paintings from Alfred's collection, including those of Whistler, Monet, Manet and Degas.

After Hill-Stead was built and Theodate and her parents moved into the home, they became friends with their high-society neighbors on Main Street in Farmington, Rear Admiral William Cowles and his wife, Anna Roosevelt Cowles, older sister of President Teddy Roosevelt. Anna took great interest in Theodate, and the two maintained regular visits and correspondence until a falling out in the mid-1920s.

Her next architectural project after Hill-Stead was to design the campus of a new school for girls in Middlebury, Connecticut, commissioned by her friend Mary Hillard. Mary had taught at Miss Porter's when Theodate was a student there and later became headmistress of St. Margaret's School for girls in Waterbury before moving the school to Middlebury. The campus, which Theodate designed in 1907, included a quadrangle centered on an interior courtyard and was completed in 1909 with the new school later renamed the Westover School.

Theodate became interested in the paranormal in late 1900 when reading books on the subject, and after the premature death of Mary Hillard's brother, John, in 1903, Theodate and Mary attempted to communicate with the deceased. In February 1904, at the suggestion of Mary Cassatt, they consulted with a psychic named Leonora Piper in Boston, and Theodate became more interested in spiritualism. In May 1915, Theodate hoped to set up a rival society to the American Society for Psychical Research. Traveling to London to attend a meeting of the British Society of Psychical Research, she boarded the steamship RMS *Lusitania* on May

1. On the day she left Pier 54 in New York, with World War I raging in Europe, the Imperial German Embassy in Washington, D.C., issued a warning to those intending to travel to Europe that any ship belonging to Great Britain was "liable to destruction."[234] But Theodate did not see or read the warning until after she had left port.

Just after lunch at sea on May 7, with the ship off the southern coast of Ireland, Theodate wondered how the *Lusitania*'s officers would ever see a periscope of an enemy submarine out in the ocean. And then, just a few minutes later, at about 2:10 p.m., a torpedo punctured the bow on the starboard side below the bridge. The instant of impact sounded like "that of an arrow entering the canvas and straw of a target, magnified a thousand times."[235] A moment later, there was a terrific explosion, with water and debris shooting into the air and down onto the *Lusitania*'s decks. In a matter of minutes, the foredeck was almost completely underwater. After she put on her life belt, Theodate slipped as she went to jump from the deck, plunging into the icy waters below. She thought of Hill-Stead, the school she had designed for Mary Hillard, and the many friends she loved—then "committed myself to God's care in thought—a prayer without words."[236]

Bobbing in the waves for over four hours, Theodate drifted in and out of consciousness until she was picked up by a rescue ship, the *Julia*. As she was suffering from hypothermia, the rescuers could not detect Theodate's pulse, and they placed her in the morgue section of the ship, to be counted among the dead. However, a survivor on board saw Theodate's eyelids flicker, and with help from the crew, Theodate regained consciousness at about 11:00 p.m., almost nine hours after the *Lusitania* sank. Miraculously, she survived.

Years earlier, Anna Roosevelt Cowles had introduced Theodate Pope to John Wallace Riddle, who had served as minister to Russia in 1905 during Teddy Roosevelt's presidency. While the two exchanged letters infrequently over the next ten years, following the sinking of the *Lusitania*, John, then fifty-one, started courting forty-eight-year-old Theodate. A day shy of one year from the disaster, the two were married at a simple ceremony at Hill-Stead in May 1916.

The previous three years had been a time of great trial for Theodate. In August 1913, her father, Alfred, died suddenly from a cerebral hemorrhage or stroke. He had been her guiding star, and his death affected her deeply. A couple of months after his passing, with her friend Harris Whittemore present, Theodate announced to her mother, Ada, that she was determined to build a school for boys in memory of Alfred. And after the sinking of the *Lusitania*, Mary Cassatt encouraged Theodate to follow through with the project, telling her, "If you were saved it is because you have still something to do in this world."[237]

In keeping the promise she made to build an "indestructible school for boys,"[238] in June 1916, Theodate bought a seven-hundred-acre parcel in Avon. No sooner had she taken the first concrete step to build the school when Theodate began having doubts as to her ability to accomplish the monumental task. Writing to her second cousin Brooks Emeny, she told him, "It may be two or three years before I begin to build, as there is so much else to be attended to. It is a very sober undertaking, and when I think of it in the gray dawn of the morning, I become quite alarmed and worried, but I shake myself out of that feeling, knowing that is the early morning feeling of dread that everyone goes through when they have a large undertaking before them."[239]

Then tragedy struck again in January 1917. Before her marriage to John, Theodate had become ward to a two-year-old orphan named Gordon Brockway, but in December 1916, Gordon, then age four, contracted polio and died just a few weeks later. In her heartache, Theodate turned her attention to her work, including a commission to restore Theodore Roosevelt's birthplace in New York City. It was Anna Roosevelt Cowles who had recommended Theodate for the project, and her design followed traditional English architecture, in contrast to the Beaux-Arts Classicism that was popular at the time.

Theodate Pope Riddle during construction of Avon Old Farms School. *Courtesy of Hill-Stead Museum Archives.*

While her plans for the school in Avon were delayed for a time by the upheaval of World War I, in early 1919, Theodate completed her architectural design of the campus and continued to buy more parcels through 1922.

In her design, she centered the buildings around a green, creating a campus she referred to as the "village at Old Farms in Avon."[240] The buildings were to be constructed in the style prevalent in the Cotswold region of England, made with steeply pitched slate roofs, low side walls, prominent chimneys and arched windows. Importantly, Cotswold buildings were constructed using locally sourced stone and lumber, and to that end, Theodate resolved that the materials for the buildings on campus would be harvested entirely from the property itself.

Theodate had strong opinions on how the school would be run. She thought educators at the time were trying to mold the students' thoughts into an ideal rather than letting them discover their own innate abilities and wanted her academy to stimulate the students' "initiative and will-power."[241] Theodate placed much of the blame on fathers: "They don't think their sons must be strong," she was quoted as saying. Instead, her school would "provide daily obstacles to be overcome by mental and physical effort."[242] Riddle believed that for nearly three centuries, American men benefited from the hard daily labor of working on a farm, and her preeminent goal was to establish that work ethic in her students. And her reference to farm work was not merely an analogy. In the early years of the school, students had to do manual labor like growing crops, raising chickens and performing carpentry work.

By 1921, Theodate had purchased nearly three thousand acres along the Farmington River, all of the land needed for the school's campus. Beginning in the spring of that year, workers cleared the land with oxen that were used to pull stumps and level the earth. Finally, in 1922, construction of the buildings began with the help of craftsmen from England who built the railroad station on present-day Scoville Road.

A source of red sandstone was found at a location just north of the campus, and when workers discovered that the sandstone was far more plentiful than they expected, Theodate changed the design of her buildings from brick to stone. With the building of her school well underway in 1923, Theodate ensured the Tudor Cotswold–style buildings would be authentically constructed, forbidding the use of levels or plumb lines. Her aim was to ensure that the school buildings blended into the landscape, adhering to a fundamental precept of the Arts and Crafts movement that was in vogue at the time.

Strong-willed, Theodate was known to be meticulous and demanding. As the school was being constructed, she prized obedience to her wishes above all else. An oft-told story is that, in assessing whether to hire a gardener, she instructed the applicant to place bushes in a flower bed upside down with the roots sticking out of the surface. Perplexed, the prospective gardener nonetheless complied and told Theodate that he was ready for her inspection. Upon seeing his work, she said, "Good. You did exactly as I asked you to do and you are hired. Now plant them right."[243]

By the summer of 1924, workers had constructed the water tower and the building that houses the chapel today, and by the fall of that year, the foundations of the quadrangle buildings were in place. By the summer of 1925, the campus was bustling with activity, with 550 men on site.

After the rock was hauled from the quarry, stonecutters, most of them Italian immigrants, went to work, "dressing" or cutting the rock into suitable shapes and polishing the resulting stones using only a peen hammer. Stonemasons were then employed to construct the walls and window arches of the quadrangle buildings using the stone blocks. A sawmill was built just south of the quarry to hew the timbers harvested from the property, and workers used traditional tools like the adze and broad axe to cut and shape the timbers. Once the rafters were in place, it was time to install the slate roof. For that effort, Theodate brought laborers over from London, England, as local workers did not have the expertise. The last of the buildings to be completed were the powerhouse in 1926 and the refectory in the spring of 1927. Finally, with a total construction cost of about $3 million, the preparatory school opened its doors in September 1927 with seventy-one boys enrolled.

She had dedicated herself over ten years to fulfilling this dream to honor her father, Alfred, and with completion of the school, Theodate Pope Riddle had accomplished her greatest architectural triumph. It took a while for her to settle on a name for her new school in Avon. Since it was a tribute to her father (and to her mother, Ada, after she passed away in 1920), Theodate initially thought she would call it the "Pope School." But by early 1921, she changed the name to the "Avon School" and eventually to "Avon Old Farms" in recognition of the name that area of town had always been known.[244]

Self-taught, Theodate earned the recognition of her peers, becoming a licensed architect in New York in 1916 and in Connecticut in 1933. She had often been reminded of the fact that people seriously questioned whether a woman could undertake such a large project. When Theodate got a letter in March 1927 from *New York Herald Tribune* art critic Royal Cortissoz complimenting her on being about ready to open the school, she recalled years earlier that, when told of Theodate's intention to build a school,

Cortissoz asked Anna Cowles, "Why don't they get a man?"[245] Now, all those doubts about her abilities had been erased, and with the completion of Avon Old Farms School, Theodate had firmly established herself as an accomplished architect, creating an "indestructible" landmark in the town of Avon.

The road to realizing her dream had been fraught with many obstacles, not the least of which was from a man she least expected would cause her trouble. Just when construction of the school was taking shape in May 1923, Theodate received a threatening letter from her old friend Joe Alsop.

21

THE SQUIRE OF AVON

Joe Alsop

Through their mutual acquaintance Anna Roosevelt Cowles, in 1905 Theodate Pope met Joseph Alsop, an Avon farmer with political aspirations, and the two became good friends. Born into a family of status and privilege, Joe Alsop attended Groton, a preparatory school in Massachusetts, before enrolling at Yale University, where he graduated with an engineering degree in 1898. After working at a Colorado ranch, he moved back to his hometown of Middletown, Connecticut, and took a job at the Russell Manufacturing Company. Then in 1903, with the help of family money, he bought a seven-hundred-acre parcel on Nod Road in Avon when he was just twenty-seven years old. Often confused with Chester Woodford's farm farther north on Nod Road, he decided to name his property "Wood Ford Farm" in honor of town founder Amasa Woodford, who had owned the land a century earlier.[246] There, Joe grew shade tobacco and raised Ayrshire cattle.

While he spent his days as a farmer, Joe soon got the itch to run for public office, following the footsteps of his father, who served in the Connecticut State Senate as a Democrat, representing the Middletown area. Though the Alsop family had been Democrats for generations, Joe quickly realized that no Democrat would get elected in Republican-controlled Avon, so he switched his allegiance to the Republican Party.

The staunch Republican Anna Roosevelt Cowles was more than willing to help Joe Alsop with his political ambitions. While she could not run for office herself due to her gender, Anna nonetheless enjoyed being active in politics. At her home on Main Street in Farmington, she frequently entertained young, politically inclined gentlemen she referred to as her "Joe-Bob's."[247] She met Joe Alsop in 1905 when he was twenty-nine and she was fifty, and the two hit it off, appreciating each other's wit and intellect. After Joe visited Anna and her husband at their Washington D.C. residence, Anna wrote to him, "I feel quite like a proud hen with a refracting duckling and you are the duckling. EVERY ONE asked for you and said such nice things."[248] With Anna's support, in 1906, thirty-year-old Joe Alsop won a seat in the Connecticut State House of Representatives and two years later was elected to the State Senate.

Joseph Wright Alsop IV, circa 1911. *From* Legislative History and Souvenir of Connecticut, *Vol. VIII,* 1911–1912.

When Theodate and John Wallace Riddle married in May 1916, they invited Joe Alsop and his wife, Corinne, to their wedding in Farmington. Before Gordon Brockway passed away, Theodate would take him to Wood Ford Farm on Nod Road in Avon so he could play with the Alsops' four children, and the two families grew close.

After serving in the Connecticut House of Representatives and State Senate, Joe Alsop became first selectman of Avon in 1922. Not yet a year on the job, he started hearing complaints from his constituents about how it was becoming nearly impossible to hire contractors or other skilled workers for anything close to a reasonable wage because Theodate Pope Riddle was paying the workers at her school as much as $1.10 per hour, driving up the market price for contractors. Joe himself was finding it hard to find workers for his farm on Nod Road, as many opted to work at the school's construction site for higher pay. Despite being a free-market Republican, Alsop wanted Theodate to rectify the situation.

In his appeal to her, he tried to soften the blow. "I am writing you this letter without the slightest desire to butt in and with the most friendly feeling" he began, but then proceeded with a most unfriendly message. Joe complained that the local mason he used just lost two of his employees to the school building project, and he asserted that at least a dozen Ensign-Bickford employees in Avon left to work at the school as well. Citizens of the town were so upset, Joe continued, that "they are all assuming an air of exceeding hostility against you," concluding in his letter, "if the present condition continues…the town's people will become your active enemies."[249]

Theodate then went to her friend Anna Cowles to help smooth over the situation and was shocked to learn that Anna herself had encouraged Joe to write the letter. "You should know what people are saying,"[250] Anna told her, trying to justify her actions. After weeks passed, Theodate sent a letter to Joe reminding him that the town would benefit from the presence of the school, and Joe did not pursue the matter further.

However, later in 1923, Joe made another disputatious move against the school, angering Theodate. While it was understood that a private school, once in operation, was exempt from paying property taxes, beginning with the 1923 grand list year, the Town of Avon began assessing the school at Joe Alsop's direction. Joe was upset that the foundation Theodate used to fund construction had not been paying taxes, arguing that the town had to provide services, including maintenance of the town roads that went through the property. What rankled Alsop is that many of the parcels Theodate bought for her school had been farms or mills that had been paying property tax, and now nearly three thousand acres of land, about 18 percent of Avon's land mass, was no longer generating revenue for the town. He had promised town residents low property tax rates, and here, Theodate had not paid any property taxes despite having bought her first parcel of land in Avon in 1916.

Given how long it was taking to build the campus, Alsop was determined to make Theodate pay taxes. He told her: "You either put boys in those buildings, and open a school, or start paying taxes on the buildings and the land."[251] In 1925, the dispute ended up in court, with Theodate arguing that the campus already met the definition of an "academy"[252] and that, in any event, the whole project served as a memorial to her father and mother and, therefore, should be exempt from tax. The judge disagreed, though he noted that the parties would need to work out a property valuation for the assessment. Theodate turned to her friend Harris Whittemore to continue the fight against the assessments, and with Whittemore representing the school, the Town of Avon ultimately agreed to lower the assessment by about half.

Feeling spurned by Joe Alsop and Anna Cowles, Theodate turned inward, refusing to respond to calls or correspondence from friends. Anna Roosevelt Cowles felt the rejection. She tried to reach out a number of times, but Theodate did not respond, believing Anna was partly responsible for the angst that Joe Alsop had caused. "If I could only avoid human contacts," Theodate observed, "I'm like an express train running at top speed." Listing those who were creating obstacles, including Joe Alsop, she said, "If people don't want trouble with me, they'd better not put stones on my track."[253]

Theodate Pope Riddle and Joe Alsop would eventually reconcile later in life, with Joe serving as a pallbearer at John Wallace Riddle's funeral, but she nonetheless stipulated in her will that Joseph Alsop was "never to have anything to do with the School."[254] Joe served as first selectman of Avon for a total of thirty-five years and was so well entrenched in the Avon establishment, he became known as the "Squire of Avon."[255] As prominent as Joe was in the community, he wasn't the only well-known and beloved citizen of Avon at the time. Another Avon man who stood in Theodate's way was an enterprising horticulturalist who created gardens so spectacular, people came from all over Hartford County to see his displays. Theodate, however, was not at all pleased with the crowd he was attracting.

22

SHERMAN EDDY'S TOW PATH GARDENS

In early 1926, Theodate Pope Riddle's on-site managers of the school became concerned about loud music in the evenings coming from an adjacent property just to the north of the campus, a place called Tow Path Lodge. On weekends, large crowds visited the ornate gardens of the lodge, clogging the otherwise quaint Old Farms Road. In the evenings, people enjoying themselves at debutante balls and other social functions danced well into the night. The noise pierced the bucolic calm that Theodate cherished for her school. The lodge was a nuisance to Theodate in other respects as well. On part of the property, there was an unsightly sheep barn right next to the school. Something had to be done to rectify the situation, but the owner was in no mood to sell.

Growing up on a farm in Simsbury, Sherman Eddy, or "Sherm" as he was known, became enthusiastic about learning all things horticultural. From 1894 to 1898, he attended Connecticut Agricultural College (later renamed the University of Connecticut), where he played football during an era when they didn't use helmets or pads.

After he left college, Sherm started out managing his dad's farm in Simsbury called J.C. Eddy & Son Farm, also known as the Hop Brook Farm. It was there that Sherman cultivated a love of gardening. The farm grew peaches and strawberries and many types of vegetables, including Sherm's favorite, asparagus.

Sherm married Grace Emily Blakeman in November 1899, and Grace moved in with him at Hop Brook Farm. Not long after the Climax Fuse factory fire of 1905, he met Ralph Ensign, president of Ensign-Bickford Company. Impressed by Sherm's ambition and initiative, Ralph offered him the position of superintendent of the Climax Fuse factory in Avon, replacing Frank Hadsell. Sherm accepted the job, and together with their young son, Sherm and Grace moved into a home in Avon next door to the Climax Fuse plant.

Sherm was quickly put to work helping to rebuild the factory after the fire, procuring stone from the Ketchin quarry in Simsbury near Tariffville. Yearning to use his talents for gardening and landscaping, on his own, he enhanced the grounds of the Climax Fuse plant in Avon with flower beds. At town parades, he and his friend Franklin Sperry would decorate their automobiles with all sorts of fresh flowers—meadow lilies, nasturtiums, orchids and white hydrangeas.

By 1915, Sherm had become a beloved figure in town, and with Grace and three young sons, things were going well. However, Sherman's life

Sherman and Grace Eddy in parade car. *Clint B. Hadsell Collection.*

Sherman W. Eddy. *Courtesy of Avon Free Public Library.*

was turned upside down in March 1919 when Grace died suddenly after an illness. She had contracted the Spanish flu after opening her home to nurse victims of the disease, and town residents mourned her loss. Grace had endeared herself to Avon—in addition to her World War I relief efforts, she was active with the local Grange and the Avon Congregational Church, and her loss was felt deeply.

Taking stock of his life and wanting to spend more time on his passion for gardening and landscaping, in July 1919, Sherm decided to build a summer home and worked with a landscape architect named Thomas Desmond on the design. He bought a property on Old Farms Road in Avon about a half mile south of its intersection with Country Club Road that had farmland, a brook and a spring that was right alongside what had been the towpath of the Farmington River canal. Sherman instantly saw the possibilities and went to work remodeling the 1786 farmhouse.

Deciding to name his summer home Tow Path Lodge, Sherm constructed the house with whitewashed stone, large timbers and a tile roof. On the grounds, he created a terrace overlooking a trout pond and installed a miniature Japanese "half-moon"[256] bridge leading to an island that he lined with ferns. The gardens were exquisite, with a dazzling display of flowers and native plants, and his lodge soon came to be known for its roses, peonies and native yellow lady's slippers. Sherm also had a large vegetable garden on the property, and each summer he would bring fresh produce into Hartford to sell on Front Street. He especially loved to grow his prized asparagus and strawberries, which he had first learned to cultivate in his youth.

To clear the land, build the pond and create the sunken garden and terraces, Sherm needed to move earth, and he did so in an unconventional manner. Leveraging knowledge he gained as superintendent of the Climax Fuse plant and using scrap product from the shop, Sherm used explosives to help remove stumps and create drainage ditches.

As a horticulturalist, he embraced the influence of the Arts and Crafts movement. Sherm's gardens at Tow Path Lodge contained abundant flower beds that blended in with the surrounding landscape, and he used natural material sourced from his property to create everything from the terraces to a bird bath made from a Native American mortar stone. Whereas Victorian gardens of the nineteenth century featured plants from all over the world, Sherm was a strong advocate for incorporating native species as much as possible into his gardens.

Missing Grace, Eddy longed for support and companionship to help through life's challenges. In September 1922, when he was forty-six, Sherm married someone he had known for many years, twenty-six-year-old Marian Spamer of Fairfield, Connecticut. He was well acquainted with Marian, as she was the niece of his first wife, Grace. The wedding venue, of course, was Sherm's Tow Path Lodge. Decorated with Ophelia and Madame Butterfly roses, the grounds for the wedding were spectacular. Sherm would go on to have two daughters with Marian in addition to his three sons from his first marriage.

As superintendent at Ensign-Bickford where he worked, Sherm was well-liked by employees at the plant, never known to "raise his voice in anger."[257] Over the years, he tried his best to improve conditions for workers there, implementing a health clinic on-site. When, on January 24, 1925, central Connecticut experienced a total solar eclipse, Sherman asked management at Ensign-Bickford if he could give his employees time off to view the eclipse without docking their pay. Management refused, leaving Sherm bewildered: "It happens only once in hundreds of years…and all they could say was 'We can't do it because it would set bad precedent.'"[258] Though he was a manager and lived in an era of formal dress, Sherm was never a suit and tie kind of guy. On being elected president of the Kiwanis Club, he dreaded having to wear a suit and starched shirt, saying, "I'd rather be horsewhipped!"[259]

At first, Sherm used the Tow Path Lodge only as his summer home but then began inviting groups to hold meetings at the property. Soon, he realized he could open the facility to the public and decided to install cooking stoves on the ground floor and set up tables and benches so people could come to picnic on the grounds. By 1924, Tow Path Lodge had become a popular destination. In June each year, hordes of visitors came to see the peonies in bloom, congesting Old Farms Road on Sunday afternoons.

Then Sherm realized that with its beautiful gardens, lily pond and views of the Farmington River Valley below, Tow Path Lodge was an ideal venue for social events, including dances. On the second floor of the lodge, he constructed a hardwood dance floor and a loft at one end where an orchestra or band could play. By 1926, Tow Path Lodge had become not only a way for Sherm to share his gardens with the public but also a business. When it came time for the daughters of upper-class families in the Hartford area to be "introduced to society," as was custom, many of them opted to hold their debutante balls at Tow Path Lodge in Avon. The balls were a huge success. On summer evenings, music and laughter rang out into the countryside and, as it turned out, well within earshot of Bill Kegley, director of the physical plant at Theodate Pope Riddle's soon-to-be-opened school.

In early 1926, Theodate concluded that something must be done about the obnoxious "dance hall"[260] next door to her school. Her vision of the school as a quaint English village, a pastoral setting for serious study, was now in jeopardy. She promptly instructed her agents to buy out Sherman Eddy and close the Tow Path Lodge.

But Eddy was a shrewd businessman, and like Joe Alsop, he was not intimidated by Theodate Pope Riddle. Realizing he was in an excellent bargaining position, Sherm held out. With the Tow Path Lodge business

Tow Path Lodge, after it was converted to a horse stable. *Courtesy of Avon Old Farms School.*

doing so well, he was willing to wait and see just how much Theodate wanted his property. The strategy worked. Theodate eventually directed that the property be purchased at whatever the cost. On October 1, 1926, Sherm sold all but 6 acres of his 150-acre Tow Path Lodge to the school at an undisclosed price.

With that purchase and the resolution of the property tax dispute with Joe Alsop, Theodate was finally rid of the troublesome pair from Avon. In what must have saddened Sherm, in 1928, Theodate dismantled the sheep barn and had Tow Path Lodge moved farther north, converting it into a stable for the school's polo ponies and riding horses.

In April 1931, Sherm decided to devote himself full time to the landscaping business, resigning his post as superintendent of Ensign-Bickford's Avon plant and buying a controlling interest of a landscaping outfit in West Hartford. In explaining the decision to his friends, Sherm joked that he "gave up a career to take up a hobby."[261] Upon the acquisition, he renamed the company Towpath Gardens Inc. given the name recognition of his Tow Path Lodge and gardens during the 1920s. His landscaping business catered to wealthy families in the Hartford area, for whom he designed ornate terraced gardens and ponds. To promote his company, Sherm attended flower shows throughout New England, often receiving gold medals for Best in Show. One of his most beloved displays re-created the scene of an old mill, with a covered bridge and wildflowers.

While he supplied customers with nonnative flowers like rose geraniums and daffodils, Sherm preferred to plant native flowers such as jack-in-the-pulpit, wake robin, blue violet and the adder's tongue. For ground cover, he liked the large, downy, heart-shaped leaves of wild ginger rather than the nonnative pachysandra. He lamented that with every passing day the land was losing its precious native wildflowers like the trailing arbutus, wood lily and hepatica. Accordingly, Sherm encouraged his Towpath Gardens customers and the public to embrace native seedlings. He could see into the future when many around him could not. Without native plant species, Sherm warned, we would lose the birds and animals that depend on them.

As his good friend John Ellsworth said about Sherman Eddy, "He loved trees and encouraged the intelligent use and culture of them around our homes….With his artistic planting, he inspired the whole community to appreciate the necessity as well as the aesthetic value of trees. He left the world a better place in which to live."[262] That was Sherm's greatest contribution—his inspiration to others. He loved trees, flowers, ferns and all things in a garden.

23

A GRAND POLITICAL ENEMY

Corinne Robinson Alsop

Wearing a blue dress adorned with a white flower on the collar, Corinne Robinson Alsop of Avon rose from her seat and stared out into an energized crowd of fifteen thousand at the Public Auditorium in Cleveland, Ohio. It was late in the evening on June 11, 1936, and though she was a little apprehensive about the speech she was soon to give, Corinne felt privileged she had been asked to second the nomination of the Republican Party's nominee for president of the United States, Alf Landon of Kansas. The first woman to have that honor at a major political party convention, Corinne was confident and poised as she stepped onto the podium at about 10:40 p.m. Told ahead of time she should keep her remarks to three minutes or less, she started, in her aristocratic accent, with levity. "I am a lady, and you have to listen to me even if I should speak three minutes and a half."[263]

A staunch Republican, Corinne detested big government and was convinced that the incumbent, Franklin Delano Roosevelt, was assuming dictatorial powers as he tried to engineer the country out of the Great Depression. She got right to the point: "Mr. Chairman, delegates to the Republican National Convention: As perhaps you have heard, this New Deal has wasted our substance in riotous spending. And we, the American people, are tired of self-styled New Dealers, and we want a square deal. We demand that the cards be dealt again in a new fashion and that in the future, no individual shall do all the dealing."[264]

The evening was the culmination of an unlikely political career. Just sixteen years earlier, Corinne did not even have the right to vote. After she fought for women's suffrage, she was elected to the Connecticut State House of Representatives in 1924, eventually serving a total of three terms. It was her husband, Joe Alsop, who had been the politician in the family, serving in the Connecticut State House and Senate and later as first selectman of Avon. But then Corinne pursued her own political ambitions, one of the first generation of women to win elected office. And on this evening in Cleveland, it was Corinne, not Joe, who stepped to the microphone in front of a throng of Republican Party delegates.

All through the evening, the crowd erupted in applause and cheers for Alf Landon's nomination. Sure, his candidacy was a long shot against the widely popular FDR, but this was a night of celebration and hope. How was it that Corinne Alsop from Avon was given the opportunity to second the nomination of Alf Landon? For the organizers of the Republican National Convention, eager to attract more women to vote for their candidate, it made sense to have at least one woman delegate on the stage to nominate Landon. But there was a more important reason Corinne was chosen for the honor. She wasn't just any Republican woman delegate. Corinne Robinson Alsop was a Roosevelt.

Born into wealth and privilege in Orange, New Jersey, in 1886, Corinne was the daughter of Douglas Robinson and Corinne Roosevelt Robinson. Her mother was the younger sister of President Teddy Roosevelt, and Corinne spent her teenage years and early twenties during Uncle Teddy's presidency. With the Robinsons firmly entrenched as members of high society, Corinne had a comfortable childhood and developed a strong bond with her mother that carried through the rest of their lives.

Growing up, Corinne was a close friend of her first cousin Eleanor Roosevelt, who was just nineteen months her senior. Eleanor had a difficult childhood. Her father, Elliott, Teddy Roosevelt's younger brother, was an alcoholic, and her mother, Anna, passed away unexpectedly from diphtheria when Eleanor was just eight years old. Before she turned ten, both her younger brother and her father also died, leaving her an orphan. After Eleanor's father died in 1894, she went to live with her maternal grandmother, Mary Hall, who was not at all endearing to Eleanor.

Corinne remembered Mary Hall as looking tired, overwhelmed by the responsibility of raising Eleanor and living in a house that Corinne saw as

Corinne Robinson Alsop. *Houghton Library, Harvard University.*

dark and foreboding. Corinne so despised the Hall home that she made excuses not to go there and later said about Mary, "She had absolutely no gaiety and no enjoyment in children."[265] While she was accustomed to life in a "proper" family of privilege, Eleanor was never entirely a part of that world; as her cousin Corinne put it, "her sadness and loneliness set her apart."[266] Given all the adversity Eleanor had overcome in her childhood, what came out of it was a deep concern for the welfare of the underprivileged—a mindset she carried with her during the rest of her life.

As teenagers, Eleanor and Corinne both attended Allenswood Academy, a preparatory school for girls in Wimbledon, London, and overlapped there for one year. After she returned to America, Corinne enrolled at a school in New York and, soon after, started making regular visits to see her aunt Anna Roosevelt Cowles in Farmington, Connecticut. Theodore Roosevelt's older sister Anna was known by her nieces and nephews as "Auntie Bye" and by her siblings as "Bamie," and she and her husband William Cowles had their principal home on Main Street in Farmington, which they called Oldgate.

Meanwhile, in 1902, Corinne's cousin Eleanor started a romance with her fifth cousin, Franklin Delano Roosevelt, whom Corinne did not admire. Franklin was known for being arrogant and a heavy drinker, and Corinne confided in her diary that he was "by no means good enough"[267] for Eleanor. In the summer of 1904, when staying at Teddy Roosevelt's home in Oyster Bay, Long Island, she wrote in her diary on July 18, "Franklin Roosevelt arrived in the morning and it was very nice to see him again. I cannot decide whether it filled Eleanor with joy or not. I think he is very crazy about her but she not about him. It is truly pathetic."[268]

On March 4, 1905, Corinne was at the White House in Washington, D.C., getting ready for her uncle's second inaugural as the family prepared for Franklin and Eleanor's wedding that would take place just two weeks later. "Eleanor, Franklin, Auntie Bye and I all went over to the White

House about 9 o'clock to see Uncle Ted start for the Capitol—he was so dear and natural with us all."[269] Two weeks later, at Eleanor and Franklin's wedding, bridesmaid Corinne had reconciled herself to the pairing, noting that "Eleanor looked perfectly charming....I do hope they will be very, very happy for if anyone deserves it, it is Eleanor."[270]

In late 1906, when Corinne was twenty years old, she herself became engaged to a man named George Draper, but after a trip to Europe in the fall of 1907, she reconsidered and broke off the engagement in the spring of 1908. When Corinne was still engaged to Draper in early 1908, she was visiting Auntie Bye at Oldgate in Farmington when she met a friend of Anna's, thirty-one-year-old Joe Alsop, and had a favorable first impression.

Through the rest of 1908 and into 1909, Corinne would see Joe when she visited Auntie Bye, and the visits became more frequent. Over time, the two developed a strong friendship that eventually blossomed into love. Corinne wrote to her mother in the spring of 1908, "I really feel that he is a friend of mine and yet the fact of his being here as Auntie Bye's friend and my not seeing him in a personal way has made it possible for it to be a perfectly natural easy thing."[271] While Joe was courting Corinne in 1908, he ran for state senator and won with the help of Anna Roosevelt Cowles.

Auntie Bye fully supported Corinne's attachment to Joe Alsop, referring to him as "a man who is as dear and high minded as they come,"[272] and in the summer of 1909 Corinne and Joe were engaged. But 1909 was not a happy year for the Roosevelt family. Tragedy struck on February 21 when Corinne's younger brother Stewart died after he fell out of a window while attending a party at Harvard University. Stewart's death was a devastating blow to the family. Corinne remembered, "The greatest sorrow of Mother's life was when my younger brother was killed when he was 21."[273]

Even though Joe Alsop was ten years older than Corinne, her mother, Corinne Roosevelt Robinson, was supportive of the marriage, writing to Joe: "I do intuitively feel that you are the man for her," adding, "Corinne is the most precious thing in the world....I feel that she has found happiness...and leave her in your keeping with a heart light in so far as her and your future is concerned."[274]

Given Stewart's tragic death, Corinne and Joe planned a simple ceremony for their November 4 wedding in New York City. Then, just three days before their nuptials, Franklin and Eleanor Roosevelt's six-month-old son, Franklin Jr., died. The wedding proceeded, but it was a solemn ceremony held in a family home. Anna Cowles felt blessed at her part in bringing Joe and Corinne together, writing to Corinne, "The wedding was the loveliest in every way that I ever have been to and we…love you more united, if, that be possible, than separately."[275]

After a ten-day honeymoon in Virginia, the newlyweds made the trip back to Connecticut, first stopping in New Haven to see Yale's football team defeat Princeton on November 13. As they drove from the Elm City to Avon after the game, Corinne got her first taste that life ahead would be far different from her upbringing. It took four hours to get from New Haven to Wood Ford Farm in Avon due to car troubles, and when she arrived at the farmhouse, she noted that with its "old portraits, disreputable, ancient rugs, battered chairs and hundreds of old and somewhat disheveled books," it looked like "a second class hotel."[276] Since Corinne was accustomed to living in luxurious homes throughout her childhood, her mother knew Wood Ford Farm would be an adjustment for Corinne, telling Joe, "She will have to learn enough in practical ways for I have failed to a certain extent I fear in practical training but I think anything she gives her mind to, be it practical management or other things, she will conquer for her will is equal to any situation."[277]

Corinne grew up in high society with all the trappings of wealth, including debutante balls, afternoon tea and evenings at the theater. The Robinsons wintered at their home in New York City; spent spring and autumn at their principal residence in Orange, New Jersey; and summered with either the Oyster Bay Long Island Roosevelts or at Henderson House, her father Douglas's family home in the Adirondacks. Compared to the refined lifestyle and luxuriant furnishings of upper-crust homes in New Jersey and New York, the rustic farm and muddy roads of Avon were a stark contrast. Corinne wrote in her diary, "When I saw the little white house, I thought as though I was in a strange dream and I laughed….For many weeks, I went about the place and the house trying to realize that it was mine and that here was to be my house for always."[278]

Joe got busy with work and politics right after they were married, and Corinne, realizing she missed being able to talk with other women, would often drive in her Model T over to Auntie Bye's for "an intimate chat."[279] Over the ensuing years, Corinne and Joe visited Anna often, and in turn, Auntie Bye traveled to Wood Ford Farm on occasion. About three months after their marriage, Corinne was expecting their first child, a son they named Joe Jr. and eighteen months after his birth, in March 1912, Corinne gave birth to a daughter they named Corinne.

Though she had a toddler and an infant, Corinne was ready to support her husband once again when he decided to run for political office in the fall of 1912, this time seeking a seat in the U.S. House of Representatives. After Teddy Roosevelt lost the Republican Party nomination for president in 1912, he formed his own Progressive Party, and for a time, Corinne Alsop and her husband joined the "Bull Moose" party, as it came to be known. The Bull Moose Party was decidedly more liberal than the traditional conservatism of Roosevelt's successor, William Howard Taft, and the Alsops enthusiastically joined the party. Married to Teddy Roosevelt's niece, Joe Alsop saw it as the perfect opportunity to run for the U.S. House of Representatives, riding Teddy's coattails.

In the 1912 election, however, Teddy Roosevelt and Taft ended up splitting the vote of the Republican electorate, enabling Woodrow Wilson to win the presidency, and Joe was unsuccessful in his bid for the House. On the campaign trail, Corinne went with Joe as he traveled through the first House district of Connecticut. "We had the most wonderful 6 weeks in the autumn" wrote Corinne. "Such a delicious time of my life. Joe and I were in perfect sympathy and we made a campaign for the Progressive Party that was more fun than anything....Though of course we lost, it was a splendid battle."[280]

Not long after the failed bid in 1912, the Bull Moose Party went into decline, and its supporters, including the Alsops, eventually went back to being members of the Republican Party. Rejoining the party just before the 1916 presidential election, Corinne and Joe remained active in politics, with both eventually serving on the GOP State Central Committee that selected presidential electors.

After Joe's unsuccessful run for the U.S. House of Representatives, Corinne resumed family life in Avon but struggled to connect with townsfolk. Her upbringing was so different from the farmers and laborers in town, and residents didn't do much to make her feel welcome. She wrote in her diary that "there is nothing but the daily happenings to the people of Avon that we have in common—our relationship stops after that."[281] When conversing with villagers in town, she reflected, "There is no stimulus of the mind... though I love to meet them and...am very fond of many of them, I do not frankly get enjoyment from social contact with them. Social and friendly contact is a very different thing. This isn't meant in the least to be snobbish and I am not snobbish at all."[282]

Well, maybe just a bit snobbish. Corinne wrote that it was difficult for "people without education or breeding to be on the same social basis as those with education and breeding."[283] Her husband, Joe, did not agree with her on that point and, in time, helped change her perspective. Joe had

Wood Ford Farmhouse. *Courtesy of Avon Free Public Library.*

learned that lesson from Teddy Roosevelt, who advised Joe not to show an air of superiority, telling him that people "with different backgrounds and education…were honestly just as sure they were right as I might be sure that I was right."[284]

As early as 1912, Corinne began working for the suffrage movement, despite the fact that many women of her privileged upbringing were against giving women the right to vote. Just a year earlier, in June 1911, Corinne joined Anna Cowles and Theodate Pope in signing a petition asking Connecticut legislators not to pass the women's municipal suffrage bill, claiming they did not wish for "the attendant burdens which it would force upon them."[285] Her attitude changed, however, when she joined the Progressive Party in 1912 and was named, along with Anna Cowles and Theodate Pope, to an executive committee of women responsible for evaluating the merits of suffrage. While Corinne and Theodate became active supporters of suffrage, Anna, or Auntie Bye, was a reluctant participant, later telling Eleanor Roosevelt that her involvement gave the committee the "faint aroma of non-suffragism."[286]

Anna Cowles liked to wield political influence behind the scenes but was strongly against women voting, arguing in 1895 that the wealthiest taxpayers were against suffrage while "the little domestic fair haired women are crazy to vote!"[287] Perpetuating a stereotype that women were not well informed about politics and likely reflecting her fear that more women voters would adversely affect Republican candidates, Anna went so far as to say that suffrage would multiply the "stupid vote."[288]

As the fight for suffrage was gaining momentum in 1918, Corinne helped organize the first group of Republican women in the state to teach them how to use their vote. Remarkably, Corinne took on this challenge when she had four young children to care for at home, including new arrivals Stewart, born in 1915, and John, born in 1916.

With the passage of the Nineteenth Amendment to the U.S. Constitution in August 1920, women voted for the first time in November of that year, and with the support of Corinne Alsop's leadership, five women in Connecticut were elected to the state house of representatives. The success of women candidates in 1920 encouraged Corinne to run for the state house in 1924 as a Republican. While the town of Avon was then a bastion of Republican support, Corinne's election was hardly assured. Many male voters still resented women running for elected office, believing that a woman's place was in the home. Despite the opposition, Corinne had just enough support, squeaking out a win by a mere twenty-nine votes. With her victory, she became the first female Roosevelt to hold political office and was assigned to the Committee on Humane Institutions.

When Corinne's first stint in the Connecticut State House ended in 1926, she decided not to run for another two-year term, but in the fall of 1928, she successfully ran again for the state legislature, campaigning for infrastructure improvements under the slogan: "Let's get the farmers out of the mud."[289]

Apart from their brief foray with the Progressive Party from 1912 to 1916 to support Uncle Teddy, Corinne and Joe Alsop were both lifelong Republicans, supporting Warren Harding, Calvin Coolidge and Herbert Hoover in the 1920s. But when Democrat Franklin Delano Roosevelt ran for president in 1932, Corinne voted for FDR, with family allegiance overcoming any concerns she may have had about Franklin's public policies. While Corinne considered herself a progressive back when her uncle ran for president in 1912, she soon regretted voting for her cousin Franklin. She opposed much of the New Deal legislation that spent money on government programs, significantly increasing the national debt.

While she appreciated the challenges of trying to lead the country out of a depression, Corinne did not like the direction the country was headed during Franklin Delano Roosevelt's presidency. In 1935, she wrote

Corinne Alsop (*standing*) on state committee. *Yale University Library.*

a letter to Theodate Pope Riddle, a supporter of the president, stating, "Your hero Franklin is having a whirl and his last pronunciamento will now tax everybody in such a way that capital will hardly exist!!" She abhorred what she called the "Soak the Rich Tax Message" that, in her view, sent "stocks tumbling and the business world shaken into a jittery condition."[290] Clearly, Corinne's fondness for Eleanor did not extend to Franklin's political leanings.

Despite her opposition to the FDR administration, she wanted to keep close ties with Eleanor. In February 1936, she and Joe stayed at the White House and visited the Freer Art Gallery with Eleanor. When their son Joe Jr. got a job at the Washington, D.C. bureau of the *New York Herald Tribune* that same year, the Alsops made a number of trips to the nation's capital.

Corinne did not want to burden Eleanor given her position as first lady, writing to her cousin, "I frankly always feel a little shy about asking you to give time when I know the many demands that you have."[291] But Eleanor was always very cordial to Corinne. When Corinne tried to apologize for treating her cousin as "Eleanor" and "not quite as the mistress of the White House,"[292] Eleanor wrote back, "For Heaven's sake, why shouldn't you treat me as Eleanor! I never think of myself as mistress of the White House with casual people, much less with my family."[293]

Eleanor Roosevelt, 1949. *Douglas Chandor.*

When FDR sought reelection in 1936, Corinne supported the Republican Party's nominee for president even if it meant voting against a close family relative. A week before the Republican National Convention, in June 1936, she told a reporter, "As to my relationship with the Franklin Roosevelts, we are and I hope we always will be friends, but I do not like their political program."[294] Later in life, she added, "I believe strongly in the two-party system. I was a Republican and I did not want to vote for Franklin."[295]

In 1936, the Republican Party nominated Kansas Governor Alf Landon to run against FDR. Like the Alsops, Landon voted for Teddy Roosevelt and the Bull Moose Party in 1912 and Alf was from the progressive wing of the party. With the country still in the midst of the Great Depression, Franklin Delano Roosevelt's New Deal was widely popular. Recognizing that, Alf supported some of FDR's measures but strongly objected to Social Security, as he believed it would not be adequately funded. In accepting his party's nomination, Alf Landon noted, "Crushing debts and taxes are usually incurred, as they are being incurred today, under the guise of helping people—the same people who must finally pay them."[296]

When seconding Landon's nomination at the Republican national convention in Cleveland Ohio, Corinne did not mince words about her disapproval of Franklin's policies. Speaking as a delegate from the First District of Connecticut, she said, "The people of our State and the people of Kansas…understand that when the government spends it is your money and my money that is being spent." She continued, "Americans hate to be coddled. They want to regain or retain their self-respect; their spirit of independence and self-reliance is vital to the body politic."[297] Though she predicted her seconding speech would last three and a half minutes, Corinne spoke for over five minutes, receiving thunderous applause.

On election night, when it became obvious that Franklin was going to win in a landslide, even winning a majority of the votes in the Republican stronghold of Avon, a gloating FDR at Hyde Park told Joe Jr. to call his mother to find out how "Corinne is taking it." When Joe Jr. reached her, Corinne was inebriated, commenting how she got the Republican candidate in Avon elected to the state legislature despite knowing "what was coming." Hearing her response, FDR quipped, "I knew Corinne was a professional."[298]

After the election in November 1936, Corinne knew she had to mend fences, writing to Eleanor: "The fact that I disagree with you politically very frequently does not change my affection one iota. I wish I could sit down with you [and Franklin] this minute and discuss anything under the sun—from politics to the last grandchild!"[299]

Eleanor was always gracious and did not hold Corinne's support for Alf Landon against her. Writing just eight days after the election, Eleanor told Corinne, "You are a grand political enemy because you do not carry it into your personal relationships and, as I don't either, it is a great relief to find it in other members of the family."[300] Ever courteous, Eleanor invited Joe and Corinne to Franklin's second inaugural on January 20, 1937, and welcomed them back to Washington, D.C., later in the year, saying "I don't think our political differences would bother us at all."[301]

During the remainder of FDR's presidency, Eleanor often invited Corinne and Joe to stay at the White House or at Hyde Park in New York, and once, in March 1943, the first lady stayed overnight at Wood Ford Farm after giving a speech in Hartford. The cousins maintained a close friendship for the rest of their lives.

Of the Alsops' four children, two of their sons, Joe Jr. and Stewart, became well-known political columnists in Washington, D.C., and their third son, John deKoven Alsop, made an unsuccessful run for governor of Connecticut in 1962. The Alsops' lone daughter, Corinne, married Percy Chubb, grandson of Thomas Caldecot Chubb, who founded the insurance company Chubb & Son in 1882. After Joe Alsop died in 1953, Corinne married Francis Cole, once chairman of the insurance company The Travelers and a prominent Hartford attorney with the Robinson & Cole law firm.

Corinne remained active in public service throughout her life. She recruited women for industry during World War I, helped organize female farm workers during World War II and was a board member of both the Connecticut chapter of the American Red Cross and of Children Services of Connecticut, the predecessor organization to the Village for Families and Children in Hartford. Empowering women to vote in 1920 and getting elected to political office herself, Corinne Robinson Alsop was one of Connecticut's pioneering women in politics.

PART VII

THE NOT SO SLEEPY HOLLOWS OF AVON

24

WILFORD WOODRUFF'S AWAKENING

As a young man, with Bible in hand, Wilford Woodruff was still searching, looking for spiritual insight, as he sat on an island in the Farmington River near the center of Collinsville, Connecticut. Deeply religious, he had been on a spiritual journey since the age of fourteen and often came to this sanctuary in the wilderness to pray for guidance. Baptized in the Lord's Barn when he was three months old, Wilford was raised in the Sleepy Hollow section of Northington. But partly due to the dissension within the Congregational Church that led its membership to split in 1818, the Woodruff family became disillusioned and explored other faiths. Wilford's father, Aphek, briefly considered joining his brother Ozem in forming the Union Baptist Society in 1817, but in time he and his family gravitated away from organized religion.

Wilford Woodruff, 1849. *Wilford Woodruff Papers.*

When the Second Great Awakening led to a revival of religious fervor in the 1820s, Wilford investigated different faiths but could not find a denomination that resonated with him. He "labored & prayed & tried to get religion" but was dismayed that "there was something in their manner of teaching & exhorting us to give our hearts to God without telling us what to do or pointing out the way so that we could understand it."[302]

Since he was a boy, Wilford had worked long days at his father's gristmill. At age twenty, he was put in charge of managing a flour mill, the first of several mills he would run. He was good at it but did not feel he had found his purpose. In 1831, Wilford was still yearning for a deeper meaning in his life when he came across a newspaper article that mentioned the publication of a book about the scriptures written by a man named Joseph Smith. When he finished reading the article, Wilford had a strong sense that perhaps, finally, he had found his calling.

Wilford Woodruff was born in Avon (then Northington) in March 1807, the youngest son of Aphek and Beulah Thompson Woodruff. Wilford, a fourth cousin, once removed, of distiller Romanta Woodruff, was just fifteen months old in June 1808 when his mother died of "spotted fever."[303] Eight months later, his father, Aphek, married Azubah Hart.

When he was old enough to help out with the family business, Wilford worked at the gristmill and sawmill that his grandfather Eldad Woodruff

Wilford Woodruff's boyhood home, Sleepy Hollow section of Avon. *The Contributor.*

built for Wilford's father in 1796. The forty-acre mill was located along what is now known as Thompson Brook, on land that is today part of Avon Old Farms School. Aphek's home and gristmill were in the Sleepy Hollow[304] section of town, in the vicinity of the two bridges that cross Thompson Brook on present-day Old Farms Road just east of its intersection with Thompson Road.

In 1817, when Wilford was ten, his father had to pay off debts he had cosigned and moved his family from Northington to Farmington center so he and his sons could work at the gristmill of Cowles, Deming & Camp. Part-owner George Cowles allowed Wilford to study at the Farmington Academy during the winter when he wasn't needed at the mill, so Wilford had more schooling than was typical for the era.

In 1827, at age twenty, he began managing a flour mill in East Avon for his aunt Helen Wheeler and went on to manage other flour mills over the next five years. During the period Wilford was operating his aunt's mill, he fell away from religion, participating in such unholy activities as playing cards and dancing.

After losing much of his wealth through bad investments, in 1830, Wilford got a job managing a flour mill for Samuel Collins in Collinsville. In the spring of 1831, however, the space occupied by the mill was needed by the fast-growing Collins Company to manufacture axes, putting Wilford out of a job. Collins was impressed with his new hire, telling Wilford he would gladly give him a recommendation, and Woodruff left for New Hartford to operate another mill there.

While working in Collinsville, Wilford became interested in Restorationism, which was a nineteenth-century movement wherein Protestants sought to "restore"[305] Christianity back to the teachings of the primitive Christian church. Although he explored different faiths, in time, he found it was more beneficial for him to pray on his own rather than attend an organized church, and when working in Collinsville in 1830, he would often go to an island in the Farmington River (now submerged) where he could pray alone.

Wilford believed that God had protected him from death on numerous occasions. Among other calamites, he fell into a cauldron of boiling water when he was three, broke both arms in separate falls while working at his father's gristmill, fractured a leg when it was caught in a wagon wheel and fell from a horse galloping at full speed, breaking his other leg. Years later, he recalled, "I can ownly [*sic*] attribute the continuation of my life on Earth… to a merciful God whose hand has been streched [*sic*] out & rescued me from death in the midst of the many dangers and hair breadths escapes."[306]

Although grateful for God's protection, since he was a boy, Wilford had questioned the doctrine taught in the Congregational church he attended with his family. As Wilford put it, "From the age of 14 to 23, my mind was often exercised upon the subject of my soul's salvation yet without submission to God or being led by his spirit." Wilford became convinced that the established churches at the time had deviated from the "pure and undefiled religion"[307] before God.

Wilford was greatly influenced by a Simsbury, Connecticut faith healer named Robert Mason, who taught him that no one individual has the authority to administer ordinances and that all have the ability, by prayer and fasting, to heal the sick by the laying of hands. Mason told Wilford, "I shall never partake of this fruit in the flesh; but you will, and you will become a conspicuous actor in that kingdom."[308] In 1831, Wilford was studying the Bible when he opened to Isaiah 56:1 and read God's message that "my salvation is close at hand and my righteousness will soon be revealed."[309]

After learning about the Mormon faith in a newspaper article in 1832, twenty-five-year-old Wilford believed he may have found the primitive Christian church he had been looking for. What impressed Wilford about Mormonism was that it taught, just as Robert Mason had prophesied, that a church should consist of "Prophets, Apostles, Pastors and Teachers"[310] all working, as stated in Ephesians, "For the perfecting of the saints, for the work of the ministry: for the edifying of the body of Christ: till we all come in the unity of the faith, and of the knowledge of the Son of God, unto a perfect man, unto the measure of the stature of the fulness of Christ."[311] Every church he attended until then had been lacking these purveyors of wisdom, and impressed with what he read, he decided to leave all behind and travel with his older brother Azmon to the town of Richland, New York. There, the two brothers bought a farm and operated a sawmill for the next two years. Then on December 29, 1833, Wilford and Azmon heard a sermon given by Zerah Pulsipher, elder of the Church of Jesus Christ of Latter-day Saints, and were so inspired by his teachings that they decided to be baptized into the faith two days later, with both "receiving the laying on of hands for the reception of the Holy Ghost."[312]

Three months later, Wilford wrote to his father, informing him that his search for truth had come to an end, declaring he had found "the everlasting gospel" and was "fully resolved to surrender my…temporarl [*sic*] & spiritual soul & body into the hands of God."[313] He told Aphek that the Mormon elders spoke with authority and could heal the sick.

Just four years earlier, in April 1830, Joseph Smith founded the Church of Jesus Christ of Latter-day Saints, a month after he published the Book of Mormon. Smith started receiving spiritual visions around 1820 and said that, in 1823, he received a vision from an angel named Moroni directing him to unearth "golden plates"[314] that included texts about the history of the ancient inhabitants of the Americas. His translation of the texts in 1828 became the Book of Mormon, and in the ensuing years, he would attract tens of thousands of followers.

In April 1834, Wilford and other brethren of the faith in Richland, New York, answered the call to "go to Zion," referring to what was known as "Zion's Camp"[315] in Kirtland, Ohio. He left his brother Azmon behind in Richland, and arriving in Kirtland, Wilford met Joseph Smith and stayed at his home. Then in January 1835, leaving Smith in Kirtland, Woodruff and other followers headed west to establish a Mormon settlement in Missouri, where Wilford was ordained an elder in June 1835.

Wilford understood the importance of his ordination and his obligation to spread the word of the Mormon faith. Back in Ohio on April 2, 1837, he wrote: "I am called to act a part in the work by being placed with the first Seventy Elders of Israel to become a special witness of Jesus Christ to all Nations [and] I need much faith, fortitude, holiness & wisdom."[316] Eleven days later, on April 13, Wilford married Phebe Carter, with the wedding taking place in Joseph Smith's home in Kirtland.

Phebe Whittemore (Carter) Woodruff. *The Church of Jesus Christ of Latter-day Saints.*

Three months after the wedding, in the summer of 1837, Wilford headed back east to proselytize in New England. This included a stop in Farmington, Connecticut, where he baptized his uncle Ozem on July 12, converting him from the Baptist Church. After traveling through New England, New York and New Jersey over the next year, Wilford returned to Avon and Farmington in June 1838 and spent eighteen days visiting his father, stepmother and other family members. During the visit, Wilford remembered that Joseph Smith had "promised me that I should bring my father's household into the kingdom of God," but when he preached the gospel to Aphek and stepmother Azubah, his message was met with stiff resistance. Wilford was convinced "the devil was determined to hinder the fulfillment of the promise" and retreated for an hour to pray alone.[317] The period of reflection achieved the desired result—he sang and shouted for joy when, on July 1, his father, stepmother and four others agreed to be baptized into the Mormon faith along the banks of the Farmington River.

A year later, in 1839, Wilford and a church apostle named John Taylor were instructed by Joseph Smith to proselytize in England, where they succeeded in converting over 1,100 people there to Mormonism, promising converts in Liverpool that they would find large tracts of land to farm in America. Soon after, Woodruff joined Taylor on the Quorum of the Twelve Apostles, considered special witnesses of Jesus Christ responsible for church governance.

In the spring of 1839, after the Mormons were pressured to leave Missouri, Joseph Smith and his followers established a settlement in Commerce, Illinois, along the Mississippi River, a place that Smith renamed Nauvoo. On January 1, 1840, Wilford Woodruff, along with other leaders of the church, made another missionary trip to Liverpool, England. After staying there for fifteen months, Wilford sailed back to America, where he once again paid a visit to his father's house in Farmington. Wilford spent much of his time there proselytizing, and on August 6, 1841, he visited the school where Mende Africans were being taught during their stay after the *Amistad* trial.

In Farmington, Woodruff approached Reverend Noah Porter about whether he could preach Mormon theology at Porter's Congregational church in the center of town. Skeptical, the pastor asked Wilford to show him the "miracles to be wrought to Convince him that our doctrine is true."[318] Wilford said he would do just that, and the two agreed to meet the evening of August 6, just after Wilford's visit with the Mendes. But the encounter did not go well. From Wilford's perspective, "Dr Noah Porter entered the room with his heart filled with madness anger & subtlety against the fulness of the gospel my testimony & Joseph Smith &c." Indeed, Reverend Porter rejected Wilford's message about the Book of Mormon, and Wilford left frustrated, having "done my duty" bearing "testimony of the truth." So disturbed was Wilford that he "repaired to the [Farmington] river & cleansed my feet with water in testimony against Dr Noah Porter In obediance [*sic*] to the commandment of God that my garments might be clear of his blood."[319]

After he cleansed himself, Wilford headed west, rejoining Joseph Smith in Nauvoo on October 6, 1841.

In May 1844, Joseph Smith sent Wilford on another missionary trip to the Northeast, where he was asked to promote Smith's long-shot candidacy for president of the United States. It would be the last time Wilford would see the founder of the Mormon church alive. The Mormons had faced hostility ever since their time in Kirtland, Ohio, and in June 1844, Joseph and his brother Hyrum were charged with inciting a riot in Nauvoo and brought to a jail in nearby Carthage, Illinois. There, on June 27, 1844, they were murdered by an angry mob while awaiting trial.

Over the next year, it became clear that the Mormons would not be safe staying in Illinois. Wilford was traveling abroad when, in October 1845, the church's new leader, Brigham Young, wrote to Wilford informing him that they would have to leave Nauvoo. Young explained that U.S. Representative Stephen A. Douglas from Illinois "told us plainly that the prejudice of the people was such that the state cannot pesably [*sic*] protect us and that it is therefore advisable for us to remove as the only conditions of peace."[320]

With that warning, Brigham Young led Wilford and 147 other Mormon pioneers out west, leaving in February 1846, a couple of years before the gold rush. Traveling by wagon train across Iowa and Nebraska, the caravan finally reached the crest of the Wasatch Range in the Utah Territory on July 28, 1847, and as they headed west down into the broad valley of the Great Salt Lake below, they stopped at the foot of the mountains. With Wilford Woodruff standing next to him, Brigham Young declared, "Brother Woodruff, drive on. Here is our home. This is the place God has pointed out for us to plant our feet."[321] The Mormons had finally reached their Zion.

Wilford quickly settled into his new life in the Salt Lake Valley, helping build the community by promoting education and supporting the establishment of theater and the fine arts. However, all was not harmonious in Salt Lake City.

While the custom of polygamy in the Mormon faith dated to the mid-1830s, it was not until Joseph Smith's time in Nauvoo that the practice became more accepted. Though Smith had only two wives before 1841, over the next three years, he married at least twenty-eight additional women. Some of them were for "eternity only," meaning that the union came into force only in the afterlife. These marriages likely did not involve sexual relations, particularly in the fourteen cases where he was "sealed to eternity" with women who were married to other men.[322] After he was already sealed in marriage to several women and girls, in August 1843, while in Nauvoo, Smith told a small number of his close associates that a decade earlier he had received a revelation from God declaring polygamy a "new and everlasting covenant,"[323] restoring a custom practiced by patriarchs of the Old Testament.

Initially, only a relatively small number of men took multiple wives, but by 1857, about half of Mormon families living in the Utah territory were polygamous. Some Mormon men and women were happy with their plural marriages, as they believed the practice strengthened family bonds, and some of the wives would eventually consider it a "blessing in disguise."[324] But many women found plural marriage to be an extremely difficult cross to bear.

Accepting the practice of polygamy espoused by Mormon founder Joseph Smith, Wilford married a total of nine women in his lifetime. On the dates of the marriages, six of the nine were less than half his age and two of them were under the age of eighteen. When his first wife, Phebe, learned that Wilford planned to take other wives, she said she "thought it was the most wicked thing I ever heard of [and] opposed it to the best of my ability, until I became sick and wretched." But through fervent prayer and acknowledging that Joseph Smith was a prophet, she came to understand that polygamy "was the will of God" and decided to "faithfully honor the patriarchal law."[325]

By the 1860s, public sentiment had turned strongly against plural marriage, and after Congress passed the Morrill Anti-Bigamy Act in 1862 followed by the Poland Act in 1874, the U.S. government sought to end the practice of polygamy by the Mormons. Ominously, the new laws gave authorities the power to criminally indict men who had multiple wives. In response, Mormon church leaders, including Wilford Woodruff, fled Salt Lake City to find places where they would be safe from apprehension.

When John Taylor assumed the role of church president after Brigham Young died in 1877, Wilford was named president of the Quorum of the Twelve Apostles and effectively "stood next in line for the church presidency."[326] With Brigham Young's passing, the controversy over polygamy did not abate. In 1875, the U.S. Supreme Court upheld the conviction of a Mormon man for polygamy, arguing that while the government cannot interfere with mere religious beliefs and opinions, it can prohibit practices. The decision marked the beginning of a decade-long battle against the Mormon Church.

Incensed by the actions of the U.S. government, Wilford defended the practice of polygamy, writing, "This testament which Joseph Smith has left Contains a revelation and Commandment from God out of Heaven Concerning the Patriarchal order of Marriage." Wilford continued, "Now after obeying this law for many years The Congress of the United States and the Supreme Judges of the Nation then Stand forth and say you shall be damned if you do obey it. Now ye Latter Day Saints what are you going to do under these Circumstances? God Says we shall be damned if we do not obey the Law, Congress says we shall be damned if we do. It places us precisely in the same position that it did the Hebrews in the firey [*sic*] furnace, or Daniel in the Den of Lions."[327] Defiant, Wilford added, "I say as an Apostle of the Lord Jesus Christ…I will not desert my wifes [*sic*] and my Children, and Disobey the Commandments of God for the Sake of accomidating [*sic*] the public Clammers of a generation steeped in sin….I would rather go to prison and to Death."[328] Wilford often wrote about the issue in apocalyptic terms, saying the U.S. government "will be rent in twain and the God of Heaven will hold them responsible for these things," adding that there would be no stopping the government "until the Nation is broken in pieces."[329]

In January 1880, Wilford was living in the wilderness of Arizona when he had a revelation that told him the apocalypse and the second coming of Christ were near, the holiness of plural marriage would be affirmed and God would inflict wrath against the United States for its prosecution of Mormons. Church leadership accepted the revelation "as the word of the Lord"[330] in April 1880.

Legislators in Washington, D.C., however, were adamant about ending plural marriage. In 1882, Congress passed the Edmunds Anti-Polygamy Act, which declared polygamy as a felony in all federal territories, including Utah, and required only proof of unlawful cohabitation to convict. The act also prevented polygamists from voting, holding public office or serving on juries and provided for confiscating church properties having a value of more than $500.

After a raid by U.S. marshals in 1884 to search for cohabitators, Woodruff and other church leaders once again went into hiding to avoid prosecution. In January 1885, Wilford fled to St. George, Utah, where he lived on a ranch and was reported to have worn a dress and sunbonnet as a disguise. When Congress further strengthened its actions against polygamy in March 1887 by passage of the Edmunds-Tucker Act, Wilford wrote that the law passed by the U.S. House of Representatives "seals their Condemnation and lays the foundation for the overthrow & final destruction of the United States government."[331] Hearkening back to the time that early Christians were mistreated for their beliefs, Wilford wrote to his daughter Emeline asserting that the church would not be facing persecution if the Mormon faith was not the "true church of Christ."[332] In the meantime, having to hide from federal authorities was hard on Wilford and his family, complicating life considerably.

After John Taylor passed away in July 1887, the Quorum of the Twelve Apostles, with Wilford as its president, met to determine who would succeed Taylor. Although Wilford would remain in hiding over the next two years, the church council named him the fourth president of the Church of Jesus Christ of Latter-day Saints in April 1889. From his humble beginnings in Northington, constant in his faith, he had risen to the highest level of the church he loved.

Now as president, he had to confront continued public outrage over polygamy. When, in May 1890, the U.S. Supreme Court upheld the Edmunds-Tucker Act, allowing federal agents to confiscate church property, Wilford was compelled to act. On September 24, 1890, eighty-three-year-old Wilford Woodruff, president of the Mormon Church, called together a meeting of the Quorum of the Twelve Apostles and convinced all present that he needed to make an official declaration stating that the church would no longer permit polygamy going forward. As Wilford put it to the council, "It is not wisdom for us to make war upon sixty-five millions of people. It is not wisdom for us to go forth and carry out this principle against the laws of the nation and receive the consequences. That is in the hands of God, and He will govern and control it."[333]

Right after he met with the Quorum of the Twelve Apostles, Wilford proclaimed to the world: "We are not teaching polygamy, or plural marriage, nor permitting any person to enter its practice."[334] Some Morman followers were skeptical that Wilford had the authority to change what Joseph Smith and Brigham Young had said was divinely directed. But Wilford held firm, explaining that his 1890 manifesto banning plural marriage came after receiving a revelation from Jesus Christ. Revelation or not, Wilford made it clear in his journal of September 25, 1890, the day after the proclamation, that his hand was forced: "I am under the necessity of acting for the Temporal Salvation of the Church. The United States Government has taken a stand & passed Laws to destroy the Latter day Saints upon the subject of poligamy [*sic*] or Patriarchal order of Marriage. And after Praying to the Lord & feeling inspired by his spirit I have issued [this proclamation]."[335]

Wilford Woodruff, 1889. *Wilford Woodruff Papers*.

Plural marriage was grandfathered for all men who had multiple wives, although some women divorced or separated from their husbands and some men stopped cohabiting with all but one wife. Despite the end of church-sanctioned polygamy, for the remainder of his life, Wilford remained married to all three of his wives who were still living.

Guiding his church away from the practice of polygamy, Wilford was steadfast in his faith and his mission to spread the word of Jesus Christ. Over a two-week period in April 1893, the aging Wilford had the privilege of dedicating the magnificent Salt Lake Temple to some seventy-five thousand followers, a testament to the growth and prosperity of the church. Though he is perhaps most remembered as the Mormon leader who ended the practice of church-sanctioned polygamy, from his humble roots in Avon, Connecticut, Wilford Woodruff remained faithful to his beliefs, inspired others through his missionary work and is remembered as one of the pioneers of a major American religion.

25

THE SHADY SIDE OF MINISTRY

Decidedly bitter, Reverend Stephen Hubbell of the Avon Congregational Church addressed his congregation for the last time on June 26, 1853. He had poured his heart and soul into being the best minister he could, tirelessly attending to the sick and presiding over countless weddings, funerals and baptisms while still finding time to prepare sermons. He knew, as a Christian, he needed to be charitable and kind, but inside he was seething at how he had been treated and could keep it in no longer.

Finally acknowledging what all had suspected, Stephen admitted his true feelings: "There have been seasons when I had little heart or relish for converse with my people—times of disquietude and sorrowful perplexity, when the stinted income allowed showed its insufficiency in the face of semi-annual bills that must be met to save my credit from dishonor." Wanting to make sure his parishioners knew exactly who was to blame for his circumstances, Stephen got more pointed, asserting he had "staggered on…impoverishing myself in ministering to a people abundantly able to place their pastor above pecuniary solitude." And he didn't stop there. He implored his congregation to repent for their sins against him, and the sooner they got to it, the better. "Some of you are far down in life's declivity—your locks whitening for the tomb, and your sun sinking to the very verge of the western hills."[336]

How did it all come to this? What began as whispers among his parishioners would quickly turn into a firestorm of controversy that would result in a hearing by the Ecclesiastical Council. This is not how a minister should be treated! Toward the end of his valedictory sermon, Stephen Hubbell asked his congregation if making a point of his insufficient salary was really such a "scandal and a crime."[337] Perhaps not. But in this case, it *was* a bit shady.

Well-groomed for his position as pastor, Stephen bristled at the blowback he got from his parishioners. He had received the best schooling, including five years at the Hawley Olmsted Academy in Wilton, Connecticut, followed by earning an undergraduate degree from Yale College in 1826. To prepare for the ministry, he enrolled at the Theological Seminary in New Haven, graduating from there in 1829. After first serving as pastor at Mount Carmel Congregational Church in Hamden and then at a church in the Wolcottville section of Torrington, Stephen was appointed minister at Avon Congregational Church in late 1840.

Soon after becoming pastor in Avon, Stephen championed the temperance movement led by Reverend Lyman Beecher of Litchfield, and he helped form the East Avon Temperance Society, inviting speakers on the subject to talk at the church. He went out of his way to accommodate his congregation, holding midweek and neighborhood prayer meetings at various locations within the parish. As he was beloved by the community, women of his congregation made a "rising sun"[338] quilt for him with each of their names stitched into the fabric.

From the perspective of his parishioners, things had gone well during the first twelve years of Reverend Hubbell's ministry, but then they felt blindsided by what happened in the spring of 1853. That year, residents of Avon looked forward to reading a new book that had just been published and was available to purchase in town. The book, titled *The Shady Side; or Life in a Country Parsonage*, was written by "a pastor's wife."[339] It was a fictional tale about the travails of a minister named Edward Vernon and his wife, Mary, living in a town called Olney. The book promised to be a light read.

The preface of *The Shady Side*, however, hinted that this novel was not entirely fictional. Dedicated by the unnamed author "to my husband, fellow-pilgrim in a path similar to that herein faintly sketched," the book offers a "simple narrative strongly suggestive of our mutual trials."[340] As citizens of Avon read *The Shady Side*, they deduced that, apart from changing the names, this was indeed largely a work of nonfiction—about real people and real events. That raised eyebrows, since it became clear that the so-called fictional tale described, in unflattering detail, residents of Avon, Connecticut. Various passages in the book seemed to depict Avon rather accurately, such as a drive in a carriage that the fictional Edward and his wife, Mary, take up to a mountain ridge that was precisely like Avon Mountain. Indeed, *The Shady Side* is, in fact, a work of thinly veiled nonfiction, and the unnamed author was quickly uncovered to be Reverend Hubbell's wife, Martha Stone Hubbell.

Martha had written children's stories for the American Sunday-School Union and decided to write *The Shady Side* as a counterpart to a popular novel written by Elizabeth Stuart Phelps in 1851 called *The Sunny Side; or, The Country Minister's Wife*. Novels gained in popularity in the 1850s, and *The Shady Side* sold over forty thousand copies in its first year.

Martha was the daughter of a prominent doctor in Oxford, Connecticut, named Noah Stone, and she was likely accustomed to a style of living beyond what a country pastor's salary could provide. In *The Shady Side*, the fictional pastor Edward Vernon attends to the needs of his congregation with little thanks for his efforts. Then, at some length, the book describes Edward's repeated efforts to ask for more pay for his services but is denied with the claim that "there is no money" in the church treasury. Speaking of Edward, the author wrote,

> *Pay-day arrived, confirming his fears. He was fifty dollars in debt; and, to add to the confusion, the society proved delinquent toward him in the same amount.... The pastor's table misses some of its wonted fare; his wardrobe tells the tale of retrenchment; his brow bears the marks of corroding care. His wife, too, is plainly and scantily attired. True, she looks well, but it is not by any adventitious aid.*[341]

The Shady Side was clearly intended to cast a light on the insufficient remuneration received by ministers throughout New England, and it did that most directly by describing the impact those financial burdens had on the fictional Mary Vernon. Of the pastor's wife, Martha wrote,

> *Having tied a white muslin apron over her plain travelling dress,* [she] *moved gracefully around, sustaining, with lady-like composure, the many searching side-glances she could not fail to see,—unfluttered by the whispers, accidentally overheard, that were not designed for her ear.*[342]

Yet even more critical of her neighbors, the author wrote of Mary,

> *The people…did not come to appreciate* [Mary's] *maturity and strength of character. Occasionally, they betrayed to Edward that they regarded her rather as his "pet" than companion.*[343]

There could be no mistake—this book was really about the plight of the Hubbells, and it cast the church's congregation in a highly unfavorable light. In her thinly disguised work, Martha Hubbell came across as self-righteous and petty. In what would be a prophetic passage, Martha wrote of Mary Vernon:

> *The gossips shook their heads, and "feared we were to have another feeble minister's wife;—this was just the way Mrs. Smith went down."*[344]

Stephen Hubbell's congregation was outraged. Fuming, the parishioners all agreed that the publication of *The Shady Side* was an insult to them that could not be overlooked—one that warranted severing the relationship with their pastor. A meeting of the Ecclesiastical Council was called for May 18, 1853, where the council was asked to dissolve the church's relationship with Reverend Hubbell. The council, however, concluded that the facts presented did not justify Hubbell's removal as minister. Parishioners refused to accept the decision, believing *The Shady Side* was "slanderous in its import against this society or some of the inhabitants thereof, unjustifiable, and without any good cause."[345] After weeks of disharmony, the rancor over the scandal did not abate, and finally, effective July 1, 1853, Reverend Stephen Hubbell agreed to leave rather than face further indignity.

In his farewell sermon, Hubbell showed some humility and regret: "A preacher…is but an imperfect man, having his own private experience, with all its variations of hope and fear, light and darkness." But ultimately, he decided he could not go quietly: "The publicity you have yourselves given the matter removes from my lips the imposition of silence."[346]

Speaking of the error of not compensating their pastor adequately, Stephen told his detractors they would one day come to regret their characterization of *The Shady Side* as an "unjustifiable, slanderous, and scurrilous publication, a book which is hailed by the united voice of the religious community as a most needed, judicious, and timely exposition."[347]

The congregation was unmoved by Hubbell's valedictory sermon. Not only did they effectively force his resignation, but when Stephen left to become pastor of the Congregational church in North Stonington, Connecticut, they were "determined to execute judgment"[348] on the Hubbell family as well, refusing to issue Martha Hubbell the letter of good standing that was customarily provided when a member left to join another church. Reverend Noah Porter of Farmington couldn't believe the small-mindedness of the Avon Congregational Church parishioners.

Asserting that *The Shady Side* was written "with great ability and pure intentions,"[349] Porter wrote a letter to John Bartlett, retired pastor at West Avon, to see if he could use his connections to convince the congregation to change their stance. Given all that transpired, it is unlikely that Bartlett was persuasive, if he even tried at all. The ordeal took a toll on Martha Hubbell. After she and Stephen suffered the loss of their twenty-year-old daughter, Mary, in June 1854, Martha died just two years later, only forty-two years old.

Later in life, Stephen Hubbell must have wondered if consenting to his wife, Martha, publishing *The Shady Side* was worth all the fuss. When he was installed at North Stonington two months after his valedictory sermon in Avon, his new congregation promised that a "sunny side"[350] awaited him. But on that day in June 1853, Reverend Hubbell left his pastorship in Avon defiant, convinced he had acted above reproach. Too bad for him that his congregation, the very people he pledged to serve, saw it differently.

26

CHERRY PARK'S ASCENSION

On the afternoon of September 12, 1894, Professor Edward Jewell, one of the "Jewell Brothers" of New Jersey, implored the crowd at the Cherry Park Fair in Avon to gather around as he began to fill up his hot air balloon.[351] When inflated, the balloon grew to 120 feet high and 88 feet in diameter and was quite a spectacle. A well-known aeronaut of the day, Professor Jewell intended to dazzle the crowd with his daring jump from the balloon.

As part of the mystical appeal of the daredevil stunt, aeronauts referred to themselves as "professors," giving the impression that they possessed some advanced scientific knowledge that enabled them to carry out their feat. But for all the bravado they conveyed, many things could go wrong for an aeronaut at a fair. The gas bag could catch fire, a strong wind or thunderstorm could suddenly blow through, the parachute could get tangled on the descent or, worst of all, the parachute might not open at all. A year earlier, another one of the Jewell Brothers aeronauts, Charles Richmond, lost his life in Trenton, New Jersey, when his parachute failed to open properly, causing him to spiral rapidly toward the ground.

The time for the professor's ascension was fast approaching, with the excitement palpable among all in attendance. At the appointed time of 3:30 p.m., Jewell heated the balloon fast so he could ascend quickly. Hanging onto a horizontal trapeze bar attached underneath the balloon, the professor lifted off, acknowledging the cheers of the crowd. When he reached a height of nearly three thousand feet, Edward Jewell looked down below to make sure he could locate his landing spot. Fortunately, in the case of Cherry Park, finding the midway of the fairgrounds below was not difficult. Just to the north was Secret Lake, with its reflection glimmering in the sun, and the only thing Jewell had to worry about was the large stand of white pines between the lake and his landing zone.

Wanting to make sure that both he, and the balloon, returned safely to earth, the professor took one last glance to make sure everything was in order. He readied himself to tip the four sandbags that would invert the balloon, bringing it back to the ground. Satisfied that everything had gone according to plan, Professor Jewell let go of the bar.

In 1882, a man named Howard Foote from Canton Center, Connecticut, and eight other men who lived in nearby towns formed an entity called the Farmington Valley Agricultural Corporation, whose purpose was to hold an annual agricultural fair on the grounds of what had been known as Cherry Park Farm in Avon. The Cherry Park fairgrounds were on a fifty-acre parcel southwest of Secret Lake along Lovely Street near present-day Craigemore Circle.

Cherry Park Farm had been the home of enslavers Shubael and Romanta Tillotson, who inherited the property from their father, Elias Tillotson. The farm may have been named after a seventeenth-century Native American called Waquaheag, whom English colonists referred to as "Old Cherry"[352] given his reported fondness for drinking cherry brandy. Secret Lake got its name from a legend about a British paymaster during the American Revolutionary War who was purportedly traveling through the Farmington River Valley when he stopped at a tavern along the Albany Turnpike in Canton. The paymaster was never seen again, and, as the story goes, the tavern owner, a fervent Patriot, suddenly became quite wealthy. In the early 1900s, it was reported that a pair of Revolutionary War–era boots were fished out of what was then known as Cherry Pond, leading to the legend that the "secret"[353] of what happened to the paymaster is buried in the pond—hence, Secret Lake.

During the 1880s, the Farmington Valley Agricultural Corporation operated the Cherry Park Fair primarily as a means for farmers to show off their livestock and produce at the end of summer. However, starting with the very first year of the fair in 1883, the organizers also held events for driving and trotting horses as well as a bicycle race. In the 1890s, the fair added new amusements to attract people, including one of the biggest thrills of the day—hot air balloon ascensions. Fortunately for the crowd, and especially for Professor Jewell, the aeronaut successfully completed his jump on that September day in 1894.

In its heyday, Cherry Park's fame was "practically boundaryless,"[354] with up to ten thousand people attending each year. Children in the neighborhood would sneak under the fence to get into the fair for free. One longtime resident named John O'Neill, the man who started O'Neill's car dealership, recalled as a boy how exciting a time the annual fair was: "I remember so well how my young friends and I looked forward to the fair—our anticipation rising to almost unbearable heights as the great day arrived and we approached the grounds."[355]

At the fair, there were also "wheelmen,"[356] who performed all sorts of feats on their bicycles. One of the first bicycle stunts at the fair featured a man riding a bike while sitting backward on the handlebars. In later years, more daredevil tricks were added. In 1904, stuntmen from Brownie & Company came to perform what they called "the most daring and thrilling ride ever attempted on bicycles."[357] A precursor to the "wall of death" that became popular at Coney Island a decade later, the daredevil would ride his bicycle

Bicycle stuntman at the Cherry Park Fair. *Clint B. Hadsell Collection.*

in circles along the inside of a large upright barrel. Prevented from falling by friction and centrifugal force, the cyclist would amaze the crowd with a feat that appeared to defy gravity.[358]

At least from the public's perspective, the annual fair continued to be a success and something the whole community looked forward to year after year. However, the fair of 1911 would be the last one held by the Farmington Valley Agricultural Corporation. During a race in either 1910 or 1911, a horse that was owned by Charles Allhouse of Granby was in an accident at the Cherry Park track and had to be put down due to his injuries. It is unclear why the Farmington Valley Agricultural Corporation would have been held responsible for the accident, but Allhouse sued the corporation and was ultimately awarded $800 in damages as compensation for his horse.

The lawsuit wasn't the only problem facing fair organizers. By 1911, annual attendance at the fair had dipped, as people from Hartford were more likely to attend other fairs that they could get to by trolley. Furthermore, the corporation had a $3,500 mortgage coming due, and so in late 1911, the three owners decided to sell the fairgrounds to settle their debts. The property changed hands a few times until Chester Stearns bought it, intending to make it his summer home. He never carried out those plans, however, and the property fell into neglect.

In the late afternoon of October 7, 1919, Michael Delaney was beaming with pride as he walked his two-year-old Holstein cows along a path on the rebuilt Cherry Park fairgrounds. Delaney, along with two other investors, had purchased the property earlier that year, intending to bring the Cherry Park Fair back to its former glory. With about three thousand people in attendance, the grand reopening was a huge success, with smiling faces all around.

Along a maple-lined avenue at the entrance to the refurbished fairgrounds was a midway, a place with booths for amusements and carnival games. Games of chance were aplenty, with patrons able to win everything from hams to a basket of roses. At one booth, there was an accordion player; the next, two cowboys showing their skill with a lasso; and at another, an Arabian dancer. Displays by aeronauts were replaced with stunts by airmen in planes. On the second day of the fair on October 8, 1919, stunt pilots performed aileron rolls and other dazzling aerobatic maneuvers to the delight of the crowd below.

In time, it became clear that Michael Delaney's true passion was more with horse racing and less with the fair, and after a few years, the Cherry Park Fair died out again. Under Delaney's direction, by the mid-1920s, harness racing became popular, where horses pulled riders sitting in two-wheeled "sulkies" and Cherry Park gained a reputation as the fastest half-mile oval in all of New England.[359]

After the harness racing era, in the mid-1940s, the park was reborn again, this time as a venue for midget car racing, until that, too, died out. Eventually, the land was sold to a developer in the early 1960s who built homes, but the Cherry Park Fair's ascension will forever be a treasured part of Avon's history.

27

VISION OF PROGRESS

Charles Stilwell

On the evening of Saturday, May 13, 1916, fifty-five-year-old Charles Stilwell was sitting quietly downstairs in his living room at Stilwell Farm in West Avon when he noticed the smell of fire. In just a few moments, smoke began to fill the room and Charles could hear the crackling of fire. It soon became clear that flames were spreading fast on the first floor and the situation was dire. His wife, Sarah, overweight and not very mobile, was upstairs when the fire started, and Charles determined he had to act quickly. Blind for the past thirteen years, he knew his way around the house but also realized that if he got up, he could risk walking into the fire. The blaze was spreading at an alarming rate, and time was running out. Charles and Sarah needed help immediately, but their two youngest sons, Walter and Howard, were attending a party next door. Fortunately, while less than a third of American homes had a telephone in 1916, the Stilwells had one for just this reason—in case of emergency.

Charles Stilwell, 1892. *Courtesy of Avon Free Public Library.*

Frantically, Charles called Walter and Howard. Screaming into the phone, he explained the situation was desperate and they must come at once. Charles could sense that soon the house would be consumed by fire, and even for an eternal optimist like Charles Stilwell, the scenario seemed hopeless. He had endured so much in life—first, the death of his sister Mary, and then the horrible accident in 1891 at Edison's lab in Ontario, Canada, that would eventually result in the loss of his sight. Yet through it all, Charles Stilwell's positive outlook never wavered. With all the scientific progress of the past forty years, he confidently predicted that in his remaining lifetime, his blindness would be cured. And yet, now, amid an inferno quickly closing in on him, a rescue appeared impossible.

Born in Newark, New Jersey, in 1861, Charles was the third child of Nicholas and Margaret Stilwell. In 1871, when he was ten years old, his sixteen-year-old sister, Mary, was punching perforations into telegraph tape at an Edison subsidiary in Newark, New Jersey, when Thomas Edison took notice of her. After a three-month courtship, the two married on a "beautiful, balmy"[360] Christmas Day in 1871 at the Stilwell family home in Newark.

In 1873, when Charles was only twelve, he got a job as a shipping clerk with Edison and lived with Thomas and Mary in their home. He continued with the firm when Edison moved his operations in 1876 to Menlo Park, New Jersey, where the inventor opened his research laboratory. In December 1877, Charles was present at the lab when his brother-in-law unveiled to the world the tinfoil phonograph, the first recording of sound ever made. It was an extraordinary invention that amazed the public—when a person spoke into a funnel and turned the handle to rotate a tinfoil-wrapped cylinder, a needle would shake and make impressions on the tinfoil, creating sound.

Two years later, in 1879, Thomas Edison began developing an incandescent bulb that could be sold commercially. He experimented with various materials to use as a filament, including platinum, uncoated cotton thread and cardboard treated with tar and lampblack, but while he had some success, none of the designs proved to have a long enough life for commercial use.

The story told in the Stilwell family is that one day in early July 1880, sitting on her veranda at her home in New Jersey, Mary Stilwell Edison was "absentmindedly stripping the split edges of her bamboo fan"[361] when she thought that bamboo might be the solution to her husband's problem of finding a suitable filament. Edison himself noted that same month

Left: Thomas A. Edison, circa 1878. *National Park Service.*

Right: Mary Jane (Stilwell) Edison. *National Park Service.*

that he experimented with bamboo "after making what may have been a serendipitous observation of the frayed edge of a bamboo fan." When he tested bamboo on July 10, 1880, the material "provided high resistance when tried in a lamp."[362] Indeed, the carbonized bamboo filament in a glass vacuum bulb proved far superior to other carbonized filaments, as it lasted 1,200 hours, becoming the standard for the Edison electric light bulb for the next ten years.

Around the same time that Thomas and Mary discovered bamboo for use as a filament, Charles was working as a glassblower at the Menlo Park laboratory. Glassblowing, necessary to create an incandescent bulb, was a complex process requiring formation of a stem to secure electrical wires and then mating the stem to the bulb to create an air-tight seal.

While working in the Menlo Park laboratory in early December 1880, Charles had the privilege of giving the actress Sarah Bernhardt a tour of the facility where she recited lines from the opera *Phèdre* on Edison's phonograph. Within a few weeks of Bernhardt's visit, on December 20, 1880, Charles married Sarah Frazee in Newark, New Jersey. They did not stay in Newark long, however, as within a year of their marriage, Charles's brother-in-law asked him to move to Canada. Though Edison developed the first commercially viable electric light bulb, the basic premise of a filament heating up inside an oxygen-free glass tube had been around since the early 1800s. Some argued that Edison's invention was merely an improvement over a similar design created by an Englishman named Joseph Swan ten years earlier. In order to satisfy a patent infringement case in Canada, in 1883, Thomas Edison built a "lamp works"[363] facility in Hamilton, Ontario, and Charles moved there with his family to be superintendent of the facility.

Tragedy struck the Stilwell family in August 1884 when Charles's sister Mary fell ill. At first, her illness did not seem serious. Then, on August 8, she took a sudden turn for the worse and it became evident that she had contracted typhoid fever. Mary's parents, Nicholas and Margaret Stilwell, telegraphed Charles in Ontario, urging him to come home at once. Charles rushed back to Newark as fast as he could, but he was "a few hours too late to see his sister alive."[364] When Thomas Edison learned of his wife's death, he cried uncontrollably, devasted by the loss. Mary's death was traumatic for the Stilwell family, and unfortunately for Charles, it would not be the last hardship he faced.

All incandescent bulbs need a vacuum inside to prevent the bulb from getting too hot and burning up the filament. In February 1891, at the Edison plant in Ontario, Charles was working with a special high-vacuum incandescent bulb when the lamp suddenly exploded, shattering into tiny pieces. The glass scattered in all directions, with some pieces projecting up into his eyes. Though Charles expected he would recover, over time, his eyesight did not improve—it worsened. By 1896, his vision tested at only 20 percent, and he was forced to leave the plant in Hamilton, Ontario, taking a sales agent job at an electric company in Shelby, Ohio. A few years later, he left Ohio to join another company back east that enabled Charles to move his family back to Newark, New Jersey. Then in March 1900, while on a sales call in New York City, Charles was stricken totally blind on Broadway and needed assistance to get back home to Newark. He regained partial vision a short while later, but by 1903, he was once again without any sight, and this time his vision did not return.

With six children to support, Charles was in serious financial straits. Desperate for income, he then made a regrettable decision. His nephew Thomas Alva Edison Jr., known as Tom, was the eldest son of Thomas Edison and Mary Stilwell Edison, and like Charles, Tom had financial troubles. In 1903, the younger Edison was boarding with Charles's family in Newark, New Jersey, when the two hatched a plan.

They decided they would market a phonograph under the name Thomas A. Edison Jr. Phonograph Company, and Charles and Tom would share the profits. Writing to Thomas Edison's confidant Joseph McCoy, Stilwell outlined his ill-conceived plan in which he outright threatened to sue Edison's National Phonograph Company for use of the Edison name once the great inventor died, hoping "that Mr. Edison would only live a few years longer."[365] McCoy, of course, went right to Thomas Edison. While angry with both of them, the inventor nonetheless had compassion for his son, who was suffering from depression and alcoholism, and for Charles Stilwell, who was blind with a large family to support. Edison struck a deal with the pair, making them sign a legal agreement prohibiting them from using the Edison name in the future while also agreeing to pay them an annual stipend for the rest of their lives—$1,890 for his son Tom and $1,350 for Charles Stilwell.

With that annuity payment, in 1907, Charles retired to live near his daughters in Avon, Connecticut. He and Sarah bought Lily Lake Farm along what is now Country Club Road, and in time, the property would come to be known as Stilwell Farm. Nearly a century earlier, the area was known as the "horse plain"[366] and was owned by Alanson Woodruff, the father-in-law of Orson Woodford, who had the fatal accident with his saw in 1855.

Charles was declared permanently blind in 1912. While it was certainly a challenge, he did not despair of his circumstances. He learned to enjoy the sound of life all around him, often listening to birds while sitting on his veranda. Charles especially enjoyed hearing his daughter Louise sing in her soprano voice and listening to the laughter that was ever-present at family gatherings.

When Walter and Howard Stilwell ran home on the evening of May 13, 1916, they saw flames visible in the windows, with parts of the roof already on fire. Rushing inside, they first rescued their father, Charles, carrying him safely outside. By now, however, flames were engulfing much of the home. Running back into the house again, they found their mother stumbling down the staircase. Acting fast, the brothers managed to escort her to the door, and just as the three of them stepped outside to safety, the house exploded in fire, with flames shooting out from the windows and the front door.

After the 1916 fire, Charles and his family needed a place to live, so they moved in with their daughter Muriel and son-in-law Ithiel Hart at a place called Sunshine Farm on West Avon Road, located on a lot across from the present-day high school. Sunshine Farm, not be confused with Sunrise Farm farther south on West Avon Road, had, at one time, been the home of Eldad Woodruff, grandfather of Mormon pioneer Wilford Woodruff. The youngest son, Howard, quickly tired of living with his sister's family and their three to four hundred chickens. In May 1917, when he was only fourteen years old and still a Boy Scout, Howard convinced a recruiter that he was eighteen and joined the U.S. Navy to fight in World War I. A survivor of the sinking of the transport ship *President Lincoln* in May 1918, Howard was one of over one hundred men from Avon who enlisted to fight in the first world war, including Bertha Dickman Brown's brother Herman Dickman and Sherman Eddy's first cousin John Eddy.

Despite all the disappointments and troubles, Charles Stilwell remained ever sanguine over the rest of his life. The invention of the radio in the 1920s gave him a wonderful new way to explore the world as he lived out his days at Sunshine Farm, always content and always the optimist.

28

BORED IN RETIREMENT

A Golf Course Is Born

In early 1925, Samuel Graham of Unionville was feeling restless. He had just retired from a successful career and had served as senior burgess of Unionville for the past four years, but he knew he needed another way to occupy his time. Going stir crazy, Samuel decided to consult with his doctor and good friend Dr. Ralph Cox of Collinsville.

A native of Nova Scotia, Ralph Cox had been a general practitioner or "country doctor" in Collinsville since 1902, treating hundreds of patients each year.[367] He originally came to Connecticut to work at the Collins Company, and after marrying a Collinsville native, he decided to become a doctor. While he served the community in Collinsville, he was also the family doctor for many residents in Avon. Ralph assisted burn victims after the Climax Fuse factory fire of 1905, treated Bertha Dickman Lynch after she was shot by her husband and made house calls caring for Joe and Corinne Alsop's children. However, at age forty-eight and still in his working years, answering a question from Samuel Graham about what to do in retirement was outside of his expertise. But he gave it a go.

Suspecting that Samuel needed some type of hobby, Dr. Cox suggested that he try farming. Enthusiastic about the idea, Graham purchased the sixty-acre Stilwell Farm, previously the home of Charles and Sarah Stilwell. Samuel soon realized, however, that farming is not retirement—even a gentleman's farm is a lot of work. He consulted Ralph Cox again, and this time they came up with a better idea: they would build a golf course on Stilwell Farm along present-day Country Club Road.

Samuel Graham and Ralph Cox set out to work right away, enlisting the support of friends, among them a "most enthusiastic"[368] Sherman Eddy. Incorporated as the Avon Country Club in October 1925, the group acquired additional acreage around Lily Pond (also known as Lily Lake). A temporary nine-hole course was put in place that year, and eventually additional parcels were acquired south of Country Club Road and east of Burnham Road to expand the course. In a November 1925 meeting held in the recreation room of Ensign-Bickford's Avon plant, the directors of the club discussed their plans for a clubhouse, and they didn't take long to decide what they wanted. The founding members loved the design of Tow Path Lodge built by Sherman Eddy along Old Farms Road, so they hired Sherm as architect to design the clubhouse in the same style. Over the winter, the land was cleared, and the layout of the course was designed and sculpted.

To help construct the clubhouse, a local stonemason named Fred Brunoli was hired. A master craftsman who immigrated from the Lombardy region of northern Italy to Avon in 1909, Fred worked as one of the stonemasons hired by Theodate Pope Riddle to construct Avon Old Farms School. Appreciating Brunoli's expertise, the Avon Country Club hired him to construct the "lighthouse"[369]-styled stone pillars that mark the entrance to the club and the money from that assignment helped him build his family a home on Eddy Street.

Fred Brunoli, stonemason. *Brunoli Family Collection.*

In the spring of 1926, before the clubhouse was finished, the Board of the Avon Country Club decided it was time to celebrate the opening of the golf course, hosting a formal dinner for all members and their spouses. Naturally, the venue they chose was Sherman Eddy's Tow Path Lodge. On the evening of the dinner, April 27, the guest speaker was none other than First Selectman Joe Alsop. An avid golfer himself, Joe at the time was president of the Farmington Country Club, and on behalf of the state's oldest golf club, he welcomed the newest.

In 1927, the Avon Country Club issued bonds to raise money for construction, and with the help of engineers from the Collins Company and Ensign Bickford, as well as a construction engineer named J. Frank Bryne, the clubhouse was completed in May 1928. With a tie to Avon's past, lumber for the clubhouse was harvested from Edwards Road on Huckleberry Hill, the same land where Romanta Woodruff had his farm and distillery in the early 1800s. Expanded to twenty-seven holes in 1967 and today known as the Golf Club of Avon, the dream of Samuel Graham and Ralph Cox serves as a legacy to the remarkable lives of Charles Stilwell and Sherman Eddy. Woven together, the stories of Avon's past represent a history of people inspired to create change—who responded in the face of adversity and, through their efforts, created the vibrant community of today.

EPILOGUE

One day in September 1913, when Chester Randolph Woodford was ninety-nine years old and still full of vigor, he took a stroll on Main Street in Avon and called on his old friend Dr. Edward Kellogg, the grandson of Avon Congregational Church's first pastor. They spoke for over an hour recounting many stories of Avon's past. Chester, a descendant of one of Avon's founding families, and seventy-one-year-old Edward had lived Avon's history and had seen remarkable changes during their lifetime. Gathering with them that day was seventy-nine-year-old Henry Bartlett, the builder of towers, and Henry shared his own cherished memories. The three had lived through the Civil War and had witnessed the community's anguish in the aftermath of the Climax Fuse fire, but they had also seen astounding progress in their lifetimes that would have been unfathomable to them in their youth. Chester could now ride in an automobile and, within a year, would be able to read at night without a candle or kerosene lamp. Fellow Avon resident Charles Stilwell could listen to recorded music on a Victrola phonograph.

The influx of immigrants who came to work at Climax Fuse in Avon and at the Collins Company in Collinsville diversified the ethnic makeup of town residents, and Avon blossomed into much more than a farming community. In the decades following the Civil War, people started to have more leisure time, visiting Henry Bartlett's tower on Avon Mountain, attending the Cherry Park Fair and dancing at Sherman Eddy's Tow Path Lodge. While in his old age Chester Woodford lamented that golf and other activities were interfering too much with church, there could be no denying that people were enjoying their free time.

Late in life, when he was sitting on his front porch on Nod Road, Chester could look up at Avon Mountain and see the Heublein Tower, the fourth one to grace the ridgeline in his lifetime. The first, the original tower built by Daniel Wadsworth, had been in existence for only four years when Chester was born in 1814. When he returned from Illinois in 1842, Chester farmed his land under the shadow of the second Wadsworth Tower until that one burned down in 1864. He also surely remembered the tower erected three years later, built by fellow Avon Congregational Church parishioner Henry Bartlett. Chester's life coincided closely with Avon's first century, and his mind still sharp, he could vividly recall the entire journey his town had taken.

Chester was a fifteen-year-old boy when Avon gained its independence from Farmington in 1830. His uncle Amasa Woodford and Truman Hawley, first cousin once removed of Reverend Rufus Hawley, guided the community in its path to independence. Avon's development was propelled by advances in transportation, from improvements made to the Albany Turnpike at the turn of the nineteenth century to the short-lived Farmington Canal and finally, the railroad that followed, bringing students to Theodate Pope Riddle's Avon Old Farms School.

The characters in the story of Avon's first century, both visionaries and victims, endured many challenges but were resolute in their determination to persevere. Henry's brother David Bartlett and fellow West Avon Congregational Church parishioner Edgar Woodford fought for the abolition of slavery, and it was the extraordinary bravery of Avon soldiers like Harrison Woodford and Leverett Holden that helped bring a beginning of freedom for Black Americans. Marrying a woman from Avon, Yung Wing persevered in his quest to modernize China despite rejection from both his native and adopted countries.

In the first decades of the twentieth century, Avon residents had emerged from a life of agrarian hardship to one of newfound possibilities. As Corinne Robinson Alsop put it, "I've lived through two eras. The death of a certain kind of society, the demise of a small New England village and its transformation into an active, bustling suburb."[370] But one thing that did not change during the town's first century was the self-reliance of its residents. Corinne adopted that ethic along with many other pioneers of the town, and through their resolve, they embodied the vitality of Avon.

NOTES

1. Acrimony Among the Faithful: The Split of the Church

1. Silliman, *Remarks Made on a Short Tour*, 31.
2. DeForest, *History of the Indians of Connecticut*, 176, 263; Bicknell, *Farmington, Connecticut*, 39–42.
3. Avon, Connecticut Land Records, Minutes of the May 5, 1830 meeting of the General Assembly of the State of Connecticut, entered July 20, 1830, by Harvey Bushnell, register, and Daniel M. Alford, town clerk, 4.
4. "'The Lord's Barn' in Cider Brook," *Hartford Courant*, September 9, 1919.
5. "'Lord's Barn' in Cider Brook"; Rettig, "History of the Avon Congregational Church."
6. Silliman, *Remarks Made on a Short Tour*, 30.
7. Minutes of Second Ecclesiastical Society of Farmington (hereafter SECF) membership meeting, May 11, 1816, Marian Hunter Local History Room, Avon Free Public Library (hereafter AFPL).
8. SECF Minutes, June 20, 1817.
9. Grant, Sermon of November 20, 1851, 23.
10. SECF minutes, December 31, 1817.
11. Silliman, *Remarks Made on a Short Tour*, 32.
12. Avon Congregational Church records, 12 of 702.
13. Johanson, "General History of Avon." This unpublished manuscript may be found in the Marian Hunter Local History Room, AFPL.
14. Silliman, *Remarks Made on a Short Tour*, 32.

2. Independence at Last: The Town of Avon Is Born

15. Avon Incorporation Papers, Connecticut State Library.
16. Incorporation of Said Town of Avon; Special Acts, May 1830, AFPL.
17. Farmington Connecticut Land Records, 2:236, May 6, 1830.
18. Howard, *Avon 1830–2005*, 5.

3. Chester Woodford's Wise Counsel

19. Taylor and Dapkus, *Antebellum Shelf Clock Making*, 115–18, 121.
20. SangamonLink, "Stephen T. Logan."
21. SangamonLink, "Stephen T. Logan."
22. "Chester Randolph Woodford, 106 Years Old," *Hartford Courant*, October 17, 1920.
23. "If You Wish for Long Life, Keep Mind Free From Worry," *Hartford Courant*, November 13, 1921.

4. Distiller of Whortleberry Hill: Romanta Woodruff

24. Romanta Woodruff diary, October 2, 1809, AFPL.
25. Romanta Woodruff diary, November 7, 1809.
26. Charlotte Cowles to Samuel Cowles, October 29, 1839.
27. Romanta Woodruff diary, October 3, 1811.
28. Romanta Woodruff diary, March 16, 1813.
29. Romanta Woodruff diary, December 4, 1811.
30. Romanta Woodruff diary, April 14, 1811.
31. "Ranaway," *Hartford Courant*, July 31, 1826.
32. "Ranaway."
33. "Ranaway."
34. "Ranaway."

5. The Insanity of It All: The Murder of Diana Derrin Woodford

35. Morgan, *Full Report of the Trial of Orrin Woodford*.
36. Morgan, *Full Report of the Trial of Orrin Woodford*, 12.
37. Morgan, *Full Report of the Trial of Orrin Woodford*, 12.

38. Morgan, *Full Report of the Trial of Orrin Woodford*, 16.
39. Morgan, *Full Report of the Trial of Orrin Woodford*, 12.
40. Morgan, *Full Report of the Trial of Orrin Woodford*, 13.
41. Morgan, *Full Report of the Trial of Orrin Woodford*, 14, 15.
42. Morgan, *Full Report of the Trial of Orrin Woodford*, 16.
43. Morgan, *Full Report of the Trial of Orrin Woodford*, 17.
44. Morgan, *Full Report of the Trial of Orrin Woodford*, 15, 16.
45. Morgan, *Full Report of the Trial of Orrin Woodford*, 17, 18.
46. Morgan, *Full Report of the Trial of Orrin Woodford*, 24–26.
47. Morgan, *Full Report of the Trial of Orrin Woodford*, 60, 61, 64, 65.

6. Those Recurring Nightmares: Orson Woodford

48. "Fatal Accident at West Avon—Prophetic Dreams," *New York Times*, April 30, 1855.
49. "Fatal Accident at West Avon."
50. Probate Files Collection: early to 1880, Orson Woodford, Connecticut State Library, 722.

7. A Matter of Conscience: David Bartlett Takes a Stand

51. West Avon Congregational Church (hereafter WACC) records, 242, 243.
52. WACC records, 242.
53. John Bartlett, Class of 1807, Yale College biographies, AFPL.
54. Northen, *Elihu Burritt*, 28.
55. "An Act to Prevent Slavery," Venture Smith's Colonial Connecticut, accessed December 28, 2024, https://venturesmithcolonialct.org.
56. WACC records, 242, 243.
57. Bartlett, *What I Saw in London*, vi.
58. Bartlett, *What I Saw in London*, 111, 116.
59. Bartlett, *What I Saw in London*, 118, 119.
60. WACC records, 248.
61. WACC records, 250.
62. WACC records, 249, 250.
63. Bartlett, *Modern Agitators*, 111, 121.
64. Bartlett, *Modern Agitators*, 39, 45, 54.
65. "Concerning Two Young Old Men," *Springfield Republican*, April 7, 1905.

8. An Inglorious Compromise: Reverend Wright's Dilemma

66. Farmington Libraries, "Twenty-One Members of First Congregational Church, Farmington to the Pastor, Deacons & Members of the Congregational Church, West Avon," April 10, 1854, Farmington Libraries (CT), The Farmington Room.
67. Reverend Noah Porter to Reverend John Bartlett, August 1854, AFPL.
68. Bardes, "Plantation Slavery in Antebellum Louisiana."
69. "Underground Railroad Sites on the Connecticut Freedom Trail," Museum of Connecticut History, accessed November 24, 2024, https://museumofcthistory.org.
70. Edwards, ed., *Farmington, Connecticut, First Church of Christ*, 6:129–31; 4:217.
71. Porter, *Two Sermons*, 5.
72. Porter, *Two Sermons*, 15.
73. Porter, *Two Sermons*, 21.
74. Porter, *Two Sermons*, 24.
75. Porter, *Two Sermons*, 24.
76. Porter, *Two Sermons*, 27.
77. WACC records, 262.
78. WACC, Minutes of West Avon Congregational Church, September 17, 1854, AFPL.
79. Hooker, *Connecticut Reports*, 349.

9. A Higher Law of Love: Edgar Woodford's Resolve

80. WACC records, 264.
81. WACC records, 263–65.
82. McLoughlin, "Establishing a Church on the Kansas Frontier," 154.
83. WACC records, 267.
84. "Widow's Pension, Mary E. Woodford, War of 1861," U.S. Civil War "Widows' Pensions," 1861–1910, Fold3, accessed November 24, 2024. fold3.com.
85. Kellogg, "Grave of Edgar M. Woodford."

10. Fighting for Emancipation: Leverett Holden and Harrison Woodford

86. Hill, *Sketch of the 29th Regiment*, 26.
87. Harrison Woodford to friends at home, December 25, 1862, AFPL.
88. Harrison Woodford to friends at home, December 25, 1862, AFPL.
89. Gordon, *Broken Regiment*, 63.
90. Priest, *16th Connecticut Volunteer Infantry*, 11.
91. Gordon, "Bad Luck Regiment."
92. Lamphere, *Experiences and Observations*, 5.
93. Kellogg, Civil War Diaries (MS 68013), September 20, 1862.
94. Harrison Woodford to friends at home, December 25, 1862.
95. Harrison Woodford to Alma Woodford, November 20, 1863.
96. Buckingham, *Life of William A. Buckingham*, 361.
97. "Colored Troops," *Hartford Courant*, November 14, 1863.
98. "Colored Troops."
99. Eaton, *Union*, 6.
100. Gilder Lehrman Institute staff, "Men of Color, To Arms!"
101. Moskowitz, "Fighting for Freedom."
102. Warshauer, *Connecticut in the American Civil War*, 134.
103. Harrison Woodford to Alma Woodford, February 20, 1864.
104. "From the 14th Regiment," *Hartford Courant*, April 22, 1864.
105. Harrison Woodford to Harvey Woodford, April 16, 1864.
106. Lamphere, *Experiences and Observations*, 18.
107. Blakeslee, *History of the Sixteenth Connecticut*, 55.
108. Oliver W. Gates diary, April 1864 (MS 78606a); Robert H. Kellogg Papers, Correspondence and Writings (MS 68013), "The Siege of Plymouth, N.C.," 3.
109. Oliver W. Gates diary, May 1864.
110. George N. Champlin diary, Connecticut State Library, 973.78, qC358, May 3, 1864.
111. George N. Champlin Diary, June 22, 1864.
112. Oliver W. Gates diary, August 23, 1864.
113. Hill, *Sketch of the 29th*, 12.
114. Newton, *Out of the Briars*, 56, 57.
115. Wallace, "Forgotten Triumph."
116. Harrison Woodford to father, mother, sister and brothers, December 18, 1864.
117. Gordon, *Broken Regiment*, 234.

118. "Reception of Colored Regiments," *Hartford Courant*, November 25, 1865.
119. "Reception of Colored Regiments."

11. Daniel Wadsworth's Monte Video

120. Platt, *Jeremiah Wadsworth*, 47.
121. Atwood, "Daniel Wadsworth and the Atheneum," 6.
122. Faith Wadsworth to Elira Lebor, 1811, Wadsworth Family Papers (hereafter WFP), 1825 Apr–1826 Oct, Box 1.
123. Atwood, "Daniel Wadsworth and the Atheneum," 2.
124. "Where Wadsworth Received Gen. Washington," *Hartford Courant*, June 30, 1894.
125. "Talcott Mountain, Notable Things About Monte Video and the Tower of Talcott Mountain," *Hartford Courant*, October 4, 1887.
126. Art Story editors, "John Trumbull."
127. Daniel Wadsworth to Faith Wadsworth, March 19, 1809, WFP, 1825 Apr–1826 Oct, Box 1.
128. Daniel Wadsworth Papers (hereafter DWP), 1749–1888, series II, III, box 4 of 4, folder 1.
129. "Talcott Mountain, Notable Things."
130. Faith Wadsworth to Elira Lebor, August 22, 1814, WFP, 1825 Apr–1826 Oct, Box 1, MS 525, Manuscripts and Archives, Yale University, Yale Archives.
131. Faith Wadsworth to Benjamin Silliman, September 8, 1811, DWP, 1749–1888, series II, III, box 1 of 4, folder 24.
132. Maria Trumbull Sullivan to Mr. & Mrs. Benjamin Silliman, September 1, 1821, Founders Papers, box 1.
133. Wallach, "Wadsworth's Tower," 10.
134. Farington, *Joseph Farington Diary*, 4:151.
135. J. Bard McNulty, *Correspondence of Thomas Cole*, xv.
136. DWP, 1749–1888, series II, III, box 4 of 4, folder B.
137. Kornhauser, *American Paintings Before 1945*, 4.
138. Kornhauser, "Daniel Wadsworth and the Hudson River School."

12. From the Edge to the Ledge: David and Clarissa Collins

139. Collins Company, *One Hundred Years.*
140. Collins Company Collection, box 2, "Memorandum of Agreement" employee contract, MS 72165, 1826–1871, folder 1.
141. Somma, "World-Renowned Maker of Axes."
142. Recollections of Huckleberry Hill Road, Marian Hunter Local History Room, AFPL.
143. Clarissa Collins to David C. Collins, September 1, 1850, David Chittenden Collins Papers.

13. "Off to the Tower!": Henry Bartlett's Dream

144. "Days of Bartlett Tower Recalled, and History of Its Two Predecessors," *Hartford Courant*, August 24, 1910.
145. "Days of Bartlett Tower Recalled."
146. "Days of Bartlett Tower Recalled."
147. "Bartlett Tower Builder Is Dead," *Hartford Courant*, December 15, 1914.
148. "Heublein Tower Is Site's Fifth," *Hartford Courant*, October 8, 1995.
149. "Talcott Mountain Tower and Grounds," *Hartford Courant*, May 21, 1887.
150. "Days of Bartlett Tower Recalled."
151. "Talcott Mountain Towers," *Philadelphia Daily Press*, circa 1867; copy maintained at the Auerbach Art Library and Museum Archives, Wadsworth Atheneum Museum of Art.
152. "Days of Bartlett Tower Recalled."
153. Wadsworth, "Towers of Talcott Mountain."
154. Wadsworth, "Towers of Talcott Mountain."

14. A Mountain of a Gift: The Robert Hoe Affair

155. "Matters of Art, The Height of the Season—Mr. Hoe's Treasures—Ingres.," *New York Daily Tribune*, February 12, 1911.
156. "The Hoe Art Exhibition," *The Sun*, February 9, 1911; "Many Old Masters in Hoe Collection," *New York Times*, February 9, 1911.
157. Comparato, *Chronicles of Genius and Folly*, ix.
158. Comparato, *Chronicles of Genius and Folly*, ix.
159. Cone, "They Scorn the '400.'"

160. Cone, "They Scorn the '400.'"
161. "The Museums on Sundays," *New York Times*, November 18, 1885.
162. "Cases Argued in Superior Court, Estate of Robert Hoe Is Plaintiff in One of Them," *Hartford Courant*, December 19, 1914.
163. Charlotte Lucile Whitehead v. Owen F. Roberts et al., 8, 9.
164. "Eugene Luther Vidal," Wikipedia, https://en.wikipedia.org.
165. "A Fine Library: Catalogue of the English Books in the Splendid Collection of Robert Hoe," *New York Times*, April 25, 1903.
166. "Robert Hoe, 3D, Dies," *New York Times*, September 23, 1909.
167. Dodge, *Tales of the Phelps-Dodge Family*, 105.
168. Anderson Auction Company, *Catalogue of the Library*, part 1, vi.
169. Friends of Heublein Tower, "Heublein Tower History."

15. The Fuse Is Lit: The Climax Fuse Factory Fire

170. Frank Hadsell Diary, August 15, 1901, AFPL.
171. "John B. Andrews, 73, Dies at Avon Home," *Hartford Times*, November 15, 1929.
172. Ellsworth, *100 Years*, 85.
173. Frank Hadsell Diary, "Review," 1903.
174. Patrick L. "Patsy" Loughman (1864–1905), findagrave.com.
175. "Ten Victims of the Holocaust in Avon," *Waterbury Evening Democrat*, September 16, 1905; Ellsworth, *100 Years*, 87.
176. Frank Hadsell Diary, The Fire—Sept. 1905.
177. "Catastrophe at Avon," *Hartford Times*, September 16, 1905.
178. "Six of One Family in Avon Disaster: Richard and Michael, Twins Fared Worst, Former Was Burned Up, Other Expected to Die," *Hartford Courant*, September 22, 1905.
179. "7 Dead, 20 Injured by Sheet of Flame in Avon Fuse Works," *Hartford Courant*, September 16, 1905.
180. "Scenes at Stricken Avon," *New Haven Journal Courier*, September 18, 1905.
181. Diana LeGeyt (1888–1905), findagrave.com.

16. A Suspect in Earnest: Avon's Double Murder

182. "The Avon Double Murder," *New Haven Morning Journal-Courier*, June 2, 1880.

183. "Avon's Tragedy: The Mystery Yet Unsolved; Mrs. Ridgeway, The Suspected Niece, Relieved from Suspicion," *Hartford Courant*, June 7, 1880.
184. "The Avon Tragedy: Clearing Up the Dark Mystery—The Double Homicide Probably the Work of an Escaped Maniac," *New Haven Morning Journal-Courier*, March 29, 1881.
185. Second Report of the Board of Trustees, 33.
186. "The Avon Murder," *Meriden Daily Republican*, March 29, 1881.
187. "A Theory Denied," *New Haven Morning Journal-Courier*, April 25, 1881.

17. Doomed Again: The Murder House

188. "Baby the Cause of Triple Tragedy, Religious Differences in Family Lead to Double Murder and Suicide," *Hartford Courant*, March 7, 1908.
189. "Baby the Cause of Triple Tragedy."
190. "Tragedy over Lent," *New Haven Morning Journal-Courier*, March 7, 1908.
191. "Brutal Avon Murder," *Farmington Valley Herald*, March 13, 1908.
192. "Mrs. Lynch May Live," *New Haven Union*, March 7, 1908.
193. "'Murder House' Ghosts Made Homeless," *Hartford Courant*, January 15, 1928.
194. "Avon's Murder House Gives Way to Progress," *Hartford Courant*, January 9, 1928.
195. "'Murder House' Ghosts Made Homeless."

18. Caught Between Worlds: Yung Wing

196. Yung Kwai Papers, notebook of recollections, MS 1795, Box 1.
197. Rhoads, *Stepping Forth into the World*, 9.
198. Yao, "Father of Chinese Overseas Students."
199. Yung, *My Life in China*, 41.
200. Courtney, *Joseph Hopkins Twichell*, 144.
201. Courtney, *Joseph Hopkins Twichell*, 146.
202. Yung Kwai Papers, notebook of recollections.
203. Yung Kwai Papers, notebook of recollections.
204. Bieler, *"Patriots" or "Traitors"?*, 7.
205. Courtney, *Joseph Hopkins Twichell*, 146, 147.
206. Yung Kwai Papers, notebook of recollections.

207. Yung Wing to Rev. Joseph Twichell, April 4, 1874, Joseph Hopkins Twichell Papers.
208. Frank Hadsell Diary, August 6, 1912.
209. "A Hartford Lady's Death," *The Day*, May 31, 1886.
210. Yung, *My Life in China*, 207, 208.
211. Yung, *My Life in China*, 201.
212. Yung, *My Life in China*, 201.
213. Yung Kwai Papers, notebook of recollections.
214. Bieler, *"Patriots" or "Traitors"?*, 8.
215. Mary Kellogg Yung to Jane Bartlett Kellogg, April 18, 1880, Yung Wing Papers.
216. Bieler, *"Patriots" or "Traitors"?*, 9.
217. LaFargue, *China's First Hundred*, 51.
218. Leibovitz and Miller, *Fortunate Son*, 175, 176.
219. Yung, *My Life in China*, 223.
220. Yao, "Father of Chinese Overseas Students."
221. Koh, "Transcript of 'Yellow in a White World.'"
222. "Death of Dr. Yung Wing," *Hartford Courant*, April 22, 1912.

19. The Fiercely Independent Fanny Whitman

223. Recollections of Seth Tillotson and Fanny Whitman, AFPL.
224. "Walnut Grove Farm," *History of Farmington Houses*, 352–53, AFPL.
225. Town Farm Road, Seth Tillotson, 6th Generation (1795–1858), AFPL.
226. Recollections of Seth Tillotson and Fanny Whitman.
227. Edwards, ed., *Farmington, Connecticut*, 4:185.
228. Recollections of Seth Tillotson and Fanny Whitman, AFPL.
229. Hurlburt, "Tillotson Farm, Farmington," *Old Houses of Connecticut, Colonial Dames Society*, January 12, 1950, Connecticut State Library, AFPL.
230. Recollections of Seth Tillotson and Fanny Whitman.

20. Going Old School: Theodate Pope Riddle's Tribute

231. Kegley, *Avon Old Farms*.
232. "Avon School Radical Departure in Teaching Methods," *Hartford Courant*, April 3, 1921.
233. Emeny, *Theodate Pope Riddle*, 6.

234. "Lusitania's Passengers Warned of Ship's Doom," *The Washington Times*, May 1, 1915.
235. Pope, "Letter from a Survivor."
236. Pope, "Letter from a Survivor."
237. Larson, *Dead Wake*, 353.
238. Ramsey, *Aspiration and Perseverance*, 7.
239. Theodate Pope Riddle to Brooks Emeny, July 28, 1916, Theodate Pope Riddle Family Papers (hereafter TPRFP), document 3243.
240. "Avon School Radical Departure."
241. "Avon School Radical Departure."
242. "Avon School Radical Departure."
243. Ramsey, *Aspiration and Perseverance*, 13.
244. "Avon School Radical Departure."
245. Royal Cortissoz to Theodate Pope Riddle, March 14, 1927, TPRFP, document 2313.

21. The Squire of Avon: Joe Alsop

246. "J.W. Alsop Dies While on Vacation," *Farmington Valley Herald*, March 19, 1953.
247. Caroli, *Roosevelt Women*, 303.
248. Caroli, *Roosevelt Women*, 124.
249. Joseph Alsop to Theodate Pope Riddle, May 9, 1923, TPRFP.
250. Katz, *Dearest of Geniuses*, 185.
251. Ramsey, *Aspiration and Perseverance*, 14.
252. "New Pope School Not Tax Exempt, Judge Marvin Rules It Isn't an 'Academy' Under Statutes," *Hartford Courant*, January 29, 1926.
253. Theodate Pope Riddle to Grace Wallace, October 18, 1923, TPRFP, document 6364.
254. Katz, *Dearest of Geniuses*, 186.
255. "J.W. Alsop Dies While on Vacation," *Hartford Courant*, March 18, 1953.

22. Sherman Eddy's Tow Path Gardens

256. "Picturesque 'Tow Path Lodge,' the Beautiful Summer Home of Sherman W. Eddy at Avon, on the Farmington River," *Hartford Courant*, October 16, 1921.

257. Recollections of Julian B. Eddy, 2, AFPL.
258. Recollections of Donald B. Eddy, 4, AFPL.
259. Recollections of Donald B. Eddy, 3.
260. Kegley, *Avon Old Farms*.
261. "Auto Show Setting This Year Novel," *Hartford Courant*, January 13, 1935.
262. "Library Given Books in Memory of Sherman Eddy," *Hartford Courant*, July 25, 1953.

23. A Grand Political Enemy: Corinne Robinson Alsop

263. Hart, *Official Report of the Proceedings*, 165.
264. Hart, *Official Report of the Proceedings*, 165.
265. "Corinne Alsop Cole's 82 Years," *Hartford Times*, December 16, 1968.
266. "Corinne Alsop Cole's 82 Years."
267. Cook, *Eleanor Roosevelt*, 1:154.
268. Corinne Robinson Alsop Cole Family Papers (hereafter CRAC) and unpublished diaries, 1903–04, July 18, 1904.
269. CRAC, 1904–05, 71.
270. CRAC, 1904–05, 74.
271. Caroli, *Roosevelt Women*, 303.
272. Caroli, *Roosevelt Women*, 305.
273. Corinne Robinson Alsop, interview with Hermann and Mary Hagedorn, November 23, 1954.
274. Corinne Roosevelt Robinson to Joseph Wright Alsop, September 25, 1909, CRAC.
275. Anna Roosevelt Cowles to Joseph and Corinne Alsop, November 6, 1909, CRAC.
276. Caroli, *Roosevelt Women*, 307.
277. Corinne Roosevelt Robinson to Joseph Wright Alsop, September 25, 1909, CRAC.
278. CRAC, 1909–14, 25, 26.
279. Caroli, *Roosevelt Women*, 316.
280. CRAC, 1909–14, 56.
281. CRAC, 1909–14, 57.
282. CRAC, 1909–14, 60.
283. CRAC, 1909–14, 57.
284. "'Guest Editorial' by Joseph W. Alsop," *Hartford Times*, November 27, 1951.

285. "Connecticut Women Don't Want Ballot: Hundreds Make Protest Against the Suffrage," *Hartford Courant*, June 1, 1911.
286. Caroli, *Roosevelt Women*, 121.
287. Caroli, *Roosevelt Women*, 121.
288. Caroli, *Roosevelt Women*, 122.
289. Caroli, *Roosevelt Women*, 325.
290. Katz, *Dearest of Geniuses*, 229.
291. Corinne Robinson Alsop to Eleanor Roosevelt, February 24, 1939, CRAC.
292. Corinne Alsop to Eleanor Roosevelt, January 10, 1936, Selected Digitized Correspondence of Eleanor Roosevelt (hereafter ERDC).
293. Eleanor Roosevelt to Corinne Robinson Alsop, dated January 15, 1936, CRAC.
294. McLaughlin, "Social Interludes Mark Visitors' Day."
295. "Corinne Alsop Cole's 82 Years."
296. Hart, *Official Report of the Proceedings*, 251.
297. Hart, *Official Report of the Proceedings*, 167.
298. Platt and Alsop, *I've Seen the Best*, 43, 44.
299. Caroli, *Roosevelt Women*, 327, 328.
300. Eleanor Roosevelt to Corinne Robinson Alsop, November 11, 1936, CRAC.
301. Eleanor Roosevelt to Corinne Alsop, September 24, 1937, ERDC.

24. Wilford Woodruff's Awakening

302. Cowley, *Wilford Woodruff*, 22.
303. Woodruff, Autobiography 1857 Draft 1 [A-5].
304. Fairchild Aerial Survey of Connecticut, AFPL.
305. Waskey, "Restoration Movement."
306. Woodruff, Autobiography 1857 Draft 1 [A-5], 3–5.
307. Kenney, *Wilford Woodruff's Journal*, 1:11.
308. Woodruff, *Leaves from My Journal*, 2–4.
309. Cowley, *Wilford Woodruff*, 29.
310. Church of Jesus Christ of Latter-day Saints (hereafter LDS), "Wilford Woodruff: Fourth President."
311. Eph. 4:12–13, KJV.
312. Kenney, *Wilford Woodruff's Journal*, 143.
313. Wilford Woodruff to Aphek Lorenzo Woodruff and Azubah Hart, March 15, 1853, Wilford Woodruff Papers (hereafter WWP).

314. Joseph Smith Papers, "Lucy Mack Smith History, 1845," 79–86.
315. Kenney, *Wilford Woodruff's Journal*, 14–17.
316. Kenney, *Wilford Woodruff's Journal*, 90, 91.
317. Kenney, *Wilford Woodruff's Journal*, 172.
318. Kenney, *Wilford Woodruff's Journal*, 74.
319. Kenney, *Wilford Woodruff's Journal*, 75.
320. Brigham Young to Wilford Woodruff, October 16, 1845, WWP.
321. Durham, *Discourses of Wilford Woodruff*, 317.
322. Joseph Smith's Polygamy, "Sealings to Legally Married Women."
323. Joseph Smith's Polygamy, "Plural Marriage Teachings."
324. Kimball, *Why We Practice Plural Marriage*, 23, 24.
325. Wilford Woodruff's Witness, "Wilford Woodruff's Wives."
326. Alexander, *Things in Heaven and Earth*, 239.
327. Kenney, *Wilford Woodruff's Journal*, 268.
328. Kenney, *Wilford Woodruff's Journal*, 289.
329. Kenney, *Wilford Woodruff's Journal*, 289.
330. Kenney, *Wilford Woodruff's Journal*, 356.
331. Kenney, *Wilford Woodruff's Journal*, 266.
332. Wilford Woodruff to Emeline Woodruff, June 26, 1886, private collection, courtesy of Earle Stone.
333. Cowley, *Wilford Woodruff*, 371.
334. B.H. Roberts Foundation, "Official Text of Wilford Woodruff's 1890 Manifesto."
335. Day in the life, entry for September 25, 1890, WWP.

25. The Shady Side of Ministry

336. Hubbell, *Valedictory Discourse*, 11, 12, 17.
337. Hubbell, *Valedictory Discourse*, 14.
338. "Avon as It Was Sixty Years Ago," *Hartford Courant*, August 31, 1915.
339. Hubbell, *Pastor's Wife*, title page.
340. Hubbell, *Pastor's Wife*, dedication page.
341. Hubbell, *Pastor's Wife*, 169, 219.
342. Hubbell, *Pastor's Wife*, 59.
343. Hubbell, *Pastor's Wife*, 50.
344. Hubbell, *Pastor's Wife*, 159, 160.
345. Congregational Church, Avon, Connecticut, *Manual, Historical Sketch and Membership Roll*, 14.

346. Hubbell, *Valedictory Discourse*, 14.
347. Hubbell, *Valedictory Discourse*, 15.
348. Hubbell, *History of the Hubbell Family*, 172.
349. "The Rev. Noah Porter Tried to Still Troubled Waters of 'Shady Side' Affair," *Farmington Valley Herald*, September 9, 1954.
350. "Rev. Mr. Hubbell," *Litchfield Enquirer*, August 13, 1853.

26. Cherry Park's Ascension

351. Cherry Park Fair flyer, "Leap from the Clouds."
352. "How Cherry Park Got Its Name," *Hartford Courant*, November 21, 1913.
353. "How Cherry Park Got Its Name."
354. "Avon Historical Society Presents 'Avon to Indy,' History of Midget Car Racing," AFPL.
355. "Harness Horses Run Again," *Hartford Courant*, May 20, 1956.
356. Cherry Park Fair flyer, "Brownie & Company."
357. Cherry Park Fair flyer, "Brownie & Company."
358. International Independent Showmen's Museum, "Wall of Death."
359. "Cherry Park, More Beautiful Than Ever, Awaits Return of Horse Racing and Fair Crowds," *Hartford Courant*, September 28, 1919.

27. Vision of Progress: Charles Stilwell

360. Baldwin, *Edison*, 53.
361. "Charles F. Stilwell, Blind Relative of Thomas Edison, Optimist Despite Affliction," *Bridgeport Telegram*, September 3, 1923.
362. Israel, Carlat, Hochfelder and Nier, *Papers of Thomas A. Edison*, 5:767.
363. Israel, Carlat, Collins and Hochfelder, *Papers of Thomas Edison*, 7:465.
364. Israel, Carlat, Collins and Hochfelder, *Papers of Thomas Edison*, 7:630.
365. Morris, *Edison*, 244.
366. Ross Family history supplied by Doug Ross.

28. Bored in Retirement: A Golf Course Is Born

367. "Dr. Cox Dies, Collinsville's Country Doctor," *Hartford Courant*, September 13, 1961.

368. Golf Club of Avon, "Avon Story."
369. Brunoli Family Collection, AFPL.

Epilogue

370. "Corinne Alsop Cole," *Hartford Times*, June 25, 1971.

BIBLIOGRAPHY

Abraham Lincoln Historical Society. "Lincoln's View on Slavery." Accessed November 24, 2024. http://www.abraham-lincoln-history.org.

Alexander, Thomas G. *Things in Heaven and Earth: The Life and Times of Wilford Woodruff, a Mormon Prophet.* Signature Books, 1991.

Alsop, Corinne Robinson. Interview with Hermann and Mary Hagedorn, November 23, 1954, and December 28, 1954. Houghton Library, Harvard University.

America in Class editors. "The Religious Roots of Abolition." America in Class, accessed November 24, 2024. https://americainclass.org.

American Battlefield Trust. "Petersburg." Battlefields.org, accessed November 25, 2024. https://www.battlefields.org.

Anderson Auction Company. *Catalogue of the Library of Robert Hoe of New York… April 24, 1911–November 18, 1912.* D. Taylor, 1912. https://archive.org.

Aptheker, Herbert. *Abolitionism, a Revolutionary Movement.* Twayne Publishers, 1989. https://archive.org.

Art Story editors. "John Trumbull, American Painter." *The Art Story*, accessed November 25, 2024. https://www.theartstory.org.

Asylum Hill Congregational Church. "CT Historical Society Exhibit." Accessed November 30, 2024. https://www.ahcc.org.

Atwood, Margaret. "Daniel Wadsworth and the Atheneum." MS 80533, May 1979, Connecticut Museum of Culture and History.

Austen, Barbara. "Yung Wing's Dream: The Chinese Educational Mission, 1872–1881." Connecticut History, October 26, 2021. https://connecticuthistory.org.

Avon Congregational Church meeting minutes, Avon Free Public Library [AFPL].

Avon Congregational Church records, 1798–1921. Genealogical Society of Utah, 1976.

Avon, Connecticut Incorporation Papers, Survey Records, Civil War Soldiers, 1828–1878, 974.62, AV75c, Connecticut State Library, Hartford.

Avon, Connecticut Land Records, Town Clerk's Office, Avon, Connecticut.

Avon, Conn. History of Avon, Avon Townwide Survey, May 1997, AFPL.

Avon town history, Recollections, n.d., AFPL.

Baldwin, Neil. *Edison: Inventing the Century.* Hyperion, 1995.

Bardes, John. "Plantation Slavery in Antebellum Louisiana." 64 Parishes. Accessed November 24, 2024. https://64parishes.org/plantation-slavery-in-antebellum-louisiana.

Bartlett, David W. *Modern Agitators: or, Pen Portraits of Living American Reformers.* Miller, Orton & Mulligan, 1855. https://archive.org.

———. *What I Saw in London; or Men and Things in the Great Metropolis.* C.M. Saxton, Barker & Co., 1860. https://archive.org.

Bartlett, M.H. *Memorial History of Hartford County, Conn., 1633–1884.* Edited by J. Hammond Trumbull. Edward L. Osgood, 1886.

Baugh, Alexander L., and Susan Easton Black, eds. *Banner of the Gospel, Wilford Woodruff.* Religious Studies Center, Brigham Young University in cooperation with Deseret Book Company, 2010.

Bender, Marjorie, Nora Howard and Jean Parker. *A Tale of Two Meetinghouses: The West Avon Congregational Church and the Avon Congregational Church and Their Communities, 1746–2019.* Self-published, 2019.

B.H. Roberts Foundation. "Official Text of Wilford Woodruff's 1890 Manifesto Ending Plural Marriage." Accessed November 26, 2024. https://bhroberts.org.

Bicknell, William H. *Farmington, Connecticut: The Geographical and Social History of an American Town.* Phoenix Publishing, 1982. https://archive.org.

Bieler, Stacey. *"Patriots" or "Traitors"? A History of American-Educated Chinese Students.* M.E. Sharpe, 2004.

Biographical Directory of the United States Congress. "Joseph Roswell Hawley, 1826–1905, Member Details: H000377." Accessed November 24, 2024. https://bioguideretro.congress.gov.

Bishop, Woodford & Co. accounting ledgers. 1838–1841 and 1843–1847. AFPL.

Blakeslee, Bernard F. *History of the Sixteenth Connecticut Volunteers.* Case, Lockwood & Brainard Co., 1875. https://archive.org.

British Broadcasting Corporation staff. "Safety Fuse for Blasting Underground." *A History of the World*, accessed November 24, 2024. https://www.bbc.co.uk.

Brunoli Family Collection. Marian Hunter Local History Room, AFPL.

Buckingham, Rev. Samuel G., D.D. *The Life of William A. Buckingham, The War Governor of Connecticut.* W.F. Adams Company Publishers, 1894. https://archive.org.

Buck, Robyn. "Understanding the Importance of Arbor in Circular Saws." Shuntool, January 10, 2024. https://shuntool.com.

Bushman, Richard Lyman. *Joseph Smith: Rough Stone Rolling.* Alfred A. Knopf, 2005.

Butler, Susan. *East to the Dawn: The Life of Amelia Earhart.* Addison-Wesley, 1997.

Camp, David N. *History of New Britain with Sketches of Farmington and Berlin, Connecticut, 1640–1889*. William B. Thompson & Company, 1889.

Caroli, Betty Boyd. *The Roosevelt Women*. Basic Books, 1998.

Champlin, George N. Diary. 973.78, qC358. Connecticut State Library.

Charlotte Lucile Whitehead v. Owen F. Roberts et al. Superior Court October Term 1912. Connecticut State Library.

Cheney, Frank W., et al. *Sixteenth Regiment Connecticut Volunteers, Excursion and Reunion at Antietam Battlefield, September 17, 1889*. Case, Lockwood & Brainard Company, 1889.

Cherry Park Fair flyer. "Brownie & Company in Their Air-Inspiring and Sensational Barrel Loop." 1904, AFPL.

———. "A Leap from the Clouds." 1894, AFPL.

Church of Jesus Christ of Latter-day Saints. "A Decade of Persecution, 1877–87." Chap. 33 in *Church History in the Fulness of Times Student Manual.* https://www.churchofjesuschrist.org.

———. "Official Declaration 1." Doctrine and Covenants. https://www.churchofjesuschrist.org.

———. "Polygamy: What Latter-day Saints Really Believe." Accessed November 26, 2024. https://ph.churchofjesuschrist.org.

———. "Wilford Woodruff." Church History Biographical Database, accessed December 6, 2024. https://history.churchofjesuschrist.org.

———. "Wilford Woodruff: Fourth President of the Church." Chap. 4 in *Presidents of the Church Student Manual.* https://www.churchofjesuschrist.org.

CIO editors. "Thomas Edison, Joseph Swan and the Real Deal Behind the Light Bulb." CIO, August 15, 2001. https://www.cio.com.

City of Alexandria, Virginia. "Fighting for Freedom, Black Union Soldiers of the Civil War." Updated April 1, 2024. https://www.alexandriava.gov.

Climax Fuse Factory Time Book. November 5, 1904, to October 20, 1906. Ensign-Bickford Collection, Simsbury Free Library, Simsbury, Connecticut.

Clint B. Hadsell Photo Collection, AFPL.

Collins Company. *One Hundred Years: A Brief Account of the Development of The Collins Company in the Manufacture of Axes, Machetes, and Edge Tools and in Commemoration of Its 100th Anniversary.* Collins Company, 1926. https://archive.org.

Collins Company Historical Memoranda and Inventory Collection. MS 72165. Connecticut Museum of Culture and History.

Collins Company records. Collection Overview, 1826–1950. Connecticut Museum of Culture and History.

Comparato, Frank E. *Chronicles of Genius and Folly, R. Hoe & Company and the Printing Press as a Service to Democracy.* Labyrinthos, 1979.

Cone, Ada. "They Scorn the '400.'" *Meriden Daily Journal*, May 4, 1889.

Congregational Church, Avon, Connecticut. *Manual, Historical Sketch and Membership Roll, 1915.* Pulaski Democrat Publishing Co., 1915.

ConnecticutHistory.org editors. "Avon Industry: From Underground to Outerspace." September 18, 2020. https://connecticuthistory.org.

———. "Talcott Mountain: A View of Early New England." July 30, 2022. https://connecticuthistory.org.

Connecticut Land Records. "The Avon Story." Town of Avon, n.d.

Cook, Blanche Wiesen. *Eleanor Roosevelt*, vol. 1. *1884–1933.* Penguin Books, 1993.

Corinne Robinson Alsop Cole Family Papers. MS Am 1785.8. Houghton Library, Harvard University.

Cornell Law School staff. "Edmunds Anti-Polygamy Act of 1882." Legal Information Institute, accessed November 26, 2024. https://www.law.cornell.edu.

Courtney, Steve. "'The Handsomest Man That Ever Was': Twain's Joe Twichell." Center for Mark Twain Studies, September 8, 2022. https://marktwainstudies.com.

———. *Joseph Hopkins Twichell, The Life and Times of Mark Twain's Closest Friend.* University of Georgia Press, 2008.

Cowles, Charlotte. Letters (1820–1866). The Connecticut Museum of Culture and History.

Cowley, Matthias F. *Wilford Woodruff: History of His Life and Labors.* Deseret News, 1909.

Dallas, John T. *Mary Robbins Hillard.* Rumford Press, 1944.

Daniel Wadsworth Papers. 1749–1888. Connecticut Museum of Culture and History.

David Chittenden Collins Papers. Manuscripts and Archives, MS 886. Yale University Library.

Davies, W.D., and Truman G. Madsen, eds. *Israel, the Mormons and the Land, Reflections on Mormonism: Judeo-Christian Parallels*. Religious Studies Center, Brigham Young University, 1978.

DeForest, John W. *History of the Indians of Connecticut from the Earliest Known Period to 1850.* Archon Books, 1964. Accessed November 22, 2024. https://archive.org.

Dodge, Phyllis. *Tales of the Phelps-Dodge Family.* Princeton University Press, 1987.

Donald B. Eddy Recollections. 1981. AFPL.

Durham, G. Homer, ed. *The Discourses of Wilford Woodruff.* Bookcraft, 1990.

Eaton, William W. *The Union: Past, Present and Future, A Speech Delivered by Hon. W.W. Eaton at City Hall, Hartford on Saturday Evening, March 3d 1860.* Published by the order of the Democratic state central committee, 1860. Accessed November 26, 2024. https://archive.org.

Edwards, Ned W., Jr., ed. *Farmington, Connecticut, First Church of Christ (Congregational) Records 1652–1938, [Farmington, Connecticut]*. 9 vols. Connecticut State Library, 1940.

Ellsworth, John E. "Ensign-Bickford Role in Avon's Development." Avon Historical Society, January 9, 1986, AFPL.

———. *100 Years: The Ensign-Bickford Company and the Safety Fuse Industry in America: A Record of One Hundred Years of Achievement, 1836–1936.* R.R. Donnelly & Sons Company, 1936.

Emeny, Brooks. *Theodate Pope Riddle, Avon and the Founding of Avon Old Farms.* Avon Old Farms School, 1977.

Engle, Paul. "Thomas Edison's Lady Glassblowers." Conciatore, March 4, 2020. https://www.conciatore.org.

Ensign-Bickford Industries Inc. staff. "Company Overview, Our History." Accessed November 24, 2024. https://ebad.com/.

Fairchild Aerial Survey of Connecticut (1934). Map including notations of sawmills on Old Farms Road, AFPL.

Farington, Joseph, R.A. *The Joseph Farington Diary*, vol. 4. Hutchinson & Co., 1924.

Farmington, Connecticut Land Records. Town Clerk's Office, Farmington, Connecticut.

Farmington Historical Society staff. "The Farmington Canal." Farmington Historical Society, accessed December 11, 2024. https://fhs-ct.org.

Farmington Libraries. "Twenty-One Members of First Congregational Church, Farmington to the Pastor, Deacons & Members of the Congregational Church, West Avon." April 10, 1854, The Farmington Room.

Finlay, Nancy. "'A Noble and Precious Life': Edgar M. Woodford, Civil Engineer, Abolitionist, and Soldier." Connecticut History, October 21, 2022. https://connecticuthistory.org.

Founders Papers. Box 1, Auerbach Art Library and Museum Archives, Wadsworth Atheneum Museum of Art.

Fowler, Karen, and Dr. William McKinney. "Noah Porter. 1781–1866, Pastor, First Church of Christ, Farmington, Connecticut 1806–1866." Unpublished manuscript, 1993. Marian Hunter Local History Room, AFPL.

Frank Hadsell Diary. Marian Hunter Local History Room, AFPL.

Friends of Heublein Tower. "Heublein Tower History." Accessed November 26, 2024. https://friendsofheubleintower.org.

Furer, Rebecca. "Simsbury at the Time of King Philip's War." Teach It, accessed January 24, 2025. https://teachitct.org.

Gates, Oliver W. Diary (MS 78606a). Connecticut Museum of Culture and History.

Gilder Lehrman Institute staff. "The Emancipator—Extra. February 24th, 1838, Anti-Slavery Convention." GLC07437. Accessed November 24, 2024. https://www.gilderlehrman.org.

———. "Men of Color, To Arms! To Arms, 1863." Broadside, Gilder Lehrman Institute of American History, accessed November 25, 2024. https://www.gilderlehrman.org.

Golf Club of Avon. "The Avon Story." AFPL.

Gordon, Lesley J. "Bad Luck Regiment: The 16th Connecticut Infantry." HistoryNet, December 9, 2016. https://www.historynet.com.

———. *A Broken Regiment, The 16th Connecticut's Civil War.* Louisiana State University Press, 2014.

Grant, Rev. Joel. Sermon of November 20, 1851. In *Centennial Commemoration of the Organization of the First Church in West Avon, Conn.* George D. Jewett, 1851.

Hamilton, Anne M. "From China to Hartford, Elsie Jane Yung's Historic Connection." *Hartford Courant*, June 14, 2009. http://hartfordinfo.org.

Harrison Woodford Letters. Marian Hunter Local History Room, AFPL.

Hart, George L. *The Official Report of the Proceedings of the Twenty-First Republican National Convention: Held in Cleveland, Ohio, June 9, 10, 11, and 12, 1936, Resulting in the Nomination of Alfred M. Landon, of Kansas, for President, and the Nomination of Frank Knox, of Illinois, for Vice-President.* Tenny Press, 1936.

Hawley-August Collection. AFPL.

Haynes, Clarence L., Jr. "What Is Excommunication and Should Churches Practice This?" Bible Study Tools, accessed November 24, 2024. https://www.biblestudytools.com.

Hill, Donna. *Joseph Smith, The First Mormon.* Doubleday & Company, 1977.

Hill, Isaac J. *A Sketch of the 29th Regiment of Connecticut Colored Troops.* Daughtery, Maguire & Co., 1867. https://www.loc.gov.

Historic Buildings of Connecticut. "West Avon Congregational Church (1818)." Accessed November 22, 2024. https://historicbuildingsct.com.

History.com editors. "Bleeding Kansas." History, April 7, 2021. https://www.history.com.

———. "Boxer Rebellion." History, updated June 26, 2023. https://www.history.com.

———. "Fort Pillow Massacre." History, last modified April 6, 2021. https://www.history.com.

HistoryNet editors. "CSS Albemarle: Confederate Ironclad in the American Civil War." HistoryNet, updated August 25, 2016. https://www.historynet.com.

History of Farmington Houses. "Walnut Grove Farm." Marian Hunter Local History Room, AFPL.

Hooker, John. *Connecticut Reports: Being Reports of Cases Argued and Determined in the Supreme Court of Errors of the State of Connecticut*, vol. 34, 2nd ed., *Tillotson vs. Tillotson, September Term, 1857*. Banks & Brothers, 1877.

———. *Some Reminiscences of a Long Life, with a Few Articles on Moral and Social Subjects of Present Interest.* Belknap and Warfield, 1899.

Howard, Nora. *Avon 1830–2005, A Brief History, Avon Telephone Directory, 2005–2006.* Avon Police Association, 2005.

Hubbell, Martha Stone. *A Pastor's Wife: The Shady Side of Life in a Country Parsonage.* John P. Jewett and Company, 1853.

Hubbell, Stephen. *Valedictory Discourse Delivered at the Congregational Church in Avon (East), Lord's Day, 26 June 1853*. Hartford, CT, 1853.

Hubbell, Walter. *History of the Hubbell Family, Containing a Genealogical Record.* J.H. Hubbell & Co., 1881. https://archive.org.

Hurlburt, Mabel Spencer. "Tillotson Farm, Farmington." *Old Houses of Connecticut, Colonial Dames Society*, January 12, 1950, Connecticut State Library. Marian Hunter Local History Room, AFPL.

Hutchins, Dawn Byron. "The Steady Evolution of a Connecticut Family Business." Connecticut History, July 22, 2022. https://connecticuthistory.org.

Incorporation of Said Town of Avon; Special Acts May, 1830, AFPL.

International Independent Showmen's Museum. "Wall of Death Is a Crowd Pleaser on Carnival Midways." March 1, 2015. https://showmensmuseum.org.

Israel, Paul B., Louis Carlat, David Hochfelder and Keith A. Nier, eds. *The Papers of Thomas A. Edison*. Vol. 5, *Research to Development at Menlo Park, January 1879–March 1881.* Johns Hopkins University Press, 2004.

Israel, Paul B., Louis Carlat, Theresa M. Collins and David Hochfelder, eds. *The Papers of Thomas Edison*. Vol. 7, *Losses and Loyalties, April 1883–December 1884.* Johns Hopkins University Press, 2011.

James Monroe Papers. University of Mary Washington, Monroe Family Genealogy. Accessed December 6, 2024. https://academics.umw.edu.

Johanson, Rev. Jerome E. "General History of Avon." Unpublished manuscript, 1949, AFPL.

Joseph Hopkins Twichell Papers. YCAL MSS 755, Beineke Library. Yale University, Yale Archives.

Joseph Smith Papers. "Lucy Mack Smith History, 1845." Accessed November 26, 2024. https://www.josephsmithpapers.org.

Joseph Smith's Polygamy editors. "Plural Marriage Teachings." Joseph Smith's Polygamy, accessed November 26, 2024. https://josephsmithspolygamy.org.

———. "Sealings to Legally Married Women; Common Questions." Joseph Smith's Polygamy, accessed November 26, 2024. https://josephsmithspolygamy.org.

Julien Eddy Recollections. 1981. AFPL.

Katz, Sandra L. *Dearest of Geniuses, a Life of Theodate Pope Riddle.* Tide-mark Press Ltd., 2003.

Kegley, William J. *Avon Old Farms, Recollections of Bill Kegley.* Avon Old Farms School, 1974. https://issuu.com.

Kellogg, Dr. E.W. "The Grave of Edgar M. Woodford." *Hartford Courant*, June 11, 1913.

Kenney, Scott G., ed. *Wilford Woodruff's Journal*. Vol. 1, *1833–1840.* Church of Jesus Christ of Latter-day Saints, accessed November 26, 2024. https://archive.org.

Kimball, Helen Mar. *Why We Practice Plural Marriage.* Juvenile Instructor Office, 1884. Accessed November 26, 2024. https://josephsmithfoundation.org.

Koh, Harold Hongju. "Transcript of 'Yellow in a White World.'" *Yale Global Online*, September 27, 2004. Accessed December 3, 2024. https://archive-yaleglobal.yale.edu.

Kornhauser, Elizabeth Mankin. *American Paintings Before 1945 in the Wadsworth Atheneum*. Vol. 1. Yale University Press, 1996.

———. "Daniel Wadsworth and Elizabeth Hart Jarvis." YouTube. Accessed December 6, 2024. https://www.youtube.com.

———. "Daniel Wadsworth and the Hudson River School." *Connecticut Explored* (Winter 2004–5).

LaFargue, Thomas E. *China's First Hundred: Educational Mission Students in the United States, 1872–1881.* Washington State University, 1987. https://archive.org.

Lamphere, George. *Experiences and Observations of a Private Soldier in the Civil War* (George Lamphere Diary). Minnesota Historical Society.

Larson, Erik. *Dead Wake: The Last Crossing of the Lusitania.* Crown Publishers, 2015.

Leibovitz, Liel, and Matthew Miller. *Fortunate Sons.* W.W. Norton & Company, 2011.

Library of Congress. "Abraham Lincoln Papers at the Library of Congress, Timeline." Accessed November 24, 2024. https://www.loc.gov.

———. "African-American Soldiers During the Civil War." U.S. History Primary Source Timeline, accessed November 25, 2024. https://www.loc.gov.

———. "England and the Printing Press: A Subject Guide." Accessed November 26, 2024. https://guides.loc.gov.

Lincoln, Abraham. The Papers of Abraham Lincoln. "Narrative Overview." The Law Practice of Abraham Lincoln, accessed November 25, 2024. https://lawpracticeofabrahamlincoln.org.

Looking for Lincoln editors. "Lincoln's Eighth Judicial Circuit, Logan-Lincoln Partnership." Looking for Lincoln, 8th Judicial Circuit, accessed November 25, 2024. https://www.lookingforlincoln.org.

Lydia Huntley Sigourney Papers. "Biographical Sketch." *Connecticut Museum of Culture and History*, accessed November 26, 2024. https://chs.org.

MacKie, Mary-Frances. *Avon Connecticut: An Historical Story.* Phoenix Publishing, 1988.

Marchant, Anita. *Yung Wing and the Chinese Educational Mission in Hartford.* Outer Sky Press, 2008.

Martin, G.C. *The Simsbury Historical Society in Cooperation with the Ensign-Bickford Company Presents Fuse Making Thru History.* Simsbury Historical Society, 1970.

Marvel, William. *Andersonville, the Last Depot.* University of North Carolina Press, 1994.

Maseda, Paola. "Designed to Heal: The Connecticut General Hospital for the Insane." Connecticut History, May 29, 2015. https://connecticuthistory.org.

Mathews, Nancy Mowlls. *Mary Cassatt: A Life.* Yale University Press, 1994.

Matulka, Rebecca, and Daniel Wood. "The History of the Light Bulb," Department of Energy, November 22, 2013. https://www.usailighting.com.

Mayer, George H. "Alf M. Landon as Leader of the Republican Opposition, 1937–1940." *Kansas Historical Quarterly* 32, no. 3 (Autumn 1966): 325–33. https://www.kshs.org.

McLaughlin, Kathleen. "Social Interludes Mark Visitors' Day." *New York Times*, June 8, 1936.

McLoughlin, Virginia, ed. "Establishing a Church on the Kansas Frontier: The Letters of the Rev. O.L. Woodford and His Sister Henrietta, 1857–1869." *Kansas Historical Quarterly* 37, no. 2 (Summer 1971). https://www.kshs.org.

McNulty, J. Bard, ed. *The Correspondence of Thomas Cole and Daniel Wadsworth.* Letters in the Watkinson Library, Trinity College, Hartford, and in the New York State Library, Albany. The Connecticut Museum of Culture and History, 1983.

Milkis, Sid, and Sarah Ong. "Transforming American Democracy: TR and the Bull Moose Campaign of 1912." Miller Center, University of Virginia, accessed November 26, 2024. https://millercenter.org.

Miller, Brenda J. "M.H. Bartlett's Tower Commanded a Spectacular View." Connecticut Explored, Summer 2008. https://www.ctexplored.org.

Minks, Louise. *The Hudson River School.* Crescent Books,1989.

Mintz, Steven. "Historical Context: The Constitution and Slavery." Gilder Lehrman Institute of American History, accessed November 24, 2024. https://www.gilderlehrman.org.

Moore, Sam. "History of the Collins Axe Works." Farm Collector, May 8, 2018. https://www.farmcollector.com.

Morgan, N.H. *A Full Report of the Trial of Orrin Woodford for the Murder of His Wife, Diana Woodford, at Avon, Conn., July 22d, 1845.* Elihu Geer, 1846, Harvard Library. Studies in Scarlet. Accessed November 22, 2024. https://curiosity.lib.harvard.edu.

Morris, Edmund. *Edison.* Random House, 2019.

Moskowitz, Talia. "Fighting for Freedom: Black Soldiers in the Civil War and Connecticut's 29th Colored Regiment." Westport Museum, June 19, 2023. https://westporthistory.org.

Moulton, Rev. J.W. *Historical Address by Rev. J. W. Moulton.* Avon Congregational Church, Avon, Connecticut, Delivered at the Centennial Celebration, September 7 and 8, 1919, AFPL.

Muller, Mary. "Marking Time: Early Connecticut Innovations Transform Clock Making." Connecticut History, February 27, 2022. https://connecticuthistory.org.

National Archives. "Dred Scott v. Sandford (1857)." Updated July 8, 2024. https://www.archives.gov.

———. "Emancipation Proclamation (1863)." Updated May 10, 2022. https://www.archives.gov.

National Constitution Center staff. "The Fugitive Slave Act (1850)." National Constitution Center, accessed November 24, 2024. https://constitutioncenter.org.

———. "Reynolds v. United States (1879)." Supreme Court Case, 98 U.S. 145 (1879), National Constitution Center, accessed November 26, 2024. https://constitutioncenter.org.

National Park Service. "Donaldsonville I, Battle Detail, The Civil War." Accessed November 24, 2024. https://www.nps.gov.

———. "Noah Porter's House." Accessed January 27, 2025. https://www.nps.gov.

Neff, Liz. Oliver Gabriel recollections, n.d., Avon Historical Society.

Newton, Rev. Alexander Heritage, D.D. *Out of the Briars: An Autobiography and Sketch of the Twenty-Ninth Regiment, Connecticut Volunteers.* A.M.E. Book Concern, 1910.

Northen, Charles A.M. *Elihu Burritt: A Memorial Volume Containing a Sketch of His Life and Labors.* D. Appleton & Company, 1879.

Oaks, Dallas H., and Marvin S. Hill. *Carthage Conspiracy: The Trial of the Accused Assassins of Joseph Smith.* University of Illinois Press, 1975.

Office of the Historian. "The Chinese Revolution of 1911." Department of State, United States of America, accessed November 26, 2024. https://history.state.gov.

Paine, Judith. *Theodate Pope Riddle, Her Life and Work.* Theodore Roosevelt Birthplace, 1979. http://www.npshistory.com.

Phyllis Eddy Beach Eddy Letters. AFPL.

Plan of the Gardens at Tow Path Lodge, Thomas M. Desmond, Landscape Architect, November 1919. AFPL.

Platt, Adam, and Joseph Wright Alsop. *I've Seen the Best of It.* Axios Press, 1992.

Platt, John D.R. *Jeremiah Wadsworth, Federalist Entrepreneur.* Arno Press, 1982. https://archive.org.

Pope, Theodate. Diary. Hill-Stead Museum Archives, Farmington, Connecticut.

———. "A Letter from a Survivor of the Lusitania." Hill-Stead Museum Archives, Farmington, Connecticut, 1915.

Porter, Dr. Noah. Letters. The Farmington Room, Farmington Libraries.

Porter, Noah, D.D. *An Historical Discourse Delivered at the Celebration of the One Hundredth Anniversary of the Erection of the Congregational Church in Farmington, Conn., October 16, 1872.* Case, Lockwood & Brainard, 1873.

Porter, Rev. Noah. Letters, Marian Hunter Local History Room, AFPL.

———. *Two Sermons on Church Communion and Excommunication with a Particular View to the Case of Slaveholders in the Church.* Tiffany and Company, 1853.

Priest, John Michael, ed. *16th Connecticut Volunteer Infantry, Sergeant William H. Relyea.* Burd Street Press, 2002.

Ramsey, Gordon Clark. *Aspiration and Perseverance: The History of Avon Old Farms School.* Avon Old Farms School, 1984.

Rettig, Barbara. "A History of the Avon Congregational Church." Avon Congregational Church, accessed November 22, 2024. https://avon-church.org.

Reverend Rufus Hawley Journal. AFPL.

Rhoads, Edward J.M. *Stepping Forth into the World: The Chinese Educational Mission to the United States, 1872–1881.* Hong Kong University Press, 2011.

Ritter, Kathy A. *Apprentices of Connecticut, 1637–1900.* Ancestry Publishing, 1986.

Robert H. Kellogg Papers. Civil War Diaries, Correspondence and Writings (MS 68013). Connecticut Museum of Culture and History.

Roberts, Kenneth D., and Snowden Taylor. *Eli Terry and the Connecticut Shelf Clock.* 2nd ed., rev. Ken Roberts Publishing, 1994.

Roosevelt, Eleanor. "My Day." January 25, 1936, the Eleanor Roosevelt Papers Digital Edition (2017), accessed November 26, 2024. https://erpapers.columbian.gwu.edu.

———. Selected Digitized Correspondence, 1933–1945. Franklin D. Roosevelt Presidential Library & Museum. Accessed November 25, 2024. http://www.fdrlibrary.marist.edu.

SangamonLink. "Stephen T. Logan (Lincoln Law Partner)." August 9, 2017. https://sangamoncountyhistory.org.

Saunders, Richard, and Helen Raye. *Daniel Wadsworth Patron of the Arts.* Wadsworth Atheneum, 1981.

Schiff, Judith Ann. "When East Met West." *Old Yale*, November/December 2004, accessed December 3, 2024. http://archives.yalealumnimagazine.com.

Second Report of the Board of Trustees of the General State Hospital for the Insane of the State of Connecticut. Thomas J. Stafford, 1868.

Seth and Fanny Whitman Tillotson. Recollections, AFPL.

Shachtman, Tom. *The Founding Fortunes: How the Wealthy Paid for and Profited from America's Revolution.* St. Martin's Press, 2020.

Silliman, Benjamin. *Remarks Made on a Short Tour Between Hartford and Quebec in the Autumn of 1819*. 2nd ed. S. Converse, 1824.

Siskind, Janet. *Rum & Axes: The Rise of a Connecticut Merchant Family.* Cornell University Press, 2002.

Smith, Joseph, Jr. *Book of Commandments, For the Government of the Church of Christ, Organized According to the Law, on the 6th of April, 1830.* W.W. Phelps & Co., 1833. https://archive.org.

Somma, Ann Marie. "World-Renowned Maker of Axes: The Collins Company of Canton." Connecticut History, April 28, 2022. https://connecticuthistory.org.

Stone, Earle. "Farmington's Wilford Woodruff: Pioneer, and Man of God." *Farmington Historical Society News*, December 2015.

Taylor, Snowden, and Mary Jane Dapkus. *Antebellum Shelf Clock Making in Farmington and Unionville Villages, Connecticut.* National Association of Watch & Clock Collectors, 2019.

Theodate Pope Riddle Family Papers, Hill-Stead Museum Archives, Farmington, Connecticut.

Third Annual Report of the Board of Trustees of the General State Hospital for the Insane of the State of Connecticut. Case, Lockwood and Brainard, 1868.

Thirteenth Report of the Board of Trustees of the General State Hospital for the Insane for the State of Connecticut. Pelton & King, 1879.

Thompson, Alice Holmes. *Avon, Connecticut: A Brief Informal History*. Avon Woman's Club, 1954.

———. *Bicentennial Commemoration Service of the West Avon Church*. December 2, 1951, AFPL.

Tillotson Family, Early Traditions and History. AFPL.

Tsesis, Alexander. *For Liberty and Equality: The Life and Times of the Declaration of Independence.* Oxford University Press, 2012.

Wadsworth Family Papers, MS 525. Manuscripts and Archives, Yale University, Yale Archives.

Wadsworth, S.C. "The Towers of Talcott Mountain." *Connecticut Quarterly*, vol. 1, January 1895 to December 1895.

Walkley, Stephen, ed. *History of the Seventh Connecticut Volunteer Infantry, 1861–1865*. n.p., n.d. Accessed November 24, 2024. https://archive.org.

Wallace, Matthew H. "Forgotten Triumph: Union Victories at the Battle of Chaffin's Farm." Black Virginians in Blue, May 15, 2019. https://community.village.virginia.edu.

Wallach, Allan. "Wadsworth's Tower: An Episode in the History of American Landscape Vision." *American Art,* 10, no. 3 (Autumn 1996).

Warshauer, Matthew. *Connecticut in the American Civil War.* Wesleyan University Press, 2011.

Warshauer, Matthew, ed. *Inside Connecticut and the Civil War.* Wesleyan University Press, 2014.

Waskey, A.J.L. "Restoration Movement." *New Georgia Encyclopedia*, updated December 4, 2013. https://www.georgiaencyclopedia.org.

Weeks, Linton. "American Women Who Were Anti-Suffragettes." NPR History Dept., October 22, 2015. https://www.npr.org.

West Avon Congregational Church. Minutes of Second Ecclesiastical Society of Farmington (SECF) membership meetings, AFPL.

———. Minutes of West Avon Congregational Church, AFPL.

———. Records of church membership admissions and dismissions, AFPL.

———. Records, 1751–1941. Genealogical Society of Utah, 1976.

Wilford Woodruff Papers. LDS Archives, wilfordwoodruffpapers.org.

Wilford Woodruff's Witness: The Development of Temple Doctrine. "Wilford Woodruff's Wives." Accessed November 26, 2024. http://www.wilfordwoodruff.info.

William Wood Papers. RG 69:35, Connecticut State Library.

Winthrop, Elizabeth. Recollections, n.d., AFPL.

Woodford, Orson. Probate Files Collection: Early to 1880. Connecticut State Library.

Wooding, Francis A. "'Cross' Young Aide Gives Tiny Avon Alsop Antidote." *Bridgeport Sunday Herald*, 1937. AFPL.

Woodruff, Romanta. Diary. AFPL. Marian Hunter Local History Room, AFPL.

Woodruff, Wilford. Autobiography 1857 Draft 1 [A-5], Document Transcript, History of Wilford Woodruff (Woodruff Autobiography), Accessed November 26, 2024. https://wilfordwoodruffpapers.org.

———. *Leaves from My Journal.* Juvenile Instructor Office, 1881.

Woodward, Walter W. "From the State Historian: Connecticut's Slow Steps Toward Emancipation." Connecticut History, accessed November 24, 2024. https://connecticuthistory.org.

Yale College biographies, John Bartlett, Class of 1807. Marian Hunter Local History Room, AFPL.

Yao, Yetta. "Father of Chinese Overseas Students—Christian Yung Wing, The First Chinese Student Graduated in the U.S." *China Christian Daily*, February 21, 2017. https://chinachristiandaily.com.

YouTube. "June 11, 1936 Broadcast of the NBC Radio Network, 1936 Republican National Convention." Accessed November 26, 2024. https://www.youtube.com.

Yung Kwai Papers. MS 1795, Yung, Kwai, 1861–1943. Beineke Library, Yale University, Yale Archives.

Yung, Wing, A.B., L.L.D. *My Life in China and America.* Henry Holt and Company, 1909.

Yung Wing Papers. MS 602, Manuscripts and Archives, Yale University Library, Yale University, Yale Archives.

INDEX

B

C

D

E

F

G

K

L

M

U

V

W

Y

ABOUT THE AUTHOR

A resident of Avon, Connecticut, Scott Lewis is on the Board of the Avon Land Trust and has given several presentations on the town's history. In addition to serving as treasurer of the land trust, he builds and maintains hiking trails in Avon. A descendant of signer Josiah Bartlett from New Hampshire, Scott serves as treasurer-general for the Descendants of the Signers of the Declaration of Independence, a national genealogy society. Prior to his retirement in 2023, Scott was a senior vice president at the insurance company The Hartford, where he served as controller and chief accounting officer from 2013 to 2023. He lives with his wife in Avon, and they have two adult children.